Researching Race and Ethnicity

To my parents, Patricia and Wimalarajah for paving the way, and to my son, Zac and his magic

Researching Race and Ethnicity

Methods, Knowledge and Power

Yasmin Gunaratnam

SAGE Publications
London • Thousand Oaks • New Delhi

First published 2003

SAGE Publications Ltd
6 Bonhill Street
London EC2A 4PU

SAGE Publications Inc
2455 Teller Road
Thousand Oaks, California 91320

SAGE Publications India Pvt Ltd
B-42, Panchsheel Enclave
Post Box 4109
New Delhi 100 017

British Library Cataloguing in Publication data

A catalogue record for this book is available from the
British Library

ISBN 0 7619 7286 2
ISBN 0 7619 7287 0 (pbk)

Library of Congress Control Number available

Typeset by C&M Digitals (P) Ltd., Chennai, India
Printed in India at Gopsons Papers Ltd, Noida

Contents

Preface and recognitions

I was born and spent the first five years of my life in Kandy in Sri Lanka, before my parents migrated to England. My mother was of Singhalese/Indonesian/Scottish descent and my father was Tamil. I still remember my excitement on the plane journey to England, my first encounter with Kellogg's Cornflakes, my mild anxiety that this was 'English food', and how my father had met us in a borrowed, tiny, green Mini car at Heathrow airport. I have a vivid memory, of some months later, of my mother giving chase to white boys from a local council estate, who used to break into the garden of our hospital flat, rented to my father as a junior doctor in the National Health Service. The boys would climb the trees, make a lot of noise and play around with apples from a tree, in ways that I found menacing. One of the reasons why I think this one incident stands out in my memory is because it was the first time that I had heard us called 'wogs'. Even though I had not heard the term before, I knew that it was racialized. I shouted back over the fence 'white wogs'. Some days later, as I was lying fast asleep in my bed, I was awoken suddenly by the noise of the window above my bed being broken. The apple that had been used to break the window lay amid pieces of broken glass on top of the bed-spread, inches away from my feet. My interest in 'race' and ethnicity, and questions of power and inequality, go back a long way.

I begin here because the different elements in this story are directly relevant to the themes that are addressed and explored in this book. First, the story encapsulates the messy and complicated interrelations between social identities – ethnicity, gender and class in this case – as they are played out in different, but always connected, postcolonial contexts. Second, it points to the relationships between the social and the individual. We always have to reckon with, and to deal with history, and the particular ways in which constructions of difference are produced and have effects at any historical moment. Yet these meanings are also dynamic and contingent, and can be negotiated, resisted and reworked by individuals. Third, the process of remembering and making sense of events is about the social embeddedness of experience and of 'voice'. That is, the story that I have narrated here needs to be read and questioned with regard to both past and present social contexts, my specific biography, and in relation to the production of evolving, contradictory and partial 'fictions' of who I was, who I have become, and who I might be. Taken together, these different elements demonstrate some of the challenges of researching 'race', ethnicity and difference, and demonstrate how social research is absolutely enmeshed in, rather than separate from social contexts. Exploring, interrogating and conceptualizing these processes is what this book is about.

There are many people who I want to thank and to recognize for their support and their contributions to my work. I have learned so much from the staff and the service users at the hospice where I did the research that forms the basis for the discussions and examples used in this book. I feel privileged to have heard these accounts, especially those from minoritized service users, whose narratives are of critical significance to current debates on 'race' and ethnicity, but whose experiences are often marginalized. So much of the research and theory on 'race', post-colonialism and multiculturalism is marked by a concern with the cultural entanglements and positioning of young minoritized people, so that the accounts and experiences of those who are old and diseased can be silenced or are devalued.

I would like to thank Gail Wilson, who provided much support and critical discussion throughout the different stages of my research, and who also offered glimpses of hope when I was trying to work and cope with new motherhood, a premature baby and severe sleep deprivation. My discussions and friendships with Gail, Helen Cylwik and Dagmar Loranz-Meyer were what got me through the barren times in an academic environment that seemed to have forgotten about history and radical politics. Colin Murray Parkes provided 'clinical supervision' during my fieldwork, which created an important space to explore and justify emotions as 'data'. Much earlier, as a teenager, it was the enthusiasm, encouragement, politics and intellectual power of Barry Sidgwick that awakened my passion for social theory. For their friendship and dialogue along the way, I would like to thank Afshan Salaria, Sara McGuire, Leena Sevak, Elaine Heffernan and David Riker. The Social and Economic Research Council funded my doctoral research.

Bob Bailey, Marjorie Bailey, Bill Bytheway, Prue Chamberlayne, Helen Cylwik, Liz Forbat, Carl Gunaratnam, Wendy Hollway, Ann Phoenix, Diane Reay and Tom Wengraf all provided comments on drafts of the chapters. Richard Bailey proof-read and contributed his 'clicking' skills to solve my computer disasters. Philip Noden has provided me with a much valued and rock-solid cyber friendship. I have learned so much from working with Gail Lewis. My discussions and my writing with Gail have really stretched and sustained me. The School of Health and Social Welfare at the Open University gave me time to work on the book, and colleagues in the Black Researchers' Group gave me continuous support. I would like to thank the women at Noah's Ark Day Nursery, and particularly Kim Jones and Cheryl Sutherland, for caring for my son Zac while I worked, and who are an integral part of the hidden chains of labour involved in this book.

I am deeply grateful to my family in England, Sri Lanka and Australia for their support over the years, particularly David, Tracy, Carl and Darrell. Bob and Marjorie have been surrogate parents and have shown a genuine interest and concern with my work and my well being. Books, art, poetry and newspaper cuttings have accompanied the steady stream of home-cooked frozen meals and chocolate over the years.

I can't begin to express the gratitude and the loss that I feel for my parents, Patricia Sourjah and Wimalarajah Gunaratnam. We all paid a price for their transgression of social boundaries; at the same time they also taught me, in their different ways, about the resourcefulness and the insightfulness that can come from the margins. This book is dedicated to them and to my son Zac, who has brought such love and brightness into my life and whose regular calls of 'Mummy, can you come down now please?' guarantee the most wonderful disruptions and fun.

Introduction – thinking through knowledge,
methods and power

Researching 'race' and ethnicity

This book is about methodology, the production of knowledge and the politics of doing research on 'race' and ethnicity, and their interrelations with other forms of social difference such as gender, class and disability. It aims to address some of the dilemmas and the 'stuck places' (Lather, 2001a) of research – not so much in the prescriptive, task-oriented style of many methods books, but in a way that is process oriented and about a thinking-through of some of the complexities, ambiguities and contradictions involved in the process of doing qualitative research that is concerned with recognizing difference and with pursuing social justice. A central concern that runs throughout the discussions in this book is how we produce knowledge about difference, and how what we know (or what we claim to know) is caught up with specific histories and relations of power (Foucault, 1977). A particular aim is to develop a critical and a theoretically informed approach to qualitative research methods, which will bring together ideas and thinking from a range of different fields, particularly post-structuralist, feminist, critical 'race', and postcolonial theory.

Put simply, a narrative thread that runs throughout the different chapters in this book is about making connections between research methods, lived experience, knowledge and politics. This theme is itself entangled with a central tension in the study of 'race' and ethnicity. This tension concerns the vigorous debates about the meanings of the categories of 'race' and ethnicity that have spanned a spectrum of approaches in the social sciences (see Aspinall, 2001; Bulmer and Solomos, 1996; Solomos and Back, 1994). These approaches can be caricatured as ranging from 'primodial' models that see 'race' and ethnicity as being characterized by 'core', inherent experiences with some degree of independence from social contexts, to social constructionist approaches that argue that 'race' and ethnicity involve socially produced, heterogeneous and dynamic *processes* of being and becoming (see Brah, 1996; Omi and Winart 1994).

'Conceptually, "race" is not a scientific category. The differences attributable to "race" within a population are as great as that between racially defined populations. "Race" is a political and social construct. It is the organizing discursive category around which has been constructed a system of socio-economic power, exploitation and exclusion – i.e., racism. However, as a discursive practice, racism has its own "logic" (Hall, 1990). It claims to ground the social and cultural differences which legitimize racialized exclusion in genetic and biological differences: i.e., in Nature. This "naturalizing effect" appears to make racial difference a fixed, scientific "fact", unresponsive to change or reformist social engineering.

[...] "Ethnicity" by contrast, generates a discourse where difference is grounded in *cultural and religious* features … [however] … the articulation of difference with Nature (biology and the genetic) is present, but displaced *through kinship and inter-marriage.*' (Hall, 2000: 222–3, emphasis in original)

Readers who are familiar with the different debates and approaches to what concepts of 'race' and ethnicity mean, will have noticed that in the discussion so far, I have used the terms together and interchangeably. This is not due to a failure to recognize any important analytic distinctions between the terms. Rather, where I use the terms together I am indicating and working with the dense interrelations between the categories (see Hall, 2000). The much used, general conceptual distinction between 'race' and ethnicity is that 'race' evokes a biological and genetic referent, and ethnicity refers to cultural and religious difference and kinship (see Hall, 2000; Mulholland and Dyson, 2001). However, such distinctions are being challenged and re-thought. Stuart Hall has argued convincingly that contemporary diasporic ways of life, and multiculturalism in particular, have served to disrupt the binary opposition between the biological and the cultural in the meanings of 'race' and ethnicity. He is insistent that:

Biological racism privileges markers like skin colour, but those signifiers have always also been used, by discursive extension, to connote social and cultural differences … The biological referent is therefore never wholly absent from discourses of ethnicity, though it is more indirect. The more 'ethnicity' matters, the more its characteristics are represented as relatively fixed, inherent within a group, transmitted from generation to generation, not just by culture and education, but by biological inheritance, stabilized above all by kinship and endogamous marriage rules that ensure that the ethnic group remains genetically, and therefore culturally 'pure'. (Hall, 2000: 223)

The important point that Hall makes is that processes of biological and cultural differentiation through the categories of 'race' and ethnicity are not two separate systems of meaning ('discourses'), but are 'racism's two registers' (2000: 223). This recognition is very important politically. It acknowledges the interrelations between the two 'registers' of biology and culture in processes of giving 'race' and ethnicity meaning and bringing them to life in the social world. And it can enable analysis and empirical research to examine how biological and cultural discourses might be variously ordered and identified with by different groups within specific social contexts.

The recognition that there can be some degree of overlap between the meanings of 'race' and ethnicity, and between the very different theoretical approaches to the categories (Smaje, 1997), is not unproblematic for empirical research. As researchers we need to be able to address and to account for the *specific* relationships between our analytic categories and subjective, social and material relations. Key questions here are: can we have an empirical approach to 'race' and ethnicity that is not reductionist and does not reify (concretize) the dynamic, interrelated and situated meanings of lived experiences of 'race' and ethnicity? How can we make decisions about the points at which we fix the meanings of racial and ethnic categories in order to do empirical research? How can we make judgements about the epistemological and the political repercussions of such decisions? How might we use empirical research to challenge and transform, rather than to reproduce, racial thinking?

SOCIAL DISCOURSES AND EXPERIENCE

In this chapter I want to give specific attention to these questions by engaging with some of the different ways in which 'race' and ethnicity have been approached in research, and the implications that such approaches have for methodological practices and the production of knowledge. Most often the differences between conceptual approaches are represented across a series of divides, such as that between the pursuit of race equality and the recognition of difference, and between theory and lived experience. I have become particularly frustrated with the often-cited opposition between social constructionist approaches and those materialist, realist or empiricist approaches that are said to be grounded in 'real' experience, as if experience somehow has a life of its own (see Brah et al., 1999; Wuthnow, 2002; Hemmings, 2002).

Alongside those such as Stuart Hall (2000), Avtar Brah (1996) and Gail Lewis (2000), I believe that social constructionist insights, particularly those influenced by post-structuralism, can be put to valuable use in understanding how experience is brought into being and has effects in specific social and interactional contexts. I also believe that to fail to recognize the contingency and the ambivalent complexity of lived experience maintains an essentialist view of 'race' and ethnicity, where experience can be seen to be wholly (pre)determined by racial and ethnic categories, that are themselves construed as unchanging 'essences', cordoned off from social, material and emotional relations (however, see Smaje, 1997 for a critique of social constructionist approaches).

In broadly similar terms, Hemmings makes a forceful case for the importance of post-structuralist epistemologies (or theories of knowledge) in making sense of the lived experiences of bisexual subjects. She argues that:

> the failure to develop models of experience as partial, fragmented, and con-
> tradictory limits our ability to make sense of and thus transform gendered
> social reality. A feminist epistemology that maintains *a priori* assumptions
> about what constitutes gendered or sexual experience, and thus subjective
> location, is necessarily attuned only to dominant gendered and sexual subject
> formations, and is ill-equipped to produce ethical research on subjects whose
> knowledges are produced from a variety of different social locations.
> (Hemmings, 2002: 38)

Hemmings's argument in relation to the need to recognize experience as partial and contradictory and to produce ethical research that is responsive to subjugated knowledges, is clearly relevant to research concerned with 'race' and ethnicity. Yet, there can also be difficulties with using post-structuralist insights in research that is concerned with social justice and with challenging racism (Alexander and Mohanty, 1997; Tuhiwai Smith, 1999). For example, in the present context of postcolonialism and multi-culturalism, 'race' and ethnicity are significant categories of meaning and of experience for all individuals. It is also the case that self and group iden-tifications among minoritized people have been, and continue to be a necessary and politically valuable tool in resisting racism and in collective mobilization (Clifford, 2000). In this regard, Alexander and Mohanty make an important point in drawing attention to how post-structuralist attempts to pluralize and disrupt the stability of categories of 'race', class, gender and sexuality can:

> foreclose any valid recuperation of these categories or the social relations
> through which they are constituted. If we dissolve the category of race, for
> instance, it becomes difficult to claim the experience of racism. (Alexander
> and Mohanty, 1997: xvii)

The conceptualization of experience and of social location have been the subject of intense enquiry and debate among feminist and postcolonial theorists (Lewis, G., 2000; Mohanty, 1992; Scott, 1992). While these con-cepts have constituted significant challenges to the use of post-structuralist ideas in research, there are researchers who have demonstrated how post-structuralist critiques of essentialism can be used in empirical research to generate more complex insights into the production of social location and experience (Brah, 1996; Lewis, G., 2000). Such work, in demonstrating the ways in which experiences of 'race' and ethnicity (among other social differences) are mediated by the continual negotiation of personal, inter-actional and social dynamics, show how social discourses can have effects upon experience and can also be questioned and contradicted by experience. As Wuthnow suggests: 'While hegemonic representations may categorize and define, there is always resistance to these definitions, and it is the subjective agency embodied in this resistance which constitutes the possibility for oppositional discourses' (2002: 194).

My approach to 'race' and ethnicity in this is book works with these tensions in the application of post-structuralist insights to qualitative research. It is concerned with using post-structuralist critiques of essentialism in research, whilst also seeking to legitimate the everyday 'situated voices' (Lewis, G., 2000) and experience of research participants and researchers as grounds for political action. In very broad terms, this approach recognizes the dynamic constitution of the meanings of 'race' and ethnicity through social discourse *and* through the subjective investments of individuals (see Brah, 1996 and Hall, 1996). It recognizes that social discourses are enmeshed in lived experience and institutional and social power relations that have emotional, material and embodied consequences for individuals and for groups. In this sense, I do not theorize social discourses as being outside of experience, subjectivity or bodies; rather, I suggest that social discourses and lived experiences are co-constituted – they intermingle and inhabit one another.

This recognition of the mutual constitution of embodied experience and social discourse can be problematic for qualitative researchers, particu-larly if we are concerned with breaking out of circular arguments and those arguments in which researchers are positioned as being outside of the flows between experience and discursive contexts. Drawing upon feminist research, I will argue for a radical reflexivity in research that involves rigorous attention to explicating the ways in which research participants *and* research-ers are socially situated (Haraway, 1988), at the same time as making our research accountable to the past (Gatens and Lloyd, 1999). My argument, in relation to this latter aspect of reflexivity, is that researchers have to examine and trace how research is entangled with wider social and historical rela-tions, and involves the ideological construction of the subject of its enquiry (Burman, 1992). The idea that research is a part of social and historical rela-tions, and produces rather than simply reflects what we are researching, is encapsulated in the conceptualization of research as a *discursive practice*.

The significance of conceptualizing research on 'race' and ethnicity as a discursive practice is that it opens up analytic opportunities for researchers to interrogate our current understandings, interests and research practices, and asks how these might be a part of what Levine has called 'epistemology as political control' (2000: 17). This process of interrogation is important for three reasons. First, it challenges radically a view of research as an unlocated and transparent reflection of some pre-existing, stable 'reality'. Second, it makes our analyses more complex as the research task becomes one in which we need to make sense of knowledge as an emergent property of the interactions between and among differently constituted and located individuals, who include the researcher (Hemmings, 2002). And third, it situates our knowledge claims in relation to historical and social relations.

CONTEXTUALIZING RESEARCH ON 'RACE' AND ETHNICITY

In developing my argument about the value of understanding research on 'race' and ethnicity as a discursive practice, it is important to put research into an historical context, so that we might understand something more about *how* the categories of 'race' and ethnicity can be thought of as *social constructs*. As several theorists have shown (Bonnett, 1998; Gilroy, 2000), there are close connections between the nature and aims of research concerned with questions of 'race' and ethnicity, and the social contexts in which research is conceptualized, developed and practised.

'Race' as a concept based upon notions of biological difference, and ethnicity as connoting cultural difference and kinship, have taken on particular, interdependent and plural meanings throughout history. Although certain approaches to researching 'race' and ethnicity have been dominant at particular historical moments, this dominance has never been all encompassing (see the pioneering work of Du Bois, 1899; 1903). The field of research on 'race' and ethnicity therefore is – and has always been – a contested and variegated one (Bonnett, 1998), and there is still considerable work to do in excavating marginalized, oppositional scholarship that has challenged and interrupted, and has also sometimes ended up being complicit with oppressive and racist forms of knowledge production.

In mapping the historical topography of research on 'race' and ethnicity, four main ideas underpin the arguments made in the following sections. These are that:

- 'race' and ethnicity are not 'objective', stable, homogenous categories, but are produced and animated by changing, complicated and uneven interactions between social processes and individual experience
- colonialism, and the 'idea of Europe', was a founding moment of racial categorization ('racialization') and of classifying and reducing ways of being to visible, embodied and hierarchically ordered forms of difference (Hesse, 1997)

- contemporary approaches to qualitative research on 'race' and ethnicity are marked by these colonial legacies of racial categorization that we need to examine, recognize, challenge and undermine
- postcolonialism, as an allegory for a movement beyond the centring of the West/North (rather than a discrete geopolitical moment), provides opportunities for developing ways of thinking and of doing empirical research that are able to work both with and against racial categories (see Chapter 2).

RESEARCH ON 'RACE' AND ETHNICITY AND HISTORY

What needs to be amplified as a starting point in this discussion is that ideas about racialized difference, as relating to 'natural', observable, physical characteristics, mental capabilities and patterns of behaviour that separate and define different groups, are relatively modern and new (Dubow, 1995). These ideas have been seen as being imbued with particular meanings in the nineteenth century (Gilroy, 2000), as a part of a colonial geopolitics (Agnew, 1999) that was also actively constructed and maintained through research (Viswanathan, 1989). Paul Gilroy's contention is that:

> the modern human sciences, particularly anthropology, geography, and philosophy, undertook elaborate work in order to make the idea of 'race' epistemologically correct. This required novel ways of understanding embodied alterity, hierarchy, and temporality. It made human bodies communicate the truths of an irrevocable otherness that were being confirmed by a new science and a new semiotics just as the struggle against Atlantic slavery was being won. (2000: 58)

In a discussion of the history of 'scientific' textbooks on the study of 'race', Gilroy has drawn attention to how scientific discourses located 'race' in selective physical characteristics (see also Manning, 1993). He states how: 'Bones, skulls, hair, lips, noses, eyes, feet, genitals, and other somatic markers of "race" have a special place in the discursive regimes that produced the truth of "race" and repeatedly discovered it lodged in and on the body' (Gilroy, 2000: 35). This empirical approach to 'race' of knowing by seeing, was also linked to what Agnew (1999) has called a 'geo-political imagination', through which 'race' in a context of colonialism was used to map and give politicized meaning to distinctions between different parts of the world, and was used to classify and distinguish differences *within* colonial populations.

Levine (2000), for example, has shown how the establishment of a census in India in the nineteenth century was dependent upon differentiation to produce the kinds of sociological knowledge that colonial officials were interested in. Paying specific attention to the rubric of prostitution and the ways in which colonialism differentiated women through 'race'-based ideas of sexual order and morality, Levine asserts that:

> Colonial definitions of sexuality served to map a geography of racial borders through a complex taxonomy of racial and ethnic distinction, in which categories were always more than innocently descriptive. It was in the interests of the authorities to represent these classifications as fundamentally descriptive and empiricist, a mere catalogue of actualities. In such a guise, nature and morality could be conflated, rather than seen as judgements which themselves produced categories of rule through racial distinction. Race, then, was that which the colonial state used in support of its rule, but which it sought to make transparent as a merely informational category. (2000: 11)

Through the racialized epistemology and methodology of the 'geo-political imagination' of colonialism, mental capabilities, morality, culture, class and gendered difference, as well as territory, were encoded and endowed with racialized meanings. However, I do not wish to represent this process as uni-directional or 'flat', without any points of interaction or disruption. As Sara Ahmed has observed: 'The encounters that characterized colonialism are not simply one-sided, or monological: encounters involve at least two cultures who, in their meeting, transform the conditions of the encounter itself' (Ahmed, 2000: 11). Yegenoglu (1998), using the psychoanalyst Lacan's (1981) concept of fantasy, has suggested that the figure of the veiled Oriental woman in eighteenth- and nineteenth-century European texts, functioned to signify the Orient as feminine, deceptive, seductive, unpredictable and dangerous, whilst also constituting a point of resistance to colonial voyeurism:

> the colonial subject's desire to control and dominate the foreign land is not independent from his scopic desire, from his desire to penetrate, through his surveillant eye, what is behind the veil. *The invisibility the veil secures for the colonial other is simultaneously the point at which desire is articulated and the ground upon which the scopic drive of the subject is displaced ...*
>
> It is the veil which enables the Oriental other to look without being seen. This not only disturbs the desire of the Western/colonial subject to fix cultural and sexual difference, but also enables the colonial other to turn itself into a surveillant gaze. (Yegenoglu, 1998: 62–3, emphasis in original)

For Yegenoglu, the veil, in signifying the articulation of both cultural and sexual difference in the Orient, threatened visual Enlightenment epistemologies based upon notions of the transparency of knowledge. So, while 'race' came to stand for embodied, observable physical differences in the nineteenth century, it also signified unseeable, 'intellectual, psychological and moral' qualities (Lorimer, 1978: 136).

Dubow (1995), in a discussion of scientific racism in South Africa, has shown how indigenous Khoisan peoples, known in derogatory terms as 'Hottentots' or 'Bosjesmans', were an icon of 'Otherness' in Western/Northern racial thinking. The brutal treatment of Saartjie Baartman, a black Khoena woman, in the name of research in the early nineteenth century, has become legendary in symbolizing the connections between the eugenics movement, colonialism and slavery. Known as the 'Hottentot Venus', Baartman was just one example of how 'the growing curiosity of the scientific and general public in Europe was to be satisfied by the exhibition of live human specimens' (Dubow, 1995: 23). Baartman was brought to London, where she was displayed in a cage in Piccadilly. Later, in Paris, her body was observed and drawn when she was still alive, dissected when she died at the age of 25, and her skeleton, brain and genitals displayed in the Musée de l'Homme in Paris for 150 years (see Dubow, 1995: 23; Erasmus, 2000: 188). There is a campaign to return her body to South Africa for burial.

What emerges from this discussion is how notions of 'race', and later ethnicity, were central to the ways in which different elements of a geo-political imagination came together in specific forms in different historical epochs. For instance, in examining Agnew's discussion of how the modern geopolitical imagination translated time into space, it is possible to see how racial and ethnic categorizations conjure up territorial distinctions that simultaneously evoke temporalized-normative distinctions between 'modern' and 'primitive' or 'advanced' and 'backward'. Of particular relevance is Agnew's point that:

The projection of temporal qualities drawn from a rendering of a specific historical experience onto territorial space, enables three political-intellectual positions. One is the tendency to essentialize places, or identify one trait as characterizing a particular spatial unit (e.g. caste in Indian, Mafia or political instability in Italy). A second is the temptation to exoticize, or focus on difference as the single criterion for comparison between areas. Similarities or global conundra are thereby eliminated from consideration (e.g. difficulties of social mobility everywhere, general barriers to political participation). The third is the tendency to totalize the comparison, or turn relative differences into absolute ones. The whole of a society is therefore made entirely recognizable in any one of its parts. (Agnew, 1999: 33)

What the work of several social theorists such as Agnew, Dubow, Gilroy, Levine and Yegenoglu demonstrates, is how racial and ethnic categories are neither 'natural' nor 'neutral', but are socially and historically produced and are heavy with political meaning (see Chapter 2). The socially embedded nature of these meanings has two main implications for an understanding of the social construction and the use of racial and ethnic categories in research. First, we are able to see that the meanings of 'race' and ethnicity are constructed relationally and are located in particular social contexts. What I mean by this is that although 'race' and ethnicity are seen as defining the identity and the very being of racialized Others in colonial and postcolonial contexts (see Chapter 5), these categories are both internally differentiated and also central to the constitution of a range of identities in Western/Northern colonial nations (Hall, 1999). As Stuart Hall has reminded us, identification is always a double-sided process, constructed *through* rather than outside differentiation (see also Kitzinger and Wilkinson, 1996 and Rutherford, 1990 for further discussions of this process of 'Othering'), and entailing:

> the radically disturbing recognition that it is only through the relation to the Other, the relation to what it is not, to precisely what it lacks, to what has been called its *constitutive outside* that the positive meaning of any term – and thus its 'identity' – can be constructed ... the unity, the internal homogeneity, which the term identity treats as foundational is not natural, but a constructed form of closure, every identity naming as its necessary, even if silenced and unspoken other, that which it 'lacks'. (Hall, 1996: 5, emphasis in original)

This is a significant theorization of processes of identity formation. It gestures to the psycho-social entanglements of difference, and also challenges the assumption that categories of 'race' and ethnicity only have relevance and meaning to those from minoritized groups (Henwood and Phoenix, 1996).

Second, the recognition of the social embeddedness of racial and ethnic categories, enables insights into colonialism as an uneven process that operated in differential ways across time and space (Thomas, 1994; Young, 1995). This recognition of the complexity of colonialism has been particularly valuable in the examination of how racial categories have also been applied to different groups of white people. For example, the British Empire and its domineering expansion, based upon systems of direct and indirect governance, began with Ireland, and produced 'a racialisation of the presumed inferiority of the Irish' (Agnew, 1999: 98). In an analysis of the letters of the anthropologist Charles Kingsley, written in the 1860s in England, Lorimer (1978) has highlighted how 'scientific' anti-Irish racism, which played upon notions of intelligence, was a significant part of debates about the extension of voting rights:

> Kingsley's emphasis upon inherited characteristics enabled him to support an extension of the suffrage in England, while at the same time claiming that Irish Celts, the population of Romance countries (*sic*), and blacks in the West Indies and America, lacked the historical experience and racial endowment for self-government. (Lorimer, 1978: 155)

Bonnett (1998), in a critical history of the conflation of European and white identities from nineteenth- and twentieth-century commentaries, has drawn attention to the historical and geographical contingency of whiteness, thereby challenging it as a 'natural', homogenous category. Bonnett's work traces the marginalization and exclusion of Chinese and Middle Eastern white identities in the formation of a European racialized whiteness, that was itself further inflected by ethnic, class and gender hierarchies. In addressing English Victorian class relations, Bonnett points to constructions of upper-class English people as being 'more white' than those from the working classes.

Modern ideas about 'race' and ethnicity can thus be understood as being produced through complicated social relations, with these ideas taking on distinct meanings within different social contexts. What is significant in noting this point, is that it recognizes the geopolitical relations through which research on 'race' and ethnicity has been a part of these social relations. For instance, in his discussion of research on 'race' and ethnicity in anthropology, Jenkins has described three significant shifts in anthropology's relationship with the 'exotically Other', in which geopolitical relations have been central to the nature of research:

> First, as early as the nineteenth century, but more commonly from the mid-twentieth century onwards, the metropolitan peripheries offered accessible and relatively exotic alterity, in the shape of residual hunters, fishers and nomads, or peasants. Subsequently, second, the exotic Other migrated to the metropolitan homelands of anthropology to become ethnic minorities; anthropologists followed them home. Third, and perhaps most radically, anthropologists have begun to pay more attention to their own cultural backyards. (Jenkins, 1996: 808)

To recognize the close relationships between research and geopolitical relations is not to suggest that all research concerned with 'race' and ethnicity was/is/will be oppressive. Rather, what I want to highlight is the need to consider the *specific* political history and the development of the relationship between theories of being (ontologies) and the production of knowledge in research. What is of critical importance for us as researchers, is that analytic attention is given to the specific relations of power that research is located in and can deploy. As Grossberg observes, 'The act of power comes not in creating something from nothing, but in reducing something to nothing ... it is precisely the articulation of difference on top of otherness that becomes the material site of discursive power' (1996: 96).

To summarize so far, my argument has been directed at challenging the 'scientific' basis of the truth claims of research on 'race' and ethnicity, by drawing attention to the ways in which the meanings of 'race' and ethnicity have been socially constructed and are historically variable. To this extent, I have argued that research on 'race' and ethnicity has been connected to geo-historical conditions of colonialism, in which knowledge about 'race' and ethnicity has been unstable and context specific, rather than universal and timeless. In moving on to examine more contemporary research on 'race' and ethnicity, I want to keep this focus upon the socially situated nature of research concerns, methods and practices.

CONTEMPORARY RESEARCH ON 'RACE' AND ETHNICITY

While research in a context of colonialism can be understood as marked by practices based upon the differentiation and control of racialized bodies (Levine, 2000), more contemporary research can be seen as being charac-terized by political concerns about questions of cultural and national iden-tity and belonging (Hall, 1993). Hesse (2000: 11–12), in a discussion of contemporary postcolonial and multicultural relations, has identified a ubiquitous 'race relations narrative', which struggles with conflicting needs to monitor, control and assimilate racialized difference as being central to forms of governance. This need to monitor, with the hope of controlling and managing 'race relations', is a real tension in contemporary research on 'race' and ethnicity, and presents significant political dilemmas for researchers with regard to the relationships between policy agenda, research questions, methodological practices and the funding of research.

It is important to recognize that the influence of the policy environment also plays a role in shaping approaches to the teaching of 'race'. In a review of teaching on 'race' and ethnicity in sociology, Mason (1996) has identified substantive changes to how the subject has been understood and taught. Of specific interest is Mason's reference to the journal *Race* that carried a report of a meeting in London in 1970 about the 'appropriate' way to teach on issues of 'race'. Mason states how:

A key point of agreement was that sociology courses should *not* be geared to the production of workers in the field. It appears that there was a strongly held view that to accept this role would mean accepting the definitions of the situation provided by organizations in the field of social policy ... In particular, there was a strong consensus, reflecting the political debates of the period, that the starting point of sociological concerns should most certainly not be the alleged problem of immigration ... Nevertheless, there was also an acknowledge-ment that many students were motivated to study the subject by their desire to be involved in the struggle for racial equality. (Mason, 1996: 793, emphasis in original)

For example, in an historical analysis of the development of surveys on 'minority' groups, Smith (1993) has shown how growing attention to 'race' in surveys, and particularly within opinion poll research in the USA, was related to the need for more information on the opinions and beliefs of African-American people as a result of civil rights activism. Before the 1950s, Smith argues, African-American people were virtually invisible in survey research in the US, with such issues as the legal and illegal exclusion of African-American people from voter registration records preventing their participation in many opinion polls. It was only with the rise of the civil rights movement and increasing debates about race equality, that the need for more information on African-American people's opinions was recognized. Indeed, Stanfield (1993a) has described the 1950s and 1960s as a 'heady time' for research on 'race relations', when 'there was a flood of federal and private foundation dollars for doing policy-related research' because of public concerns about desegregation and the civil rights movement. Shosteck, in describing his survey on 'respondent militancy' in the late 1960s among African-American people, has written how:

> In 1968 the Reverend Martin Luther King had been assassinated, the country was convulsed with civil disorder, cities from coast to coast literally were burning. The firm with which I was then associated was commissioned to survey the racial situation in Indianapolis ... Our task was to evaluate the potential for civil unrest, to determine the reasons for that potential, and to provide recommendations for preventing unrest if an outbreak appeared imminent. (Shosteck, 1977: 37)

In similar terms, there were also a number of English surveys such as the one by Daniel (1969) on *Racial Discrimination in England*,[1] that were initiated in the context of political concerns about racism and the 'integration' of 'Commonwealth immigrants' in England, following 'race riots' and racist violence. In 1971, Derek Humphry and Gus John first published *Because They're Black*, a qualitative study commissioned by the Runnymede Trust, an independent foundation set up to promote 'public education on race relations', following the stabbing of a young African-Caribbean man in Handsworth and rising complaints from African-Caribbean people about police harassment. Based upon participant observation, interviews and case studies in Handsworth, a multiracial, working-class area in the English Midlands, John describes how he set out to 'give the black people a chance to voice *their* view of *their* situation' (p. 10, emphasis in original). This was a position that John has framed as being in opposition to the politically ineffective, quantitative approaches to researching 'race' that were predominant at this time:

> We seem to be overwhelmed with academic social science on race relations, using the market research approach and doing little more than quantifing the obvious. While I am the first to recognize the limitations of an impressionistic study, I also feel it necessary to emphasize that what people think in a situation such as that in Handsworth is of utmost importance. It both determines

their stance to society and motivates their actions. Dare we dismiss lightly
their interpretation of the situation? (Humphry and John, 1972: 10)

There can be little doubt that the Handsworth study sought to challenge
the political ineffectiveness of quantitative approaches to 'race relations'.
Yet the focus upon the need to hear the 'voices' of 'black' people also constructs particular relations between minoritized groups and wider social
relations. In John's statement, we can see an approach to qualitative
research on 'race' and ethnicity in which the subjectivity of those from
'minority' groups is seen as an integral part of 'race relations', and which,
if ignored and left un-interrogated, could threaten social order and cohesion (see Chapter 3). In this approach, the traditional, scientific model of
research, based upon distant observation and the classification of 'race'
through the body, is displaced by an approach that is concerned with the
relations between 'race', subjectivity and proximity in research (see
Chapter 4). There is a concern with getting close to what minoritized
people think and feel, and with discovering the links between thought and
action/behaviour. The role of research on 'race' and ethnicity in such a
context then becomes to develop strategies, methods and practices that
can gain access to the experiences and the opinions and attitudes of those
in minoritized groups (see Chapters 6 and 7).

The conceptualization of 'race' and ethnicity *as* subjectivity is still
prevalent in current debates, particularly in relation to ethnic commonalities and differences between the researcher and research participant (see
Chapters 3 and 4). However, debates about the meanings of racial and
ethnic categories continue to be highly significant. For example, there was
considerable debate preceding the 1991 Census in the UK, which was the
first British census to ask a question about ethnicity. Researchers such as
Ahmad and Sheldon (1991; 1993) argued that the process of operationaliz-
ing ethnicity into distinct categories for the census was a reductionist,
political process, implying:

> the acceptance of some notion of homogeneity of condition, culture,
> attitudes, expectations, and in some cases language and religion within the
> groups identified on an ethnic basis. (Ahmad and Sheldon, 1991)

Despite the categories in the 1991 Census conflating a number of different
elements such as culture, geography, nationality and skin colour, the
ethnicity data from the census has since been used in examining and in
challenging inequalities, particularly in public services (see Dyson, 2001).
For instance, Simpson (1997) has suggested that the demographic data
from the 1991 Census was critical to locality based, secondary analysis in
helping to save specific government funding to support the schooling of

Terminology to describe different racialized groups is highly contested. In this book, I do not use the term 'ethnic minority' in any unproblematic, descriptive sense. I prefer to use the term either in quotation marks or else, more often, I use the term 'minoritized' to give some sense of the active processes of racialization that are at work in designating certain attributes of groups in particular contexts as being in a 'minority'. Brah has also argued that the term 'minority' discourages a 'multi-axial' analysis of power that questions the simple 'minority/majority' dichotomy:

the numerical referent of this dichotomy encourages a literal reading, reducing the problem of power relations to one of numbers, with the result that the repeated circulation of the discourse has the effect of naturalising rather than challenging the power differential ... A multi-axial performative conception of power highlights the ways in which a group constituted as a 'minority' along one dimension ... may be constructed as a 'majority' along another ... In other words, 'minorities' are positioned in relation not only to 'majorities' but also with respect to one another, and vice versa. Moreover, individual subjects may occupy 'minority' and 'majority' positions simultaneously, and this has important implications for the formation of subjectivity. (Brah, 1996: 187–9)

children with English as an additional language in Bradford, an ethnically diverse area in the North of England.

With regard to a new question on religion asked in the 2001 Census of England, Scotland and Wales, Aspinall (2000) has argued that the question, in enhancing and making more complex data from the ethnicity question, can be used to develop service provision, and to monitor and review the implementation of anti-discriminatory initiatives. Of particular relevance to this discussion are the relations that Aspinall describes between government policies and growing awareness of the interrelations between religious and ethnic identifications:

The government's policy agenda encompasses several major new inter-departmental initiatives, including tackling social exclusion and poverty, urban regeneration, educational reforms, and health improvement. Its broader interests in communitarian approaches have given rise to the recognition of the essential and increasing involvement of faith communities as collaborators in urban revitalization and policies to tackle social exclusion. (2000: 593)

Information generated through tightly defined categories of ethnicity, such as the census data, has been used in challenging forms of racialized inequality. Nevertheless, it is important to recognize that these categories are far from benign descriptors. By this I mean that definitions and categories of 'race' and ethnicity can also serve to *construct* racialized identifications, experiences, forms of governance and the meanings of social inequalities, not in any simple sense but through the interaction of different domains of social relations.

In the quotation from Aspinall above, it is possible to see how the recognition of religion as a form of identification for certain individuals and groups comes at a time when 'faith communities' are playing an increasing role in the implementation of government policies. This, together with a shift to a 'top-down' generation of topics in the funding of research (Lewis, J., 2000), can serve to ensure that particular definitions of the meanings of ethnicity predominate. But, it is also the case that forms of racism and discrimination based upon religion are on the rise (Richardson, 1999), and religious identifications can also take on varying levels of significance in relation to changing local and global relations (see Eade's (1997a) work on young 'Bangladeshi Muslims' in London). For instance, there has been both an increase in Islamaphobia reported by British Muslims following the destruction of the World Trade Centre in New York in 2001 and strong identifications with religion among young British Muslims (ICM Research, 2002). Religious identification can thus be an important, but also a changing part of the lived experience of different groups, in which traditions, practices and beliefs can vary between individuals, making generalization difficult (Hall, 2000).

In recognizing a context-related, and also complicated use of categorical approaches to 'race' and ethnicity, I do not wish to suggest that we should accept such approaches as part of a pragmatic research practice (see Smith, 2002). Rather, in pointing to areas of complexity and ambiguity, I want to uncover and examine how we might work with the contorted relations between research and lived experience (see Chapter 2). These relations are at the heart of the 'everyday' dilemmas that researchers encounter and in which there can be several levels of tension, from the funding of research to epistemological concerns.

Trends in the funding of research, for example, stress the need for social science research to be seen as 'relevant' and 'useful' for addressing 'everyday' concerns – with 'usefulness' being interpreted in relation to the need to build and support policy and practice (Lewis, J., 2000). At the level of epistemology there can be related tensions between the need to work with highly defined categories of ethnicity in order to undertake research that challenges social inequalities, and the recognition that such categories are socially and historically contingent and situated (see Modood et al., 2002 and Smith, 2002 for a debate about ethnic categories in research). These tensions are further intertwined with lived experiences of 'race' and ethnicity (see Chapter 2) and with identity politics (Clifford, 2000).

DANGEROUS CATEGORIES

This broad discussion of examples in the history of research on 'race' and ethnicity is relevant in thinking about how we conduct qualitative research on 'race' and ethnicity today. The horror of eugenics in its nineteenth-century versions is, thankfully, no longer with us. Yet the drive to categorize 'race' and ethnicity, and to apply these categories to groups defined primarily by their 'race'/ethnicity (and more recently religion) still lingers (see Chapter 2). In recognizing the historical contingency in the meanings and use of racial categories, I want to foreground what I see as a fundamental political and methodological danger of an unproblematized reliance upon categorical approaches to 'race' and ethnicity in qualitative research. This danger relates to how categorical approaches can serve to reify 'race' and ethnicity as entities that individuals are born into and inhabit, and that are then brought to life in the social world, rather than 'recognizing' race and ethnicity as dynamic and emergent processes of being and becoming. The conceptual 'fixing' of 'race' and ethnicity is dangerous in terms of the limitations that it can place upon analysis, and because it can serve to produce and reproduce wider forms of essentialism, stereotyping and racism (see Chapter 2).

My argument is that at the beginning of the twenty-first century, the drive to racial categorization needs to be understood in relation to complicated postcolonial relations that are played out on a global stage and have a localized impact upon our research (see Chapter 8). By postcolonialism, I am not referring to a singular and definitive overcoming of colonialism, such as that often represented in the post-1945 breakdown 'of direct rule, governance or protectorship by an imperial power' (Hall, 2000: 213), and the reconfiguration of colonial power into new modes of transnational interdependence, multicultural social formations and more diffuse forms of governance.

As critics of concepts of postcolonialism have pointed out, such an understanding of postcolonialism is flawed both in its totalizing impetus and in the assumption of a clear-cut 'post' (McClintock, 1995; Radhakrishnan, 1996). Rather than using postcolonialism to refer to a specific historical moment, I use the term to refer to the ruptures and shifts in epistemology that are made and are required when we engage with, and recognize the fundamental distinction between the 'West/Rest' that underpins contemporary global relations (Sayyid, 2000), and which marks all identities. As Ahmed states:

> post-colonialism is about re-thinking how colonialism operated in different times in ways that permeate all aspects of social life, in the colonised and colonising nations. It is hence about the complexity of the relationship

between the past and present, between the histories of European colonisation and contemporary forms of globalisation. That complexity cannot be reduced by either a notion that the present has broken from the past ... or that the present is simply continuous with the past ... To this extent post-coloniality allows us to investigate how colonial encounters are both determining, and yet not fully determining, of social and material existence. (Ahmed, 2000: 11)

RESEARCH THROUGH THE POST-COLONIAL

Drawing upon Ahmed's conceptualization of postcolonialism as a signification of material and epistemological encounters between the past and present, I want to highlight two central challenges to methodology and epistemology in trying to break out of the constraints of racial thinking. For the sake of clarity, I will address these challenges through the concepts of relationality and multi-sited research.

Relationality

When applied to research on 'race' and ethnicity, I use the first concept of *relationality* to refer to the epistemological break with thinking of 'race' and ethnicity as unitary, hermetically sealed, homogenous categories of difference. Engaging with the relational production of 'race' and ethnicity involves recognition of the long, differentiated and convoluted history of colonialism that has meant that all contemporary social differences are marked by and are constituted through 'race', and that consequently 'race' is also marked by and constituted through its relationships with other social differences. In this sense, categories of gender, sexuality, class, age or disability, for example, are also understood as categories that carry racialized meanings.

The recognition of this discursive interlacing of social differences means that the 'majority'/'minority' binary, which is so prevalent in racial thinking, is disrupted (Brah, 1996), so that whiteness is de-centred as a 'pervasive normative presence' (Bonnett, 1996: 97), as we come to understand it as a racial category, i.e., socially located, internally differentiated and unstable. My understanding is that research that thinks through the postcolonial, is research that is involved in a 'race riot' at the epistemic level, overturning the understanding of 'race' and ethnicity as neutral, unitary and ahistorical categories, and demonstrating the social construction of the categories and their connections to other categories of difference.

A closely related epistemological break engendered by an engagement with the concept of relationality, concerns the erosion of a system of knowledge production and analysis based upon categorization, coherence and stability, and a move towards a recognition of more contextual, contingent and ambivalent forms of knowing. If we recognize that post-coloniality and related processes of globalization and multiculturalization are unsettling the traditional binary meanings of 'race' and ethnicity, and that these categories are always inscribed by multiple forms of difference, then categorization as we know it is disrupted. We can no longer equate 'race' with biological difference, or ethnicity with place-based culture (Bhabha and Comaroff, 2002). Research on 'race' and ethnicity must now develop analytic frameworks that are capable of addressing the relational and situated nature of identities, and their production, negotiation and contestation at the social and subjective levels.

Brah's conceptualization of *diasporic space* provides a good example of what forms such a critical analysis might take. In relation to 'race' and ethnicity, Brah has used the concept of diasporic space to recognize how the dynamic movement and negotiation of culture is reconfiguring the meanings of ethnicity, and other forms of social difference, for *all* individuals and groups. Hence, 'diasporic space' is used to refer to 'the entanglement ... of the genealogies of dispersion with those of "staying put"' (Brah, 1996: 209). Using England as an example, Brah suggests that difference is played out and negotiated at many levels so that:

> African-Caribbean, Irish, Asian, Jewish and other diasporas intersect among themselves as well as with the entity constructed as 'Englishness', thoroughly re-inscribing it in the process ... in the post-war period this Englishness is continually reconstituted via a multitude of border crossings ... These border crossings are territorial, political, economic, cultural and psychological. (1996: 209, emphasis in original)

In terms of methodology and epistemology, diasporic space as a product and a producer of postcolonialism can be understood as being both about changing social, historical and inter-subjective relations, *and* the gaps that are forced open and created within knowledge. In this respect, it is not so much that the task of researching 'race' and ethnicity is getting more complicated – it is that key analytic approaches and concepts have to be challenged and transformed (see Chapter 2).

What this means in relation to social research is that it is not enough to address the marginalization and the pathologization of minoritized experiences in research, by simply focusing analytic attention upon these experiences, or by attending to the inadequacy of racial and ethnic categories in research by an obsessive expanding and refining of categories (Barker et al., 1994). Such practices can reverse processes of analytic marginalization, but they continue to constitute 'race' and ethnicity through the same discursive system, based upon fixed binary categorizations between a normalized, dominant whiteness and negatively valued, pathological or deviant 'Others'.

My contention is that research needs to examine and to map the specific contextual meanings and emergent properties of 'race' and ethnicity, and it needs to break down binarism by uncovering and working through the tense entanglements, interdependencies and junctions between categories and social relations. What such a theoretical project involves when applied to research on 'race' and ethnicity is a reflexive, analytic doubleness (see Chapter 2). This doubleness entails being able to address the historical particularity *and* the plurality of racialized and ethnicized difference, at the same time as interrupting binary systems of knowledge production. It also means tracking the production and effects of social difference across geographical and cultural spaces (see Chapter 8). It to this process of analytic mapping that I now turn.

Multi-sited research

The second analytic challenge in researching 'race' and ethnicity is the move beyond the vacuous relativism that all experiences of 'race' and ethnicity are socially constructed and relational. This move will seek to uncover the *specific* nature of the practices involved in producing particular forms of social difference at particular moments, while making these practices accountable to histories of colonial relations and to our own 'semiotic technologies' (Haraway, 1988: 579). Hence, the epistemological challenges of thinking and working with 'race' and ethnicity as socially constructed, relational categories brings us to methodological practices and to an ethics of connection and responsibility in research, in becoming accountable for what we do and the knowledge that we produce. I have found Marcus's (1998) concepts of multi-sited research and of complicity of great value in this respect, because of the potential they offer in connecting a postcolonial analytic with local research practices.

I have devoted Chapter 8 to a discussion of how the concepts of multi-sited research and complicity might be used in qualitative research on 'race' and ethnicity. For the purposes of this discussion, I want to highlight a concern with multi-sitedness as a cartographic strategy that seeks to examine research relationships with continual reference to history, and to a complicated web of spatial and social relations. This means moving beyond banal acknowledgements of relationality. It means moving towards a focus upon specific embodied practices and interrelations in research, towards the detail of how difference is produced and has effects within specific sites, and towards an examination of how these forms of difference might be connected across very different social spaces and experiences. In this sense, a multi-sited analytic – and complicity with its concern with a practice of care and connection in research – is critical to a methodology that seeks to connect experience, knowledge and ethics. What I want to examine throughout this book is what such a circle of experience, knowledge and ethics might look like, and what practices will need to accompany it in its subversive application.

A SUMMARY OF THE BOOK

In so far as the chapters in this book attempt to interrogate methodological and epistemological legacies, *and* to challenge and transform existing approaches to researching 'race' and ethnicity, they are all concerned with the role of research in transforming the racial order. Chapter 2 builds upon the analytic themes in this chapter, and addresses the fundamental epistemological and methodological tensions in research on 'race' and ethnicity, in terms of what Radhakrishnan (1996) has called the 'treacherous bind'. The 'treacherous bind' names and describes the dangerousness and the contradictions of our continued use and reliance upon racial and ethnic categories that can be complicit with racial typologies and thinking. Rather than condemning all research on 'race' and ethnicity as ultimately oppressive, I argue that what we need is a 'doubled' research practice that is capable of working both with and against racialized categories, and which is able to make links between lived experience, political relations and the production of knowledge.

Part II of the book is dedicated to an examination of debates about 'interracial' research in quantitative and qualitative research. These debates occupy a significant epistemological and methodological space in empirical research concerned with 'race' and ethnicity, and as such are a key site for the production of racialized discourses and practices. In this sense, I do not see the debates and the dilemmas about racial/ethnic matching and about 'commonality' and 'difference' in empirical research as simply reflecting our individual, methodological connundra. As Billig et al. (1988) argue, dilemmas are cultural products, which have a history based in the tensions and the contradictions of modern ideologies.

It is with this recognition of the *social* nature of our individual dilemmas that I have examined the debates on interracial interviewing. My argument is that the literature on interracial interviewing does more than just describe methodological 'problems' and concerns with regard to researching 'race' and ethnicity. I argue that the literature – as an example of research as a discursive practice – is also produced by and produces racialized and ethnicized social relations. I will demonstrate how the process of research, being actively involved in the production of the social meanings of 'race' and ethnicity, takes place at two main levels: through the racialized (gendered and classed) occupational structures of social science institutions that structure the micro-interactions of research encounters, and through the epistemological assumptions that are made, and then acted upon, about the nature of racialized subjectivity, inter-subjectivity and difference.

Chapter 3 uses American debates about 'race-of-interviewer-effects' in survey research to track relations between the construction of 'race-of-interviewer-effects', the social and historical context of the research and the micro-interactions of survey interviews. By examining critically the suggestion that research participants are less willing to tell interviewers from another racial group what they 'really think', I uncover and address assumptions about a single 'truth' and about the unreliability of the racial-ized research subject that pervade the literature. Chapter 4 focuses upon debates on interracial research and ethnic 'matching' in qualitative research, and examines the contributions to the debates from feminist and minoritized researchers. Through this examination I problematize the privileging of 'race'/ethnicity in interview interactions, and address the ambivalent repercussions that this privileging has had for racialized occu-pational structures and relations within the academy.

While all of the chapters engage with experiences of research and with practice, those in Part III of the book are centred upon empirical research. In these chapters, I draw upon my experiences of ethnographic research on the production of 'race' and ethnicity in a hospice setting (Gunaratnam, 1999)[2] to examine in detail some of the analytic, ethical and methodological challenges that can be faced in qualitative research concerned with 'race', ethnicity, difference and social justice. The aim of these chapters is to pro-vide an *in-depth* examination of different aspects of the doing of research. In order to take this 'in-depthness' seriously, I have concentrated upon a small number of examples which provide a close-up working through of key methodological, epistemological and ethical dynamics and dilemmas.

I have used this analytic approach in order to make explicit some of the detail that can be glossed over in broadbrush approaches. This detail includes attention to my own methodological practices and interrelations within research encounters, and their implications for the generation of knowledge. These are dynamics that have traditionally been marginalized and/or seen as not legitimate for discussion in books on methodology. However, this position is being challenged radically by feminist researchers (Haraway, 1988; Reay, 1996b; Ribbens and Edwards, 1998; Visweswaran, 1997) and researchers working with more psycho-dynamic models of the research process (Hollway, 2001; Hollway and Jefferson, 2000). My inten-tion in making explicit my own practices and interactive movements in the case study examples is not an introspective 'navel-gazing'. It is about challenging the hygienic, transcendent 'view from nowhere', and about making more transparent the fine-grained detail in which research is situated and constructed, and can also be judged.

That the case studies are drawn from research based in a hospice is highly significant. It means that the examples that I use in Part III often concern experiences that are marginalized or are unrecognized within popular and academic discourses. Postcolonial theory, for example, has only recently begun to address disability (see Quayson, 2002; Thomson, 2002), and a significant focus in the discipline remains upon 'youth' – where 'race' and generation have also come to stand for able-bodied and physically healthy. In addressing the construction and negotiation of racialized identities that are particularly marginalized, an underlying theme in Part III explores the challenges to epistemology and methodology of recognizing and engaging with a diversity of racialized experiences.

Chapter 5 focuses upon the 'problem' of how we can analyse racialized identifications and how we can address 'race'/ethnicity in accounts where it is not talked about in direct ways, or where it is embedded. In this regard, the chapter addresses a very basic and general analytic concern – how we can approach the analysis of 'race' and ethnicity in the research partici-pant's account. The chapter describes and uses an analytic approach sug-gested by Knowles (1999) of disassembling 'race', by examining the ways in which it acquires meaning through different narrative themes in accounts of individual lives. This analytic approach is read through a theoretical understanding of 'race' as a 'metalanguage' (Higginbotham, 1992) that can be both hyper-visible and invisible in its intersections with other social differences.

Chapter 6 examines the production and interpretation of noticeable insecurities of meaning in research encounters. I argue that attention to ambiguities of meaning can provide researchers with valuable analytic and ethical insights into the nature and the negotiation of social, interactional and biographical difference in research encounters. The discussion is based upon the analysis of an insecurity of meaning from a qualitative interview with a working-class, black, African-Caribbean man 'Edwin', who had prostate cancer. Through this discussion, I make explicit an interpretive process based upon movements of contextualizing, de-contextualizing and re-contextualizing ambiguous meanings. The chapter engages with ethical concerns and dilemmas, through a discussion of researcher accountability to the 'refusing subject' (Visweswaran, 1997), where ambiguities of mean-ing can also convey a resistance to and a negotiation of the subject posi-tions that are produced and made available in the research encounter. In relation to Edwin, these subject positions are examined through discur-sive relations between emotions and the body in constructions of black masculinities.

Chapter 7 draws attention to the often neglected spatial dimensions of qualitative research interactions, through discussions of what have been defined in the methodological literature as 'threatening' or 'sensitive' topics. Engaging with this literature, I suggest that the production of threatening topics should be seen as a dynamic co-construction between the researcher and research participant, within the psycho-social spaces of research interactions. My theorization of psycho-social space builds upon the work of the social theorist and social geographer Henri Lefebvre (1991), who has highlighted the active construction of social space and the power relations that are involved in this process. I argue that it is only by situating and tracing the production of topic threat within research interactions that we can uncover and examine some of the interrelations between emotions, social space and difference.

The final chapter, Chapter 8, uses a discussion of complicity and multi-sited research (Marcus, 1998) to bring together the politics of care and connection that I have suggested should be an integral part of research concerned with 'race' and ethnicity. In this chapter, particular attention is given to an exploration of relations of complicity between the researcher and research participant, as a way of mapping the micro-interactions of research encounters into broader contexts. This cartographic strategy is seen as being particularly important in terms of situating and connecting the research encounter to broader global processes.

Ultimately, all of the discussions in the book hinge on examining and making explicit the different ways in which questions of 'race' and ethnicity are central to all qualitative research. An additional aim of the discussions is to explore how we might produce and develop methodological, epistemological and ethical practices that, in uncovering and attending to 'race' and ethnicity as socially produced categories, can provide a means of disrupting and challenging the oppressive power relations that can flow from racial thinking.

SUGGESTED READING

J. Stanfield (1993) Methodological Reflections: An introduction. In J. Stanfield and R. Dennis (eds), *Race and Ethnicity in Research Methods*. Newbury Park, CA: Sage, pp. 3–15.

L. Tuhiwai Smith (1999) *Decolonizing Methodologies: Research and Indigenous Peoples*. London: Zed Books and University of Otago Press (Chapter 1).

F.W. Twine (2000) Racial Ideologies and Racial Methodologies. In F.W. Twine and J. Warren (eds), *Racing Research, Researching Race*. New York: New York University Press, pp. 1–34.

NOTES

1. The Daniel study is notable because, in addition to two surveys carried out with 'immigrant' and 'white' samples, the study also used a series of 'situation tests' to examine racism in the areas of housing, employment and 'commercial services' in six English towns. In these tests:

first a coloured immigrant, then a white immigrant of Hungarian origin, and finally a white Englishman applied for what seemed to be available to all people irrespective of colour or ethnic origin. In each test the three applicants had equivalent occupational qualifications or housing require-ments. The results from the housing tests speak for the whole survey: when applications were made for private letting or purchase, the West Indian was discriminated against on two thirds of the occasions when the Englishman received a positive response; the white alien [sic] was also discriminated against, but on many fewer occasions. (Daniel, 1969: 13)

2. This research combined forms of observation, participant observation, 32 one-to-one interviews with 23 hospice service users from African, African-Caribbean and South-Asian backgrounds, and 14 group interviews with hospice staff (the majority of whom were white women). Hospices provide care and support for people with terminal, and sometimes chronic illnesses. I became interested in exploring 'race' and ethnicity in hospice care because of my own experiences of caring for my mother when she was diagnosed with cancer of the pancreas in 1992. She died seven weeks after her diagnosis, at home and with support from a hospice 'home care' team.

A 'treacherous bind': working with and against racial categories

SUMMARY

This chapter engages with debates about the use of racial and ethnic categories in research, and discusses concerns about the ways in which processes of categorization can reinforce and reproduce racial thinking. Through this discussion I also address relationships between theory on 'race' and ethnicity, empirical research and lived experience. The chapter will help you to think about how you might develop a research practice that is able to work against the limitations of categorical approaches to 'race' and ethnicity.

In this chapter I want to address a critical and – for some researchers – a fundamental tension in research concerned with 'race' and ethnicity: that is, how our reliance upon, and our use of racial and ethnic categories in research, can itself be involved in reproducing dominant conceptions of 'race' and ethnicity (Smith, 2002; Stanfield, 1993c). By 'dominant conceptions' I am referring to particular political formations of social meaning (discourses) that produce 'race' and ethnicity as discrete, homogeneous, fixed categories of difference, with 'race' functioning primarily, though not exclusively, as a signifier of biological difference, and ethnicity as signifying cultural difference and heritage (Hall, 2000). Yet, this is only part of the story, and context is everything. It is also the case that these very categories, when mobilized by socially marginalized individuals and groups in asserting claims to personhood, can be less about a preservation of oppressive racial hierarchies and can be more about ambivalent, situated and strategic moves to transform such hierarchies (Clifford, 2000; Yegenoglu, 1998), and to invent new discursive positions within them (Mama, 1995).

This chapter will provide a critical discussion of these issues and their implications for qualitative research concerned with uncovering and addressing the complex, dynamic and socially situated effects of racial and ethnic categorizations. I will argue that researchers are in a 'treacherous bind' (Radhakrishnan, 1996) in researching questions of 'race' and ethnicity, because we are thinking with concepts at the limit (Derrida, 1981). In this respect, I point to the need for a 'doubled' research practice (Lather, 2001b), in which researchers need to work both *with* and *against* racial and ethnic categories at the levels of epistemology and methodology. This doubled research practice will be elaborated by reference to conceptual approaches and their application in empirical research, which will provide examples of the opportunities and the problems that researchers can face.

WORKING AGAINST ESSENTIALISM

A central tension that I want to highlight at the outset of this discussion is how researchers can work with the inadequate racial and ethnic categories that are to hand, whilst also finding ways of identifying and disrupting the ways in which these same categories can 'essentialize' (Said, 1985) 'race' and ethnicity, where:

> To essentialise is to impute a fundamental, basic, absolutely necessary constitutive quality to a person, social category, ethnic group, religious community, or nation. It is to posit falsely a timeless continuity, a discreteness or boundedness in space, and an organic unity. It is to imply an internal sameness and external difference or otherness. (Werbner, 1997: 228)

Processes of essentialism and their uses in research can be witnessed in the driving impetus to categorize the bodies, experiences, practices, and even the thoughts, of individuals and groups in relation to 'race' and ethnicity. A glance through journal articles concerned explicitly with 'race' and ethnicity – nearly always in relation to groups racialized as 'ethnic minorities' – provides numerous examples. There are articles that claim knowledge about 'the perceptions of Pakistani and Bangladeshi people', or 'the needs of the Chinese community', or 'the African experience' where the narratives/experiences of some individuals are used to represent all of those in the racial/ethnic category (Narayan, 2000), erasing differences within the categories. At the same time, whiteness is naturalized and left to stand as a de-racialized (and also often a de-ethnicized) norm, with 'race' being the defining property and experience of 'Other' groups.

These categorizing tendencies and their repercussions are not simply confined to the realm of knowledge production. They also affect our 'beingness' (the ontological), from the intricate and surprising detail of everyday interactions, to policy-making and wars. In constituting individual and group experiences and identifications, racial and ethnic categories have implications for how we understand and challenge the complexities of racism at these different levels. For example, our analytic approach to the meanings of the categories, and their intersections with other social divisions, affects how we might recognize and make sense of different experiences of racism among minoritized people and how these differences might affect group identifications and political mobilization (see Elam and Chinouya, 2000). The risks of essentializing 'race' and ethnicity in research are thus caught up at many different levels with the 'racial order' (Omi and Winant, 1994), and have implications for the nature of research that is concerned with uncovering oppression.

An important point that underpins my argument here is that the categorizing of *all* social identities, for example in relation to gender, class, sexuality or disability, is an essentializing and reifying political process in which the categorizing of 'race'/ethnicity, while specific, is not exceptional:

> Any attempt to think about social identities is based on an erasure of internal difference and divisions … How populations are classified and formed into clusters is ultimately a political process. All social identities are heterogeneous since they do not have an essence that can guarantee their homogeneity. Thus, it would be impossible to ground empirically the homogeneity of social identities … Homogeneity is an effect of articulatory practices, an articulation that rests upon exclusion and not the uncovering of some deep underlying essence. (Sayyid, 2000: 40)

What is of importance, then, in how we work with categories of 'race' and ethnicity in research, is the analytic attention given to how essentialism can construct particular racialized effects at any given time, and how these racialized effects may intersect with, and/or obscure other forms of social and personal difference. Why and how, for example, might the category 'Chinese' come to stand for the experiences of a diverse group of people, and in doing so also come to signify some degree of homogeneity and stability of experience? What effects does such homogenization have upon the economic, social, political, interpersonal and emotional lives of people identified as being in that group? And what effects does such homogenization have upon how we might examine, understand and represent these economic, social, political, interpersonal and emotional dynamics?

Using the work of social theorists who have addressed the complexities and the contingency of 'race' and ethnicity as one part of a wider, heaving dynamic of social differentiation (Brah, 1996; Hall, 2000;

Radhakrishnan, 1996), I want examine how research might engage with and work against the erasures and exclusions of categorization at the level of knowledge production and in the recognition of multiple forms of beingness.

THE 'TREACHEROUS BIND': RESEARCHING 'RACE' AND ETHNICITY

No sooner do we mention 'race' than we are caught in a treacherous bind. To say 'race' seems to imply that 'race' is real; but it also means that differentiation by race is racist and unjustifiable on scientific, theoretical, moral, and political grounds. We find ourselves in a classic Nietzschean double bind: 'race' has been the history of an untruth, of an untruth that unfortunately is our history ... The challenge here is to generate, from such a past and a present, a future where race will have been put to rest forever. (Radhakrishnan, 1996: 81)

The 'treacherous bind' of 'race' and its close relationship to racism is an ever-lurking presence in research. It has implications for all researchers who are concerned with social difference and with how research can be used to challenge racism and oppression. As Hall (1996; 2000) notes, 'race' – and related concepts such as ethnicity, identity, diaspora and multiculturalism – are so 'discursively entangled' (incapable of 'pure' meaning) that they can only be used 'under erasure'.[1] Following Derrida (1981), Hall's reference to concepts operating 'under erasure' signals a *deconstructive* approach that recognizes our relation to concepts that have passed their analytic sell-by date, that are no longer 'good to think with', but which have yet to be replaced.

For Hall, in the interval, 'there is nothing to do but to continue to think with them – albeit now in their detotalized or deconstructed forms, and no longer operating within the paradigm in which they were originally generated' (1996: 1). Recognizing 'race' as a concept that operates 'under erasure' – a concept that cannot be thought of in the 'old way' as representing essential, discrete differences between groups, but which we still need in order to address and dismantle racism[2] – speaks to the dangerousness (the 'treacherous bind') of research on 'race' and ethnicity evoked by Radhakrishnan (1996).

Let me unpack some more of this line of theorizing in relation to current debates and scholarship. 'Race' has now been discredited as a category of 'real' biological difference (hence the scare quotation marks that surround it; see Gilroy, 2000; Jones, 1981), and has been theorized as involving political processes of classification (Miles, 1982; 1989; Omi and Winant, 1994). The demise of 'race' as a purely 'objective', descriptive category connoting 'natural' biological difference, together with the increasing influence of post-structuralist and post-colonial scholarship, has led to theoretical approaches that have conceptualized 'race' and ethnicity as socially constructed, relational and socially located (Brah, 1996; Lewis, G., 2000; Radhakrishnan, 1996). That is, 'race' and ethnicity have been seen as variegated *social* categories that are in a constant state of production and negotiation with other forms of difference, and within specific social, historical and interactional arenas, whilst also serving to constitute these arenas.

In this regard, 'race' and ethnicity are not positioned in isolated and ranked opposition to other forms of differentiation. They are always seen as co-constituted and reconstituted through their interrelations with other social categories (Bhattacharyya et al., 2002; Lewis, G., 2000), *and* with regard to specific configurations of power which both differentiate and situate the meanings of particular racial and ethnic categories in relation to others (Brah, 1996).

Winant, in an exposition of 'racial formation theory', has made clear some of the relations between processes of 'race' made through categorization and classification, and the production of the 'racial order':

racial formation theory suggests that race has become a fundamental organizing principle of contemporary social life. At its most basic level, race can be defined as *a concept which signifies and symbolises sociopolitical conflicts and interests in reference to different types of human bodies*. Although the concept of race appeals to biologically based human characteristics (so-called phenotypes), selection of these particular human features for purposes of racial signification is always and necessarily a social and historical process. There is no biological basis for distinguishing human groups along the lines of 'race', and the sociohistorical categories employed to differentiate among these groups reveal themselves, upon serious examination, to be imprecise and arbitrary. (Winant, 1994: 270, emphasis in original)

THEORY, METHODS AND EXPERIENCE

There are three main methodological points that I want to make in relation to these deconstructive and anti-essentialist approaches to 'race' and ethnicity that, I believe, offer us a more effective and ethical way of working with the 'treacherous bind' of racial and ethnic categories in qualitative research. First, to examine and to uncover processes of racialization and ethnicization in research (how racial and ethnic categories are produced and given meaning), whilst also wanting to address the fictional nature of 'race' and ethnicity as pre-given, homogeneous categories of difference, is an ambivalent and a complicated position for a researcher to be in. What I mean by this is that our very concern with naming and examining 'race' and ethnicity (often in order to uncover oppressive relations of power), always runs the risk of reproducing 'race' and ethnicity as essentialized and deterministic categories that can (re)constitute these very power relations. In addition, our theoretical concerns, and how we do research, are related to us as individuals, to our social location (as racialized, gendered and classed for example) and to our 'speaking selves' (Probyn, 1993), which also need to be accounted for in the production of knowledge. There is no way of getting away from these complicated relations, although there are ways in which we can use them theoretically and methodologically in practices of reflexivity that 'allow us to become answerable for what we learn how to see' (Haraway, 1988: 583).

Second, as those who have engaged critically with social constructionist approaches have argued, there is something of a perverse relationship between the theoretical recognition of 'race' and ethnicity as social categories that contain and overflow with multiple meanings, and 'the real, present-day political and other reasons why essentialist identities continue to be invoked and often deeply felt' (Calhoun, 1994: 14, quoted in Ang, 2000: 2). What I am referring to here are the convoluted relationships between social theory and lived experiences of racialized identities and identifications. It is not simply a case of working through the tensions and contradictions in the relationships between theory and experience (Ang, 2000) – of addressing, for example, how at the time I was writing this chapter, I was singled out and stopped by an Indian man and his daughter in the middle of London and asked where India House was. When I told them I didn't know, the man laughed and said 'You're not Indian are you?', to which I replied without any hesitation, 'No. I am Sri Lankan'.

These very real contradictions refer to just one aspect of the relation between theory and experience that I want to call attention to. The other is about how the essentialism of research methods based upon rigid categorizations, which give primacy to one form of difference over another, can at times tap into the essentialism of common-sense experiences and feelings about identities. As much as I feel uncomfortable in recognizing it, methods that employ essentialist categories of 'race' and ethnicity do have some level of resonance with lived experiences and this is something that we need to both address and interrogate rigorously. As I have argued in Chapter 1 with regard to census categories of ethnicity, the degree of resonance between the categories and lived experiences and identifications can be influenced by political and funding agenda (Aspinall, 2000). However, this is not to suggest an uni-directional causal pathway between social structures and lived experience.

The third point, and very much related to the preceding one, is that despite theoretical understandings of 'race' and ethnicity as relational and socially constructed, there is still a voracious appetite for approaches that freeze, objectify and tame 'race'/ethnicity into unitary categories that can be easily understood and managed. In health service provision for example, where much of my research has taken place, there has been a proliferation of what I have called 'fact-file' approaches to 'race' and ethnicity (Gunaratnam, 1997). These approaches include not only the pamphlets, books and training resources that contain compartmentalized information on different ethnic and religious groups, but also policy-driven approaches that want tidy, no-nonsense (often described as 'practical') information and research about the racialized/ethnicized care needs of different groups. Within such a context, where funding is also often given to research into the needs of specific ethnic groups, without a problematizing of ethnic categories it can be difficult for researchers to challenge or resist the essentialist assumptions that are a part of funding criteria.

Categorical approaches, based upon reified and reductionist conceptualizations of ethnicity, are also prevalent – and are desired – within the social sciences, but not in such obvious ways. For example, a longstanding and persistent area of debate in research on 'race' and ethnicity is that of interracial research (see Chapters 3 and 4). Researchers want to know, and some researchers also want to advise others, about what they should do when their research involves working across racialized and/or ethnicized differences. Can 'white' researchers ever gain access to the 'true' feelings/attitudes/opinions and stories of racialized Others? Don't minoritized research participants feel more able to talk to researchers from a similar racial/ethnic background? Should specific efforts be made to match the 'race'/ethnicity of the researcher and research participant (see Papadopolous and Lees, 2002)?

It is not difficult to see how approaches detailing methodological strategies, practices and 'solutions' – how some research participants voiced their preference for researchers of their own 'race'/ethnicity, confessional stories of what really made a difference – have an eager audience. Yet, when we recognize that 'race' and ethnicity are socially produced, that their specific effects both constitute and are negotiated through other social differences, and that research encounters are themselves very layered (see Bhavnani, 1993; Hollway and Jefferson, 2000), then highly prescriptive 'solutions' to the challenges of researching 'race' and ethnicity become untenable. It is with regard to these complicated dynamics that we need to develop research that both recognizes *and* disrupts essentialism in the ways in which racial categorization can be produced, encouraged and put to work in research. We need to recognize and care about lived experiences of 'race' and ethnicity, and we also need to resist and challenge the appetite for essentialism in research.

DOUBLED RESEARCH

In order to develop a theoretical and political approach to researching 'race' and ethnicity which addresses the tensions, contradictions and dilemmas that I have identified, it is helpful to think of and approach research as a 'doubled-practice' (see Lather, 2001b). For me, this means challenging and seeking to transform the essentialism of categorical approaches to 'race' and ethnicity in research. It also means connecting theory with lived experience, where the claiming of personhood through categories of 'race', ethnicity, gender and sexuality, for example, needs to be recognized and examined critically as part of a potential move towards social transformation. Through this critical recognition I think that we can begin to explore possibilities for a future 'politics of radical indeterminacy' (Radhakrishnan, 1996: 62), outside racial thinking.

Radhakrishnan, in an attempt to conceptualize ethnicity through post-structuralism, has suggested that:

> The theory that we are looking for may have to fulfil all of the following requirements: it must divest itself from economies of mastery and yet empower the 'ethnic' contingently and historically; it must generate critical statements even as ethnicity is affirmed, endorsed, and legitimated; and it must be able to conceptualise the 'postethnic' as a radical and necessary extension of the 'ethnic'. (1996: 65)

What Radhakrishnan draws attention to so beautifully are two analytic movements. First, the ethical need for intellectual projects to move outside of an abstracted mastery, and to connect with local struggles and with experience. And, second, the need for reconciliatory work between two temporalities of 'short-term ethnicity' (marked by 'oppression, memory and enforced identity') and 'radical ethnicity' ('heterogeneous difference'). In other words, an approach to 'race' and ethnicity that works against the essentialism of racialized difference in the 'here' and the 'there', and the 'now' and the 'then', whilst working for an 'empowerment and enfran-chisement of contingent, heterogeneous "identities"' in the future (Radhakrishnan, 1996: 71). The move is one which seeks to outstrip systems and processes of categorization and through this process breaks down the possibilities of categorization itself.

I am aware that all of this can sound 'good' but idealistic and abstract, in a way that can seem far removed from the 'reality' of research and every-day life. What does it mean for the way we do research and how we approach 'race' and ethnicity in the projects we are involved with? How can we move towards a dynamic analytic practice, when we also have to define and fix the meanings of 'race' and ethnicity in order to do empiri-cal research? In taking these questions seriously, and in order to make this discussion less abstract, I want to examine examples of qualitative research that point towards what a doubled research practice might involve, conceptually and empirically.

TOWARDS DOUBLED RESEARCH

In this section I will examine approaches to empirical research and analysis used by Avtar Brah (1996), Gail Lewis (2000) and Kum-Kum Bhavnani (1993) that I have found extremely valuable in working with and thinking about how we might negotiate the 'treacherous bind' of racial and ethnic categories in research. Avtar Brah's theorizing of 'difference' provides a sophisticated analytic framework for working with categories of 'race' and ethnicity in ways that are neither reified nor reductionist. Gail Lewis's interpretation and application of Brah's approach to empirical research enables us to examine and evaluate the use of such a conceptual framework in practice; and Kum-Kum Bhavnani's focus upon methodology and the process of doing research provides examples of how we might produce more complex representations of the production of 'race' and ethnicity within research projects.

Avtar Brah: conceptualizing 'difference'

In her 1996 book *Cartographies of Diaspora*, Brah offers a layered reconceptualization of 'difference' through the four modalities of 'experience', 'social relation', 'subjectivity' (how individuals make sense of themselves at both conscious and unconscious levels) and 'identity'. For Brah, the analytic value of this approach to categories of difference, is that it enables us to break down the totalizing effects of categories and to examine how difference is animated and brought to life. In terms of 'race' and ethnicity this means examining how racialized boundaries are produced, their content, their consequences and salience for individuals and social groups, and their associations with other forms of difference – none of which can be taken as pre-given. What Brah's analysis emphasizes is the simultaneous distinctiveness and connectivity of collective and individual experiences of 'difference', where:

> These sets of 'differences' constantly articulate, but they cannot be 'read off' from each other ... how a person perceives or conceives an event would vary according to how 'she' is culturally constructed; the myriad of unpredictable ways in which such constructions may configure in the flux of her psyche; and invariably, upon the political repertoire of cultural discourses available to her. Collective 'histories' are also, of course culturally constructed in the process of assigning meaning to the everyday of social relations ... The same context may produce several different collective 'histories', differentiating as well as linking biographies through *contingent specificities*. In turn, articulating cultural practices of the subjects so constituted mark contingent collective 'histories' with variable new meanings. (1996: 117, emphasis in original)

Within such an analytic schema, the once-and-for-all privileging of a single category of difference, in any one site of social life, is displaced in favour of a more multi-dimensional framework in which the constitution of difference is intimately and variously connected to subjective and social elements. What is so valuable about Brah's approach is that her attention to subjectivity brings questions of being and of experience into consideration, but always within a context of historical, social and material relations. This means that the linear connections between 'Pakistani's' and 'their perceptions', or whatever other factors we are interested in tying to 'race'/ ethnicity, are broken as we are forced to account for the specificities of the ways in which 'we are both structurally located and actively occupy a number of subject positions open to us' (Lewis, G., 2000: 133).

Difference in Avtar Brah's (1996) analytic approach is conceptualized in relation to discourses and practices across four dynamics:

- *Difference as experience*: 'a notion of experience not as an unmediated guide to "truth" but as a practice of making sense, both symbolically and narratively, as a struggle over material conditions and meaning' (p. 116).
- *Difference as social relation*: 'refers to the ways in which difference is constituted and organised into *systematic* relations through economic, cultural and political discourses and institutional practices. That is to say that it highlights *systematicity across contingencies* ... the concept of social relation [does not] operate[s] at some "higher level of abstraction" referencing the "macro" as opposed to the "micro-context" ... these spheres have always been interlinked, but they articulate in quite unique ways in the present historical moment' (pp. 117–18, emphasis in original).
- *Difference as subjectivity*: 'Subjectivity – the site of processes of making sense of our relation to the world' (p. 123).
- *Difference as identity*: 'identity may be understood *as that very process by which the multiplicity, contradiction, and instability of subjectivity is signified as having coherence, continuity, stability: as having a core – a continually changing core but the sense of a core nonetheless – that at any given moment is enunciated as the "I"* (pp. 123–4, emphasis in original).

In summary, Brah's concern with the relationship between different modalities of difference and the construction and negotiation of meaning, turns attention to 'the processes whereby a category is invested with particular meanings *without* ourselves taking recourse to discursive strategies that take meaning as pre-given' (1996: 245, emphasis in original). In terms of doubled research, this strategy means that although we might use particular categories of ethnicity, such as 'Pakistani' or 'Ugandan', in order to do research with individuals and/or social groups who might identify or be identified with these categories, we can neither take for granted the meanings or the effects of these identifications, nor can we ignore their relationships to other categories of difference, such as age, disability and gender.

Drawing upon Brah's conceptualization of difference, my argument is that while there must be temporary moments of closure in the defining of racial and ethnic categories in order to do research, these points of closure must also be opened up again in the process of doing research and in analysis. They must be opened up in ways that enable us to look at and hear *how* 'race' and ethnicity are given situated meaning within accounts, and how meanings can be both secured and made more ambiguous and uncertain (see Chapter 5). Who, for example, is included and who is excluded in these processes of meaning construction and identification? How are the categories internally differentiated? How do particular ethnic identifications relate to others?

Gail Lewis: difference and empirical research

The value of Brah's approach, understood as a doubled research practice, and how it might be applied to empirical research, can be witnessed in Gail Lewis's study (2000) of 'black women' social workers in England. In this study, Lewis uses Brah's conceptualization of difference in interpreting aspects of her qualitative interviews with 32 'black and Asian' women social workers. In addition, Lewis argues that Brah's formulation of difference can be used to enable social workers to recognize ethnicity in their work as a socially produced category that carries multiple meanings. At the heart of Lewis's analysis is the 'charting of a set of connections which move from the macro-social, to central/local government relations, to local/professional discourses' (p. 205). Through her interviews with the social workers, Lewis instigates an intricate destabilization of categories of social identity in which she draws particular attention to the mutually constitutive nature of the categories of 'race' and gender in the women's accounts, and to the co-construction of accounts within the research relationship.

In her analysis of her interviews with the social workers, Lewis examines how dominant professional discourses of 'race' and ethnicity within social work had the effect of positioning minoritized service users and social workers in essentialized categories. Specific attention is given to how policies of 'same-race' placement for the adoption and fostering of black children within social services departments opened up the recruitment of black social workers, who were positioned as having the necessary 'cultural knowledge' that departments needed. However, what Lewis then goes on to demonstrate are the nuances of how the women negotiate and contest these racialized positionings in their everyday working lives. Whilst some women adopted and used essentialist notions of the difference between 'black' and 'white' people to give meaning to their workplace relations and professional practice, others challenged the homogenizing effects of racial categories.

By locating the interview accounts within micro-interactional *and* broader social and organizational contexts, and by then using her analysis to uncover the points of difference within individual accounts, Lewis is able to show the

> impossibility of a foundational or essentialist view of 'race'/ethnicity or one which abstracts these categories from the social and occupational formations in which these differences are enacted. (2000: 154)

What is of particular interest in Gail Lewis's work is her two-sided approach to difference – as an analytic resource for researchers in making sense of the multiple and shifting meanings of social identities within empirical research, and as a tool that can be used by practitioners (in this case social workers) in challenging essentialist notions of 'race' and ethnicity in their work. In relation to this latter point, Lewis argues that reconceptualizing difference in social work through Brah's modalities of experience, social relation, subjectivity and identity, will allow for the recognition of 'race' and ethnicity as being in a constant state of becoming, for both service users and social workers themselves:

> What will be at play at in any social worker/client encounter is not only the complex intersection of relations of power along numerous axes within which the client is positioned and which structure her life – but also the set of complexes which position and structure the social worker's life ... The factors which act to bring any to the fore in a given circumstance cannot be predicted or reduced to any assumed primary or foundational modality. (2000: 132)

Although Lewis is discussing the social worker/service user relationship here, the points that she makes are extremely relevant in considering practices of ethnic matching in qualitative research (see Chapter 4). That is to say, the move to challenge essentialism at the conceptual level becomes much more than 'merely' theoretical. Reading Lewis's approach within the context of a doubled research practice thus enables significant connections to be made between the recognition of the multiple meanings of difference in relation to the conceptualization of 'race' and ethnicity, *and* in relation to methodological practices. These connections lay important foundations for exploring the different layers involved in doubled research and for connecting theory with practice.

Kum-Kum Bhavnani: 'reinscription, micropolitics and difference'

Kum-Kum Bhavnani's work provides a further example of an approach to qualitative research that seeks to challenge essentialism and to make links between analytic approaches and methodological practices. In an article in the *Women's Studies International Forum* in 1993, Bhavnani used an engagement with Donna Haraway's (1988) work to identify criteria and principles in implementing the goal of 'feminist objectivity' in empirical research. In developing Haraway's conceptualization of feminist objectivity as 'situated knowledges', requiring 'positioning', 'partiality' and 'accountability', Bhavnani used her own experiences of qualitative research with African-Caribbean, South-Asian and 'white' British young people to develop the three criteria of *'reinscription'*, *'micropolitics'* and *'difference'* that, she suggests, can be used to evaluate feminist research. Bhavnani's central concern, that within feminist research 'points about racisms, exclusion and [the] invisibility of women of colour' (1993: 96) should not become silenced, provides considerable scope for the criteria to be used in developing and evaluating methodological and analytic practices in research informed by questions of 'race' and ethnicity.

- *Reinscription:* for Bhavnani, feminist research should not be complicit with dominant representations that can reproduce social inequalities. Bhavnani suggests that researchers need to ask themselves two main questions: 'Does this work/analysis define the researched as either passive victims or as deviant?' 'Does it reinscribe the researched into prevailing representations?' (p. 98).
- *Micropolitics:* refers to whether the research findings discuss the micropolitical processes involved in the research: 'what are the relationships of domination and subordination which the researcher has negotiated and what are the means through which they are discussed in the research report?' (p. 98).
- *Difference:* Bhavnani suggests that researchers ask: 'In what ways are questions of difference dealt with in the research study – in its design, conduct, write-up, and dissemination?' (p. 98).

Drawing upon her own research, Bhavnani describes how she avoided reinscribing the young people within dominant representations as 'politically apathetic', by refusing to take their views about politics at face value, and by using the narrative links made by the young people within their accounts as a way of understanding how they positioned themselves in relation to wider social discourses about political opinions. How Bhavnani did this can be seen in following extract:

The suggestion was implied by many of the interviewees that their views about, for example, the Labour Party were not legitimate because the speaker did not see her/himself as intelligent. Thus intelligence came to be seen as a necessary requirement for being able to comment on parliamentary parties. This link between democracy and 'intelligence' provided by the interviewees led to an unexpected opening. That is the young people in this study were not necessarily politically apathetic, but rather, these young people understood the playing out of democracy in relation to levels of intelligence, and thus defined themselves as not intelligent enough to present *legitimate* opinions about political parties. Not that there was not interest there – just an implicit and explicit wondering whether their views were legitimate. (1993: 100, emphasis in original)

In relation to micropolitical interactions in research, Bhavnani focused upon the multifaceted nature of the power relationships between herself and the young people in the study, which had 'structural domination and structural subordination in play on both sides' (p. 101). By highlighting 'race', gender and class differences, and how these differences cross-cut the power asymmetry in research roles, no one site of difference is given exclusive analytic attention in making sense of the research relationships. Bhavnani is thus able to use an engagement with these complex interrelations to critique matching strategies in research (see Chapters 3 and 4), and also to make links between theory and methodological practice. Moreover, she has also suggested that when such micro-interactions invert 'usual' power relations in research, such as in Bhavnani's interviews with young white men, the play of differences can enable a 'sharper' engagement with power relations which can be glossed over when broad commonalities are focused upon. A key point of relevance in Bhavnani's discussion is the value of not only noting and bringing research interactions into view, but also of connecting them explicitly to the process of knowledge production (see Chapter 4).

Bhavnani's third principle in pursuing the goal of feminist objectivity is that of asking in what ways issues of difference have been identified and dealt with in a research project? The example that Bhavnani uses is that of differences in the ways in which young people talked about racism. While many of the white research participants suggested that racism was a 'natural' part of life and 'human nature', Bhavnani points to how some of the young 'black' people identified contradictions within racist discourses, and how others suggested explicit strategies for negotiating and challenging racism. In making sense of these differences, Bhavnani asserts that:

In suggesting that patterns of racist behaviour can be altered and eliminated, there is a consequent implication that, therefore, racism is not natural. That is, it is implied that racism in a result of social definitions rather than a biological inevitability of 'human nature'. It is this discontinuity of both identity and experience which can be generated if a sense of difference is built into the research process. (p. 103)

In this extract we can see shadows of Brah's more complicated conceptualization of 'difference as social relation' and its patterned and varying connections to the domains of subjectivity, identity and experience. However, at an analytic level, what Brah, Lewis and Bhavnani's approaches all provide, by breaking down the defining, encompassing nature of categories of 'race' and ethnicity, are ways of attending to the complex effects and mediations of ethnic and racial categories *in situ*. In this attention to localized dynamics, the discursive connections that ethnicity and 'race' maintain with the wider social and historical context can be traced and mapped. At the same time, we are also able to address how racial and ethnic categories are inflected and differentiated in the local, although it might appear *as if* they had unchanging, transcendent qualities and meanings.

This is a point that Homi Bhabha, in a published conversation with John Comaroff (2002: 22), has described as being particularly difficult to 'work on' experientially for the 'subject', and to 'work out' and represent analytically and theoretically for the researcher. A key point in relation to my argument about the value of a doubled research practice, is how anti-essentialist approaches can enable us to examine more fully the complexities and the heterogeneous effects of racial and ethnic categories for both researchers and research participants.

The examples of empirical research from Gail Lewis and Kum-Kum Bhavnani that I have highlighted as offering researchers valuable insights into a doubled research practice, were undertaken as doctoral research projects. Doctoral research can often afford researchers certain levels of autonomy – to define our research objectives, methodology and research outcomes – that can be far more restricted in commissioned, 'contract' research. In the next section, I want to examine a study funded by the UK Department of Health, to explore the particular possibilities and the constraints facing those seeking to work with and against racial categories in externally commissioned research.

ELAM AND CHINOUYA: A FEASIBILITY STUDY FOR HEALTH SURVEYS AMONG BLACK AFRICAN POPULATIONS

The Elam and Chinouya (2000) study that I am going to look at was a 'Stage Two' study of a three-stage research project conducted by the Joint Health Surveys Unit for the Department of Health. The aim of this qualitative study was to examine the feasibility of extending national health surveys to include black African populations living in the UK. The study consisted of in-depth interviews with 44 representatives of organizations working with people from Ghanaian, Nigerian, Somali and Ugandan community groups in London and Manchester.

What is noteworthy about this study is that right from the beginning of the research report, the researchers highlight the diversity and the difference within and between the defined ethnic groups in the project. In relation to the nature of diversity within populations, for example, the report draws attention to differences in migration histories; generational relations; experiences of education and employment; gender relations; family structures; ethnic sub-groups and 'tribes'; and identifications with being African. By addressing historical, social and subjective differences in the study populations, what the researchers make visible as the starting point of their analytic explorations are the variations within each racialized category. Thus, in relation to differences in experiences of migration, the report addresses the Somali population, describing them as consisting of more recent, involuntary migrants seeking asylum in the UK. Yet, this general description is immediately disturbed by the following caution:

> However, the types of people who have migrated from Somalia over the past fifteen to twenty years have varied as different sectors of the community have been affected by the changing nature of the conflicts in Somalia. During this time, changes in legislation for asylum seekers has had an impact on the type of support offered to people coming to the UK. (Elam and Chinouya, 2000: 3)

By pointing to racialized patterns of social relations and experience, and by then making these patterns more complex and contingent, the researchers do not use racial and ethnic categories in ways that gloss over intra and inter-group difference. Rather they strive to uncover difference at play within specific social spaces and historical moments. In the study we can see how the category of gender, for example, is not given meaning simply by reference to differences between men and women, but is also a category that is shown to be riven by ethnic, migration and class difference. In relation to 'race'/ethnicity, the study also makes it possible to discern differences in the forms of essentialism deployed in the self-identifications of African community groups and individuals within racialized contexts, and those used in the violations of racism (see Bashi, 1998; Werbner, 1997) against different African populations.

For example, despite the diversity pointed to within and between different ethnic groups, the Elam and Chinouya report notes how in interviews with 'community' representatives there was 'a strong desire to present communities as unified groups or at least moving towards unity' (2000: 18). Elam and Chinouya link this emphasis upon unity to recent events and the wider historical context, including religious views, colonial and post-independence experiences of government that emphasized national, rather than regional/tribal identifications, and experiences of being a minoritized group in the UK where there were reported advantages of 'overcoming differences and working together' (p. 19). Although the

Elam and Chinouya report rarely names racism directly, but instead tends to discuss it through more general references to social inequalities arising from experiences of migration, unemployment and poor housing, the study does enable insights into the tensions surrounding the essentialism of ethnic and racial identifications in lived experience.

This point – of research being able to address and to recognize situated differences in the use and deployment of essentialism – is an important one in working with the 'treacherous bind' of racial and ethnic categories. Pnina Werbner (1997), has provided a theoretical framework for making sense of these differences in forms of essentialism, through her distinction between *objectification* and *reification* in her work on racist violence. In Werbner's analysis, modes of objectification that are used in the self-identifications of minoritized people, are a 'rightful performance or representation of multiple, valorized and aestheticised identifications' (1997: 229). Reification, however, is theorized as ultimately 'representation which distorts and silences'. Forms of objectification, that Werbner sees as characterizing the 'everyday' identifications of minoritized individuals and groups (an identification with being 'African' for instance), are seen as representing a 'positive politics' that construct moral and aesthetic communities, that, over time, are contingent, shifting and strategic in their relation to other communities. In contrast,

> the communities essentialised by the perpetrators of violent acts of aggression are not imagined situationally but defined as fixed, immoral and dangerous. In being demonised they are reified. (1997: 230)

Werbner does not explore in any detail the exclusions that are also entailed in processes of objectification. Nevertheless, she has acknowledged the ambivalence of both 'everyday ethnicity' and racism, and their entanglements with complicated subjective relations of envy and/or desire across the Self/Other boundary. Her underlying argument is directed at the need to distinguish and recognize the 'violating ambivalences of racism' based upon subordination, exclusion and/or annihilation in specific sites of experience. The point that I want to make in relation to this discussion is that addressing and recognizing the situated nature of different forms of essentialism in the use of racial and ethnic categories and identifications, is an important part of a doubled research practice. This recognition can enable more layered and complicated understandings of the highly specific meanings and effects of 'race' and ethnicity in lived experience, which in turn can serve to challenge categorical thinking and to close the gaps between theory and lived experience.

However, a doubled research practice does not simply involve analytic challenges, but can also produce points of tension in the ethical position of the researcher in relation to funding agencies, relationships with research users and participants, the methods that we use and how the findings of research are used and represented (see Chapter 6). As I noted in Chapter 1, the funding of research – and also the funding of community services – can be based upon very rigid categories of ethnicity. Research that attempts to challenge the rigidity of categorizations employed among the users of research (such as government departments, charities, public sector bodies and voluntary groups) and research participants can be particularly threatening. Indeed, research studies rarely build in enough time for the development and sustaining of meaningful levels of involvement with users and research participants over the lifetime of a project (for an exception see Kai and Hedges, 1999; see also Lather and Smithies, 1997). There can also be difficulties with modes of funding that promote a 'closeness' with the users of research, yet do not address either the political tensions that such relationships can produce or how the views of some groups can get prioritized over others (Rappert, 1997).

Rappert makes the important point that:

> Attention paid to critical thinking or theoretical sophistication may suffer so as to secure long-term links. In situations of conflicting users' agendas, trying to conduct research in such a way as not to offend is, to say the least, practically, intellectually, and morally a difficult task to sustain. (1997, para 6.1)

From what is reported in the Elam and Chinouya study, it is not clear how these issues were dealt with throughout the study, and the research report is silent about the 'micropolitics' (Bhavnani, 1993) of the research relationships. Reflexivity and attention to the micropolitics of research relationships are issues that are rarely reported on in government-funded research, except in relation to ethnic matching strategies between the researcher and research participant(s). Interestingly, however, the Elam and Chinouya report highlights and challenges the essentialism of ethnic matching strategies, advocated by community representatives for the next stages of the study, where the researchers had recommended partnerships with community organizations and 'community researchers'. Elam and Chinouya note that:

> There was an expectation that research conducted by community members would be genuine, non-judgemental and tailored to community needs. However, benefits of matching need to be balanced against generational differences; regional animosity; and a reluctance to talk openly for fear of personal circumstances reaching community members in the UK and those in home towns of Africa. The latter concern arises from the strong links many Africans have with relatives in Africa; the desire to protect dependants living in Africa from problems people have in the UK; the stigma attached to poor health in general and to poor mental health, TB, and HIV in particular; and concerns that poor health may impede asylum applications. (2000: 9)

Doubled research, in its desire to challenge essentialism can thus face a series of difficulties and tensions, such as negotiating the differences in opinion about the meanings of 'race' and ethnicity between researchers and research users and participants. One way of engaging with such tensions is for research to become actively involved not just in the negotiation of users' views once a research project has begun, but also in their construction throughout the life of a study (Woolgar, 1997), when the views of researchers can also be subject to change as a result of the process.

Although the Elam and Chinouya study (2000), does not address these dynamics in relation to the researchers' own experiences in the project, the researchers do advocate the use of participatory models of research in the development of Stage Three of the study, and in engaging with diverse experiences within the study populations. Among the initiatives that Elam and Chinouya recommend are:

- that the identification of people of black African origin and their recruitment for surveys should be carried out in partnership with community organizations and community researchers
- multiple approaches to recruitment should reflect the diverse experiences within populations and ensure that approaches can meet the needs of those who are most 'isolated and vulnerable', such as people with chronic and stigmatized illnesses and those who do not speak English
- an involvement of community language speakers
- The composition of focus groups should be sensitive to preferences for single sex groups and generational, religious, tribal and political divisions.

In making these methodological suggestions, Elam and Chinouya go on to place models of participatory research within a wider political context, stating that:

> participation in survey research also rests on notions of citizenship and community responsibility. When people are not treated as citizens in many aspects of their lives it is unlikely that they will perform as citizens in other respects. People have to believe that the research will benefit their community. If the community is poorly treated or does not receive feedback or see any benefits, this belief will be difficult to sustain. (2000: 9)

The Elam and Chinouya research moves a considerable way beyond the crude essentialism that can characterize research on 'race' and ethnicity, by recognizing some of the complex differences that can inscribe racial categorizations. By addressing intra-group differences, such as those relating to migration, gender and religion, and also how these differences can be part of a constant process of change and negotiation, the study is able to convey some of the dynamism and socially located nature of the effects of lived experiences of 'race' and ethnicity.

However, in relation to Bhavnani's three criteria (Bhavnani, 1993), it is significant that, despite the importance given by the study to the process of doing research, the researchers fail to address the micropolitical inter-actions between themselves, the funding agency and the 'community rep-resentatives' involved in the project, and the implications of these for the production of the research 'findings'. Government-commissioned research can actively discourage attention to reflexivity on the part of researchers, however the failure to recognize and make explicit the micropolitics of research and their relations to knowledge production can serve to repro-duce research as the 'view from nowhere'.

This approach to research can enact a significant split between the positioning of research participants, who are constructed as having ethnic-ity, gender, class and so on, and researchers, who are positioned as dis-embodied and dis-located – except in discussions of ethnic matching. At an analytic level the complexities of the meanings of difference and how they are produced *through* research relationships can be both obscured and com-partmentalized. This obscuring and compartmentalizing process is a parti-cular concern in qualitative research, where research relationships have been seen as a valuable object of analysis in themselves, and as providing a means for investigating the production and negotiation of difference.

CRITICAL KNOWLEDGE

This discussion of examples of research that bring to the fore some of the complexities and difficulties of working with the 'treacherous bind' of ethnic and racial categories, brings us to the question of 'methodological economies of responsibility' that are a central concern in this book, and relate to how we might 'produce different knowledge and ... produce knowledge differently' (Lather, 2001b: 200).[3] This concern is, of course, much wider than the question of ethnic and racial categories, and relates to epistemological and political ambitions and the practical doings of research.

The point that I am making relates to the epistemological need to deconstruct ethnic and racial categories, *and* the simultaneous need to keep questions of the experience of categories – for *both* researchers and research participants – in view and open to examination. That is, to engage with lived, heterogeneous experiences of 'race' and ethnicity, beyond any simplistic sense of them being pre-given or 'authentic', whilst also recognizing the limi-tations of representing such dynamic and emergent experiences either 'objectively' or 'fully'. Rather, the hope is to create a critical methodological project, outside of the mastery talked about by Radhakrishnan (1996), in which social location as an unavoidable part of a situated production of knowledge is explored and connected to the deep complexities, inventiveness and hesitations of lived experience for research participants and researchers.

Judith Butler's (1993) work on gender performativity and its relation to the construction of the body, is instructive in working our way through the enormity of the conceptual, methodological and political questions that can confront us in taking up such a project. What I have found particularly valuable in Butler's work is how she has manipulated and exploited, irreverently, the limitations and paradoxes of the essentialist/constructivist divide in debates about the status of the body. One particular aspect of Butler's dense and complex theorizing that is significant to this discussion, is her drive to imagine against the ontological constraints imposed upon bodies, and to expand options for bodily life. An analytic device through which she does this is by working with purposeful contradictions. For example, in challenging ontological claims that legitimize certain bodies and ways of being, Butler makes the claim that there *are* abject[4] bodies – bodies whose existence and beingness is not recognized. She therefore institutes a discursive domain of being for those for whom it does not exist:

> it is not as if the unthinkable, the unlivable, the unintelligible has no discursive life; it does have one. It just lives within discourse as the radically uninterrogated and as the shadowy contentless figure for something that is not yet made real. (Meijer and Prins, 1998: 281)

Butler's approach is to 'hold out for' a conceptual apparatus which will enable abjection to 'operate' in ways that allow it to come out of the discursive shadows, but which does not allow it to become rigid, normative and paradigmatic.

In relation to this discussion of 'race' and ethnicity, it is important to think about and to envision what we might be 'holding out for' politically and conceptually, and how we might intervene in current methodological and political debates, particularly where they can appear to be so heavily reliant upon essentialism. How might we, in Butler's terms, contribute to the production of a discursive domain that will enable recognition of the complexities and contingency of ethnicity, as in Radhakrishnan's (1996) 'radical ethnicity', and in which we can transform an impoverished racialized vocabulary and imagination?

For Lather, the doubleness of such a goal lies in creating subversive variations within the repetition of categorizations. In relation to this discussion, it means recognizing that we cannot at present talk about 'radical ethnicity' within the current language and meanings of 'race'/ethnicity, without at some level repeating the essentialism of categorization. In this sense, 'The task is not whether to repeat but how to repeat in such a way that the repetition displaces that which enables it' (Lather, 2001b: 204).

In epistemological and methodological terms, what matters to me is how we might develop ways of thinking and working with categories of 'race' and ethnicity in qualitative research that question and disrupt categorization, and in the process bring about different ways of knowing, doing and being. In research, this can include strategies that avoid reinscribing research participants into prevailing representations (Bhavnani, 1993), or that draw attention to whom and to what becomes racialized/ethnicized and who/what is left outside racial/ethnic categories (Bonnett, 1998). In the same analytic breath, it can mean uncovering the power dynamics of processes of representation that work to try and fix the meanings of 'race' and ethnicity and obscure its interrelations with other social divisions (Brah, 1996; Lewis, G., 2000). It can mean staging analytic encounters between the people and the stories that appear to 'fit' readily into categories and those that are marginal and unsettle categorization (see Chapter 5). As I have argued earlier, such methodological practices are not so much about expanding existing racial and ethnic categories, but about risking and enabling subversive, marginalized and multiple representations of difference.

CONCLUSIONS

The doubled research practice that I have begun to outline here is one that is feeling and thinking its way through hugely uncomfortable, contradictory and challenging concerns. It is a practice that can go against the grain of current approaches and appetites that want clear, generalizable knowledge about 'race' and ethnicity, often under the guise of wanting to make 'real', 'practical' and inclusive changes.

In engaging with critical methodological and epistemological debates, and by using and interrogating my own experiences of research, I have kept in mind my own feelings and the experiences of peers and of students, of being lost and overwhelmed by research. In this sense the book is 'practical', in that I have tried hard to make explicit analytic frameworks, ethical questions and methodological processes that I have worked with/against in my own research. However, in recognizing that racialized fields and social relations are complex, dynamic and changing (Twine, 2000), I also recognize that these frameworks, questions and practices need to be worked upon and re-formulated in relation to research in different contexts.

There will always be a diverse range of approaches to research on 'race' and ethnicity of course, but for me, the value of a doubled research practice can be judged in relation to three main points. First, whether an approach is able to illuminate the heterogeneity, areas of ambiguity and the partiality within any category of difference, so that any individual or social group cannot be understood by reference to a single category of difference. Second, whether it is able to take account of the relational nature of social difference. And third, whether it can enable us to recognize the systematic patterning *and* the specific contingency of the connections between individuals and social contexts.

SUGGESTED READING

V. Bashi (1998) Racial Categories Matter Because Racial Hierarchies Matter: A commentary. *Ethnic and Racial Studies*, 21(5): 959–68.

A. Brah (1996) *Cartographies of Diaspora: Contesting Identities*. London: Routledge (Chapter 5).

S. Hall (1996) Introduction: Who needs identity? In S. Hall and P. du Gay (eds), *Questions of Cultural Identity*. London: Sage, pp. 1–17.

NOTES

1. Hall elaborates upon deconstructive approaches in an essay entitled 'Who needs identity?', where he argues that

   the deconstructive approach puts key concepts 'under erasure' … the line which cancels them, paradoxically, permits them to go on being read. Derrida has described this approach as thinking at the limit, as thinking in the interval, a sort of double writing. 'By means of this double, and precisely stratified, dislodged and dislodged writing, we must also mark the interval between inversion, which brings low what was high, and the irruptive emergence of a new "concept", a concept that can no longer be and never could be included in the previous regime' (Derrida, 1981). (Hall, 1996: 1–2)

2. This tension also runs throughout the fierce debates about the status of 'race' and ethnicity as analytic categories. These debates continue to rage in the social sciences. For an overview of some of these debates see Mulholland and Dyson, 2001; Smaje, 1997; Smith, 2002; Solomos and Back, 1994.

3. This discussion owes much to the work of feminist researchers who have questioned, troubled and re-thought the boundaries between theory and experience (see Lewis, G., 2000; Mohanty, 1992; Probyn, 1993; Scott, 1992).

4. Butler has always resisted the demand for examples because she has not wanted examples to become normative. However, in conversation with Meijer and Prins, scholars from the University of Utrecht, Butler has said that the abject body

   relates to all kinds of bodies whose lives are not considered 'lives' and whose materiality is understood not to 'matter'. To give something of an indication: the US press regularly figures non-Western lives in such terms. Impoverishment is another common candidate, as in the domain of those identified as psychiatric 'cases'. (Meijer and Prins, 1998: 281)

Debates and dilemmas in 'interracial' research

TWO

Faking 'race' or making 'race'?
'race-of-interviewer-effects' in survey research

SUMMARY

The North American survey research on 'race-of-interviewer-effects' marks a significant point of failure in the reliability of survey methodology in its attempts to know racialized difference. The research suggests that standardized survey questions and interview inter-actions are not 'race' neutral. Studies claim that research participants are less willing to tell interviewers from another ethnic/racial group what they 'really' think with regard to their attitudes and opinions about 'racial' topics. Through a discussion of this literature, this chapter will contest assumptions that certain racialized research participants are 'faking' the reporting of their attitudes, beliefs and experiences in interracial interviews. Rather than faking 'race', I argue that race-of-interviewer-effects are part of a dynamic process of making 'race' that makes possible new ways of understanding the production of racialized difference.

- The chapter will help you to think about some of the methodological, epistemologi-cal and political issues that are involved in approaches to interracial interviewing in both quantitative and qualitative research.
- A particular concern in this chapter is to examine the epistemological assumptions upon which race-of-interviewer-effects have been conceptualized, and how these assumptions relate to notions of racialized inter/subjectivity and 'truth'.

[...] the historical images of African-Americans role-playing and accommo-dating whites have surprising relevancy today. Symbolic of normal everyday interactions with whites, African-Americans are pressured by white inter-viewers to conceal their true political beliefs to the extent that they would disassociate themselves from black issues, and alternatively, appear more docile and accommodating. (Davis, 1997: 320)

An underlying assertion in the survey literature on interracial interviewing is that racialized difference between the research participant and interviewer can affect the 'genuineness' and 'accuracy' of what research participants say (Rhodes, 1994), particularly with regard to 'racial topics'. In research into survey methodology, the examination of interracial interviewing in the US in the 1950s and 1960s, which focused largely upon minoritized research participants, led to the concept of 'race-of-interviewer-effects' (RIE). This concept has been used to refer to the 'response bias' and 'measurement error' that has been recorded in the 'adjustment' that people make to their opinions and attitudes when questioned by an interviewer from another racial or ethnic group.[1]

There has been no comparative research in Britain into 'race-of-interviewer-effects' on the scale of the US research, however practices of ethnic matching in surveys in Britain have a long history and continue to be used. Ethnic matching has been justified largely with reference to the need for cultural and linguistic matching (see Nazroo, 1997; Rudat, 1994).

A survey into racism in Britain as early as 1966 (Daniel, 1969) used interviewers from Pakistani, Indian, 'West Indian' and Cypriot groups to interview research participants from the same ethnic backgrounds. In an appendix to the report of the survey, we are told:

> Prior to the main study a series of studies were carried out to develop the questionnaire and assess the use of white and coloured [sic] interviewers. The results showed that the success rate in terms of achieved interviews was somewhat higher for coloured interviewers. For some of the Indian and Pakistani informants the use of coloured interviewers was obligatory because of the language barrier. After the experience of the pilot studies the decision was taken to use immigrant interviewers for the entire sample. (Daniel, 1969: 248)

This chapter will provide an in-depth discussion of the North American RIE literature, particularly the early studies, through which RIE were first conceptualized. My argument is that this literature, and the research studies that investigated RIE (and which continue today, see Davies, 1997; Webster, 1996), provide valuable insights into research as a discursive practice (see Chapter 1), through which ideas about racialized subjectivity, difference and whiteness are produced and secured. By using the RIE studies as an example through which I can examine these complicated processes, I want to demonstrate and make visible the ways in which methodological practices, epistemological assumptions and the organization of social research are all a part of the social construction of 'race' and ethnicity that need to be recognized and investigated. In this sense, the chapter is highly relevant to contemporary discussions of interracial research in both quantitative[2] and qualitative research (this latter area is the focus of Chapter 4), particularly in relation to how interracial research has been constructed as a 'problem'. In contemporary research it is not unusual for research studies to exclude minoritized research participants, because they are seen as being difficult to access and because of language and cultural differences. The representation of minoritized research participants in research studies can also be marginalized. The UK's annual national 'Health Survey for England' (HSE), funded by the Department of Health, in order to help plan health services and promotion, provides such an example of marginalization. Elam and Chinouya have described the particular under-representation of black African people in the survey that interviews around 17,000 adults and 4,000 children in their homes:

> Despite the large scale of the HSE, in 1996 only 131 people taking part in the survey described themselves as having black African origins or other black ethnic origin ... In addition, about 1% of the overall non-response was due to households which could not be interviewed because they did not speak sufficient English. The low numbers of black Africans surveyed restricts the extent to which inequalities in health present among black African ethnic groups can be investigated. (Elam and Chinouya, 2000: 13–14)

The RIE research needs to be situated in this wider problematizing discourse of interracial research that continues to characterize contemporary research. In exploring the social, methodological and interactional dimensions of RIE, this chapter has been structured around the discussion of five main areas relating to:

1. The relations between 'race' and emotions in interracial research and RIE.
2. The relevance of discussions of RIE for qualitative research on 'race' and ethnicity.
3. A discussion of the research from some of the US studies into RIE.
4. The social and institutional context of the survey research and how these have contributed to the construction of RIE.
5. Epistemological assumptions about the research subject in survey research and how such assumptions are given different meanings through 'race'.

'RACE' AND EMOTIONS IN INTERRACIAL RESEARCH AND RIE

My examination of the research into RIE has been driven by two particular concerns that are themselves related in specific ways to the role of emotions in research. The first area of concern regards interracial research as a source of considerable anxiety for researchers; the second relates to assumptions about the emotionality of racialized research participants, and how these assumptions are related to broader attempts to manage and/or suppress emotions in survey research.

The whole area of interracial research is one that causes considerable emotional and methodological anxiety to researchers (see Anderson, 1993; Montero, 1977; Myers, 1977; Watson and Scraton, 2001). Despite RIE being comparatively small in comparison to other 'response effects' in survey research (Sudman and Bradburn, 1974), RIE can serve to justify these anxieties, by appearing to provide 'evidence' about the difficulties and the barriers to interracial communication. It is important to question this 'evidence', and the epistemological assumptions that can go with it, which are based upon particular ideas about racialized subjectivity and ideas about a single truth. I will do this by exploring the methodological 'ruins' (Lather, 2001a; 2001b) of survey research in the wake of RIE, to look at what we can learn from the failures of the research to produce 'valid' and 'reliable' knowledge about the nature of racialized difference.

Within survey research, 'race' and/or ethnicity have been conceptualized as 'objective', fixed qualities that individuals 'have' by virtue of biology and/or culture. 'Race' and/or ethnicity are assumed to have the same, stable meanings within groups, which can be examined and understood by asking standardized questions and manipulating tightly controlled interview conditions. What I want to suggest is that RIE serve *both* to secure such understandings of 'race' and ethnicity, *and* to make them shudder at the methodological and epistemological levels. At a methodological level, the variability in the reporting of opinions according to the 'race' of the interviewer, undermines the standardizing, generalizing impulse of surveys (see Box 3.1 for further explanation of the need for standardization in surveys and concerns with interviewer effects). At an epistemological level, the apparent defensiveness of the racialized research participant in not disclosing their 'real' thoughts and feelings on 'racial topics' in interracial interviews, suggests important emotional and interactional dimensions to 'race' and ethnicity that have implications for the conceptualization of 'race' and ethnicity as objective (largely demographic) categories.

My second concern is with how the conceptualization of racialized research participants as concealing their 'true' opinions about 'racial topics' posits a certain kind of 'research subject', raising questions about how racialized subjectivity is defined and what assumptions are implied. I will argue that the racialized research subject of the RIE studies is not only conceptualized as social (i.e., constructed by demographic difference, Hollway and Jefferson, 2000), but s/he is also acknowledged as having a limited, defensive emotionality. This research subject is one who is assumed to have a racialized un/consciousness and who is assumed to be deeply threatened by racialized difference. It is a research subject who is anxious and emotional, and whose responses therefore cannot be trusted.

Group working in survey research (Hyman et al., 1954), the scale of data generation, and the nature of the interview as a complex, inter-personal encounter, have all been seen as leading to the need for highly organized systems of the training, control and coordination of interviewers by survey organizations (Hoinville and Jowell, 1978). In terms of interviewing, this is manifested in the need for standardization between individual interviewers. The goal of standardization is to increase the reliability of data through the elimination of 'interviewer-related-error' (see Schaeffer and Maynard, 2002), one source of which has been identified as relating to the demographic characteristics of the interviewer.[3] According to Fowler and Mangione (1990: 98), 'The hope for standardisation … is that … interviewer characteristics are irrelevant and do not affect the answers that are obtained.' (See Suchman and Jordan, 1990 for a critique of standardization.) This approach to interviewing is in marked contrast to those who have suggested the epistemological value of RIE as an opportunity to examine the ways in which knowledge is situated (Phoenix, 2001).

Box 3.1 Standardization and the concern with interviewer effects

In the context of these assumptions, what I want to suggest is that there is a fundamental contradiction in the acknowledgement of the emotionality of the racialized research subject of survey research and how emotions are approached in survey methods and in analysis. For example, approaches to the standardization of interviews in survey research are based upon the need to, at best, de-emotionalize the interview and, at second best, to manage and/or suppress the emotions of both interviewers and research participants. Holstein and Gubrium have captured many of the methodological characteristics of survey interviews in their observation that:

> The interview conversation is … framed as a potential source of bias, error, misunderstanding or misdirection, a persistent set of problems to be controlled. The corrective is simple: if the interviewer asks questions properly, the respondent will give out the desired information … there is a highly sophisticated technology that informs researchers about how to ask questions, what sorts of questions not to ask, the order in which to ask them, and the ways to avoid saying things that might spoil, contaminate or otherwise bias the data. (1998: 113–15)

Yet, what the RIE research suggests is that the 'race' of the interviewer and the nature of particular racialized topics have emotional meanings in the interview that defy and confound the rationalist approaches of survey research. Work that I have done with Gail Lewis on emotional labour and the production of 'race' in social care organizations, is directly relevant to my argument here about survey methods and RIE. In theorizing the complexities and contradictions of emotional labour and processes of racialization in social care organizations, we have argued that

> systems and practices in social care organisations are based upon the suppression, repression and regulation of emotions that feeds [sic] into and off specific forms of the defensive splitting of emotions around racism for both practitioners and service users. (Gunaratnam and Lewis, 2001: 135)

Drawing upon this work I will argue that, despite an acknowledgement of the emotional dimensions of inter/subjectivity in certain areas of survey research (I am specifically thinking about RIE and more generally about research on 'threatening topics', see Chapter 7), surveys are centred upon the 'suppression, repression and regulation' of emotions in research (see also Gubrium and Holstein, 2002). More than this, I also think that there is a relation between such emotion management in the interview, and wider, emotional defensiveness in relation to 'race', ethnicity and racism. With regard to RIE, my argument is that there are connections between approaches to emotions in survey research and how RIE are produced and given meaning in the micro-interactions of survey interviews. This point runs throughout the following discussion, and I will return to it in more detail in the section on epistemology towards the end of the chapter.

HOW RELEVANT ARE DISCUSSIONS OF 'RACE-OF-INTERVIEWER-EFFECTS' FOR QUALITATIVE RESEARCH?

Despite my claims about the critical methodological and epistemological issues that are raised by RIE, you might still find yourself wondering how this survey research is relevant to qualitative research on 'race' and ethnicity? Why, in a book about qualitative methodology, have I devoted a whole chapter to a discussion of debates in quantitative research that originated more than half a century ago in the United States? How are the issues significant today, not only to researchers outside the US, but also to researchers using different qualitative methodologies?

In order to begin to address these questions in a less abstract way, I want to return to the point and place in which I am writing – England in mid-2001. A significant part of political attention to 'race relations' at this time has been due to the so-called 'race riots' in the north of England (see the 'Cantle' Home Office Report, 2001, for a government response to the 'riots'). In this discussion I want to focus upon the events that took place in Oldham.[4] Oldham near Manchester, has relatively large Pakistani and Bangladeshi populations. The overall unemployment rate is 4 per cent, but is 16 per cent among Pakistani people, and 25 per cent among Bangladeshi people.[5] In the summer of 2001, there were 'riots' in Oldham that were seen as having been started by 'Asian' youth. The media coverage produced a number of different images of 'race relations' in Oldham. These representations included claims that attacks by 'Asian gangs' had made parts of the town no-go areas for white people; that Asian youth were able to 'get away' with criminal activities because of police fears about allegations of racism if they intervened; and that racist attacks on Asian people were not taken seriously by the police. Following the 'riots' in May 2001, the national organizer of the far-right British National Party stood for election in the area, and Oldham was the focus for activities by other far-right groups such as the National Front, which had marched there in 1987.

'This has been a momentous year for race relations in the UK. In early summer, riots raged in Oldham and Bradford. Young British-Asian men fought the police as decades of simmering resentment exploded in an ugly rage. And in June, the BNP secured its best ever result in a General Election, gaining more than 11,000 votes in Oldham. A couple of months later, Fisat Dag, a 22-year-old Kurdish asylum seeker, was murdered in Sightholl, Glasgow. And away from these domestic events, the savage attack on America heightened tensions between different communities around the world as well as in Britain.'
    The *Observer*, 25 November 2001, 'Race in Britain'

What I want to do now is to ask you to consider the questions below that I have adapted from an American survey which investigated RIE[6] (Schuman and Converse, 1971). These questions were posed to African-American people by white interviewers in Detroit in 1968, following 'urban riots' and the assassination of Martin Luther King. I want you to imagine these questions being asked of Asian people in Oldham, by white, British interviewers (let us assume that some of these interviewers can speak different Asian languages such as Urdu, Hindi, Punjabi and/or Bengali) shortly after the 'riots'. Make a note of the issues and the feelings that they raise for you:

1. Do you personally feel that you can trust most white people, some white people, or none at all?
2. Would you say that because of the disturbance, Asians in Oldham now feel more ready to stand up for their rights, less ready to stand up for their rights, or that there hasn't been much change?
3. Some people feel that the summer's disturbance was a step forward for the cause of Asian rights. Other people feel that it was a step backward

for the cause of Asian rights. Which opinion comes closest to the way you feel?

4. Suppose there is a white shopkeeper in an Asian neighbourhood. He employs white shop-assistants but refuses to employ Asian assistants. Talking with him about the matter does no good. What do you think Asians in the neighbourhood should do to change the situation?

5. Some leaders want to organize Asians into groups to protect themselves against any violence by whites? Do you think it is worthwhile or not?

6. How do you feel we should refer to this summer's disturbance in Oldham? Should it be called a riot, a rebellion, or what?

7. Have you ever taken part in any kind violent protest?

I have thought myself into this interview situation, and have gone through the questions several times in order to make the RIE studies come alive for me. I have become aware of two main points while doing this activity. First, how racial categorizations and thinking can already be present, specified and produced within research before any encounter with research partici-pants has even taken place. By this I am referring to the productive power of racializing discourses within the questions themselves, which I will dis-cuss in more detail below. Second, how despite the standardizing drive of surveys (the need to keep interview conditions the same), survey research can generate *situated* knowledge, even though the complex nature of this knowledge can be obscured in quantitative analysis. By situated knowledge I mean the ways in which knowledge is inscribed by, and not separate from, its social location and context. In terms of this discussion, I am refer-ring to how difference as experience, social relation, identity and subjec-tivity (Brah, 1996, see chapter 2) can be an integral (but hidden) part of the ways in which survey research is conceptualized, and how questions are asked, interpreted and responded to within the interview at particular times and in particular places.

What I want to suggest is that the meanings circulating within the RIE questions (such as those above), and also when the questions are asked, in what order, to whom and by whom, can serve to racialize the interview encounter in highly specific ways. More generally, it is also very likely that responses to the same questions can change over time. A fundamental question here is how is it possible to make judgements about the truth-value of responses to such questions? (Box 3.2 provides an example from the Schuman and Converse study about how the researchers approached this issue.) For example, in the Oldham case, if I was asked the same ques-tions a week later by an Asian interviewer, and gave different answers to the questions, which responses would reflect my 'true' opinions and feel-ings? How much could any variance in my responses be related empirically to the 'race'/ethnicity of the interviewer alone?

'To settle the general issues of validity we would need somehow to obtain independent evidence as to attitudes and facts reported by respondents. For factual information such data are theoretically possible, but there is nothing of a factual nature in the present study that we are able to validate. From past studies there is one piece of evidence implying that more valid information comes from black interviewers. Price and Searles (1961) and later Pettigrew (1964) report that respondents were more often able to identify political leaders when asked to do so by black interviewers ... Assuming that the interviewers themselves performed in the same way, this result seems interpretable only in terms of suppression or repression of knowledge by black respondents when confronted by white questioners.'

'From our own data we have been able to devise only one hypothesis that bears directly on the issue. There are three interrelated assumptions: (1) the *attitude* of militancy should be positively associated with *behavior* indicative of militancy; (2) if the behavioral measure of militancy does not vary by race of interviewer, it can be assumed to be equally valid in *both* interviewing situations; (3) the *attitude* of militancy can be interpreted as more valid in situations where its relationship to militant *behavior* is stronger.'

'Our behavioral question asked whether the respondent has "ever taken part in any kind of nonviolent protest for civil rights". It does not show any difference by race of interviewer. Moreover, this behavioral measure of militancy is indeed positively associated for the total sample with an attitudinal measure of militancy ... when we separate out the two race-of-interviewer situations, we find a higher correlation between protest behavior and militant attitudes among those interviewed by blacks ... We therefore conclude that militant attitudes are more validly measured in the black interviewer situation.'
(Schuman and Converse, 1971: 59–60, emphasis in original)

Box 3.2 Validating 'real' responses in the Schuman and Converse 1971 study

Debates on interracial interviewing in qualitative research are useful in attending to the epistemological issues raised by such questions (see Chapter 4 for a more in-depth discussion about these debates). A British researcher, Rhodes, has argued that even though 'race' has an effect upon interview interactions and what research participants say, it is inappropriate to evaluate such differences in terms of their 'truthfulness'. Writing about the British context of white people interviewing research participants of African descent, Rhodes states that:

Critics of the practice of cross-racial interviewing argue that racism is an inherent feature of British social life. Black people's mistrust of white people in general will, therefore, be extended to the white researcher or interviewer, preventing access or, if access is obtained, distorting the quality of communication which ensues. The analysis assumes a single 'truth' which can be tapped through respondents' accounts and that the accounts given to the white interviewer will be a distortion of that 'truth'. Accounts are treated as either accurate or distorted representations of a single reality rather than as situated and contingent, creative mappings of a complex and multi-faceted reality or realities. (1994: 548)

The points that Rhodes makes reflect the influences of post-structuralism, which has challenged ideas about a stable, single 'truth' and has emphasized the contingent nature of meaning (Derrida, 1976; 1981). These points also have relevance with regard to the RIE studies. However, there are important differences between interracial interviews in quantitative and in qualitative research. The emphasis upon the standardization and the reliability of survey interviews constitutes a particular form of knowledge production based upon controlled, over-determined repetition.[7] Although I have theorized RIE as serving to disrupt this process of repetition through 'race'-related variation, there is limited information within the literature about the situated meanings of such variation, or the ways in which racialized difference might be given 'subversive' meaning in questions that (appear to) show no RIE.

Despite some of the careful research designs of the RIE studies in attempting to understand the complexities of the causes of RIE, the studies are grounded in rationalist, emotion-stripping approaches to researching 'race' and ethnicity. Such rationalism is characterized by positivist ideas about 'the disinterested observer seeking objective truth with universal validity that is based on the notion of a reality independent of human thought and action' (Huber, 1995: 204). Hence, many of the RIE studies are based upon an underlying assumption that the 'race' of the interviewer can be an obstacle that 'gets in the way' of the valid and reliable reporting of the research participant's 'true' opinions and experiences of 'race' and racism (see Chapter 4).

These rationalist approaches to research have been coming under growing criticism for their failure to address the irrational, unconscious, emotional dimensions of inter/subjectivity in research. Hollway and Jefferson (2000), for example, have drawn upon the ideas of the psychoanalyst Melanie Klein to theorize both research participants and researchers as 'defended subjects', whose sense of self is organized with regard to unconscious defences against anxiety. Box 3.3 provides further explanation of Klein's ideas about subjectivity. In addition to these unconscious dimensions of inter/subjectivity, for Hollway and Jefferson the research 'subject' is conceptualized as psycho-social, with anxiety being connected to social processes and discourses:

> unlike some psychoanalytic usages, anxiety is not treated simply as a psycho-logical characteristic. Though it is a feature of individuals, it is not reducible to

psychology: anxiety and the defences which it precipitates are complex responses to events and people in the social world, both past and present ... The concept of an anxious, defended subject is simultaneously psychic and social. It is psychic because it is a product of a unique biography of anxiety-provoking life-events and the manner in which they have been unconsciously defended against. It is social in three ways: first, because such defensive activities affect and are affected by discourses (systems of meaning which are the product of the social world); secondly because the unconscious defences ... are inter-subjective processes (that is, they affect and are affected by others); and thirdly, because of the real events in the external, social world which are discursively and defensively appropriated. (Hollway and Jefferson, 2000: 24)

What is valuable about Hollway and Jefferson's approach is that it enables a more complex reading of the responses of research participants and researchers, within the micro-interactions of the interview. Within this

---

The 'paranoid-schizoid' position and the 'depressive' position are two concepts that are central to Klein's approach to defensive anxieties. Gail Lewis has provided a clear summary of Klein's approach:

> For Klein (1975) the self is forged out of defences against anxiety and these defences are inter-subjective in that they come into play in interpersonal relations. Such interpersonal relations are, for Klein, present from the very first moments of life and manifest in the baby's search for her/his mother's breast. This action already figures as a pre-conscious awareness of a need for something outside of itself and it is this that both signals and provides the grounds upon which an individual's fundamental social character develops ...

> The problem is that negotiating this process of emergence to individuality through sociality and simultaneously acquiring the ability to make and sustain fulfilling and constructive relationships requires an ability to recognize and contain pain, loss, separation and difference. It involves dealing with negative feelings as well as positive ones. It is from this nexus that the defence of *splitting* emerges in which people are divided into loved and hated, good and bad parts (or groups). Associated with what Klein called the *paranoid-schizoid* position, splitting works as a defence against anxiety in at least two ways. First, by dividing a person (the 'object') to whom one has contradictory and ambivalent feelings into two separate parts, creating part objects of those elements associated with feelings of love and warmth, and different part objects for those elements associated with denial, hatred and fear. Second, this mechanism of splitting also works as a way of avoiding rather than working through those aspects of the self that are hated and feared. (Gunaratnam and Lewis, 2001: 142, emphasis added)

'For Klein, the attainment of psychic integration of good/bad, positive/negative approximates a state of wholeness' (2001: 144). This position has been called the *depressive* position and refers to the holding of ambivalence. (Gunaratnam and Lewis, 2001).

Box 3.3 Klein and defensive anxieties

frame, research participants' accounts are seen as being *co-produced* through the interview interaction in ways that are not always either conscious or rational, but which have biographical, emotional and discursive dimensions. In linking Hollway and Jefferson's account of the 'defended subject' to processes of racialization, it is possible to theorize how such psychosocial dynamics might also produce racialized difference as an emotional experience, a social identity and a practice (Gunaratnam and Lewis, 2001). What I want to suggest is that attention to constructions of 'race', ethnicity and difference through the emotional, when placed alongside attention to social processes, can enrich our understanding of the complex nature of the racialized dynamics in RIE. Yet this understanding is also a restricted one, because of the methodological approaches of the RIE studies that have provided limited information on the interactional components – or what Bhavnani (1993) calls the 'micropolitics' of the research (see Chapter 2). There are, therefore, many aspects of the nature of the micro-interactions of the RIE studies that we don't know about.

However, this chapter is not about setting the RIE studies up as a 'straw person', to be knocked down by the superiority of qualitative approaches to 'race' and ethnicity. Rather, my general interest is with exposing and facing up to the political nature of knowledge production (Gill, 1998), which confronts both quantitative and qualitative research on 'race' and ethnicity. I believe that RIE, in embodying the so-called 'defects' (Schuman and Converse, 1971) of survey research, provide valuable opportunities to examine and to transform the ways in which knowledge is produced about racialized difference. In this respect it is not enough simply to identify how knowledge about 'race' is both socially situated and contingent – it must also be held to account with regard to oppressive social relations in the past and in the present.

THE RACE-OF INTERVIEWER-EFFECTS RESEARCH

In order to begin exploring the connections between 'race' and interactional and social processes in the RIE studies, it is necessary to examine some of the studies in more detail. In this section, I give specific attention to a study by Schuman and Converse. Box 3.4 provides examples of some of the questions used in the survey by Schuman and Converse (1971) that used 'white' and African-American interviewers to interview a sample of African-American people living in Detroit in 1967. It will give you a flavour of some of the differences between questions that were said to produce the greatest and least differences in RIE.

In general terms, the US survey research has been seen as providing a somewhat varied and 'erratic' (Schaeffer, 1980) picture of RIE. However,

Questions with racial content that showed greatest difference by race of interviewer

Do you personally feel that you can trust most white people, some white people, or none at all?

Would you say that because of the disturbance Negroes in Detroit now feel *more* ready to stand up for their rights, *less* ready to stand up for their rights, or that there hasn't been much change?

Do you think Negro parents can work better with a Negro teacher or a white teacher?

Some leaders want to organize Negroes into groups to protect themselves against any violence by whites. Do you think this is worthwhile or not?

In your church has money ever been collected at Sunday service for the Civil Rights movement?

Do you think Negro teachers take more of an interest in teaching Negro students than white teachers do?

Do you think city officials in Detroit are *more* willing to listen to Negro demands since the disturbance, *less* willing to listen, or hasn't there been much change?

Questions with racial content that showed least difference by race of interviewer

Have you ever taken part in any kind of violent protest for civil rights?

Now that Martin Luther King is gone, who do you think is the single most important Negro leader in the country?

Do you and the white families that live around here visit each other's homes, *or* do you only see and talk to each other on the street, or do you hardly know each other?

Do you think you were ever refused a job because of being Negro?

Do you think there are many, some, or just a few places in the city of Detroit where a Negro could not rent or buy a house because of racial discrimination?

Do you think you have ever been discriminated against when you were trying buy or rent a particular house or apartment?

Do you feel that you personally have missed out on getting the kind of job you want and are qualified for because of race?

Box 3.4 Examples of questions used in the Schuman and Converse study (1971: 54–5, emphasis in original) there are three types of questions that have been identified as most likely to show RIE. The questions are those with an 'explicit "racial" content, those with social desirability or prestige implications, and those inquiring about support for established political and economic institutions' (Schaeffer, 1980: 407). One general but consistent suggestion from the literature is that the answers that research participants give to questions relating to *opinions* on particular 'racial issues', tend to reflect their attitudes more closely when interviewers are of the same 'race' as the research participant. This 'finding' has also been reflected in studies such as those conducted by Schaeffer (1980) and Campbell (1981), which examined RIE with regard to the data produced by 'black' and 'white' people interviewing both 'black' and 'white' research participants.

Schuman and Converse have suggested that in their Detroit survey, questions dealing with 'hostility' and 'suspicion' towards white people and 'identification with black militancy' showed large RIE. However, in over 90 per cent of the questions asked in their survey, there were said to be no significant RIE (even with 'race' – related questions). It was questions that involved the expression of 'direct' opinions about a racial group, i.e., questions that the researchers categorized as 'racial topics' that were found to show the greatest recorded effects. Schuman and Converse state that:

> Although in some sense any topic can have racial connotations, we have drawn an operational distinction between questions that employ racial terms bluntly ... ('Negro,' 'white,' 'race,' 'discrimination,' 'Detroit riot') and those that do not. We *assumed* that the respondent's awareness of his interviewer's race would be particularly heightened with questions that broach racial matters directly. (1971: 50, emphasis added)

In beginning to interrogate these assumptions about what constitutes a 'racial topic', with regard to the preceding discussion, it is important to reiterate how the historical and ideological meanings of language used in questions can operate to racialize the meanings of topics and interview encounters. The timing of the studies and the biographical and emotional meanings of 'race' in the interview interaction also need to be taken into account. So it is relevant that while the Schuman and Converse study was concerned with RIE, it examined these in relation to expressions of 'anti-white sentiment and militancy', 11 months after 'a major urban riot' in Detroit, and two weeks after the assassination of Martin Luther King. In other words, the study was conducted and located within a particular social context, in which questions of racial difference were in the spotlight – and were also a point of real tension – in the lives of the people living in Detroit.

Questions that ask African-American people about 'hostility' and 'suspicion' towards white people and 'identification with black militancy' at a time of racialized violence and 'unrest', are questions that do not only enquire into racialized identifications. They are also questions that *construct* a particular form of racialized inter/subjectivity. Thus, in the questions in the Schuman and Converse study, we can see the double movement of highly emotionalized and also discursive processes of race-making that contradict the rationalist approaches of survey research. By this, I am referring to how the Schuman and Converse questions signify 'race' through a defensive and a discursive splitting between a 'them' and an 'us'. This splitting can be seen as being produced through the design of the survey questions themselves, whilst also being given particular meanings in the interactions between interviewers and research participants within the interview. The critical point that I want to make is that the different emotional and social dimensions of these meanings cannot be adequately represented by the rationalist and categorical approaches of survey research.

It is important to note that not all surveys are based upon quantitative approaches alone; they can include ethnographic work (Kurokawa-Maykovich, 1977), phases of pre-survey qualitative research (see Hyman et al., 1954) or qualitative post-survey evaluations of the interview (Tizard and Phoenix, 1993), that can provide valuable information about interview interactions. One British study that discusses interracial interviewing, and which used qualitative post-interview discussions where research participants were encouraged to talk about their feelings about the interview, is the 'Social Identities' in young people study (Tizard and Phoenix, 1993). This study explored the social identities of 'race', gender and class in a sample of 248 'mixed-parentage, black and white', 14–18-year-olds and 70 of their parents. Of particular relevance to the discussion of RIE questions in the US studies is an example Ann Phoenix draws attention to, of criticism about the nature of the survey questions from a 'black' mother who was highly critical about the study, and told Phoenix:

> Some of the questions you could actually *feel* was a white person asking them, and some of them were so stupid that you could get the feeling that somebody was trying to get inside black people to find out what it is like. (Phoenix, 2001: 207, emphasis added)

The timing and the use of survey methods to examine the intimacies of racialized subjectivity by Schuman and Converse, and other RIE studies, is something that has great relevance to this discussion, bringing to the foreground issues of methodology, epistemology and ethics. These issues call attention to the connections and contradictions in quantitative approaches to 'private' racialized subjectivity, at times when minoritized people were denied full citizenship and were excluded from, or were marginalized in their participation in, various forms of public life (including employment by social science institutions). Motivated by the need to know (and to manage) racialized subjectivity when organized resistance to racism was growing (Smith, 1993), RIE can also be interpreted as a resistance by research participants to an easy accessing and categorizing of the meanings of racialized difference. In this regard, we might ask what right researchers have to enquire into intimate details about subjective experiences of racialized difference, and how they might earn this right (see Briggs, 1986 for a discussion of the 'right to know' in ethnographic research). It is also important to note the tensions between research into highly 'sensitive' and also highly complex areas of subjectivity and experience, and the nature of survey methods that, through their categorizing of responses, seek to define, control and limit what is knowable about lived experiences of 'race' and ethnicity.

Because there is much that we don't know about the ways in which minoritized research participants have reacted to being the increasing focus of the attention in social research, my discussion of RIE can be read as suggesting a certain lack of agency at the group level of the 'communities' in which surveys were conducted. This was certainly not the case, and there are some documented cases of resistance to research. One example that found, a multi-method project (Bengston et al., 1977) on older people from five ethnic groups ('black, Mexican-American, white, American Indian and Oriental') in Los Angeles, details how political pressure from community representatives from 'black and Mexican-American' groups led to the suspension of project funds at an early stage in the research. Community representatives objected to not being involved in the preparation of the grant proposal and to their tokenistic representation on the project advisory group. Comments from the representatives in terms of the objectives that they had defined for the project included the points that:

> the ultimate goal of the research project was to develop relevant information about aging ... A second goal ... was to have input into all the different phases of the research, from the policy-making level down to simple decisions ... A third goal was training of minority students ... Time and time again we have been told there are no professionals from our community. It is our belief that we have a strong responsibility to help push open the door at the universities for our young people. They are our future and they must be given an opportunity to educate themselves ... Another goal was the accessibility of the findings and the use of such information to improve the condition of the community. It was a prime concern that community groups be provided with the research findings so that proposals might be written and funded to bring services to the community ... Along with these goals, it was also the aim of the community group to establish communication between the university and East Los Angeles. Our community has suffered greatly from a lack of knowledge about how systems work and how they have failed our community ... It was believed that with this research project both the university and the community system would become more knowledgeable about each other. (Bengston et al., 1977: 81)

At a broader level, it is relevant that the RIE research itself gained prominence during the 1960s when the Civil Rights and Black Power movements were at their peak (Twine, 2000). Drawing attention to changes in the participation of African-American people in surveys, Smith (1993) has argued that, in the period before the 1960s, African-American people were frequently not asked their opinions on 'race'-related topics, because their responses were seen as being 'obvious'. Smith notes how this pattern of racialized exclusion from research changed with the Civil Rights movement[8]:

> Although exceedingly slow, by the 1960s a realization was developing among scholars that studying responses to questions about race relations in tradi-tional national surveys was not producing much knowledge about public opinion among Blacks. In part this realization was forced on survey researchers (especially the academicians) by their collective failure to warn the nation of the impending racial crisis, leading to widespread collective civil rights activity and to the race riots that followed. (Smith, 1993: 220)

In overview, it is possible to see that the survey research that first concep-tualized RIE presents us with a number of interesting, but problematic issues. At a general level, it alerts us to the construction and expression of particular forms of racialized difference within the interview, yet it also masks its own role in the production of such difference, and the extent to which this role has also been part of wider racialized social relations. In order to make more sense of these complicated processes, it is important to examine critically the relationships between the micro-interactions of the interview, the social context and racialized divisions in social science institutions. I will do this with regard to the US survey research, to demon-strate how attention to the wider social location of research, particularly with regard to institutional practices, can throw further light upon the nature of RIE. This process will, in turn, problematize the ways in which research methods and analyses produce, and are produced by, racializing categories and discourses.

SOCIAL SCIENCE INSTITUTIONS AND RACE-OF-INTERVIEWER-EFFECTS IN US SURVEY RESEARCH

The US RIE research was itself located within specific racialized, gendered and classed relations within the social sciences. Social exclusion and dis-criminatory practices in education and in employment have served to determine the types of interviewers used in survey research, obscuring the extent to which relations of 'race', gender, age and social class are a part of interview relations even before an interview has taken place. Fowler and Mangione have described how:

The vast majority of interviewers used in social science research in the United States are white females who have completed at least 4 years of high school education ... Moreover the pools of potential interviewers who are male, minority group members, or have not completed high school are comparatively limited ... For these and other reasons, there is a problem in disassociating the effects of interviewer demographic characteristics from differences due to experience, training or interests. (1990: 99)

In relation to my argument that RIE are a part of a situated, racial formation, it is important to explore how some of these institutional factors are entangled in the research on RIE, and also how they link to the social context in which the research was carried out. In the study by Schuman and Converse (1971: 47), the 'black' interviewing staff were said to consist mainly of 'older female professional interviewers employed by the Survey Research Center of the University of Michigan', and were described as 'moderate-appearing, middle-aged women' (p. 60). It is highly likely that many of these interviewers were recruited through black churches, which were commonly used by researchers to recruit black interviewers (Shosteck, 1977). The white interviewers in the Schuman and Converse study were described as young (in their twenties), graduate students, half of whom were male and half female. Schuman and Converse note that, 'Both black and white interviewing staffs were rather clearly middle class in economic and social terms' (1971: 47).

Many of the studies on 'race-of-interviewer-effects' provide scant information on the recruitment and training of minoritized interviewers into studies. A notable exception is a paper by Axelrod et al. in *Public Opinion Quarterly* in 1962, which provides a rich account of a range of issues relating to the recruitment of African-American interviewers for a survey on 'Negro Political Participation in the South'. The paper highlights the practical and political 'challenges' experienced by the study managers in recruiting and training African-American interviewers. These included the additional financial costs of recruitment, concerns about offending existing white interviewers, and difficulties in finding 'suitably qualified' individuals. The authors' commentary about their choices in recruiting interviewers and the reassurances that they felt they had to provide in training is both interesting and disturbing. For instance, Axelrod et al. state that in recruitment, 'efforts were made to eliminate both "race men" – Negroes [*sic*] active in agitational movements ... and "Uncle Thomas" types – the sophisticated accomodationists whose efforts to get along with paternalistic white leaders are resented by fellow Negroes' (1962: 258). The authors also state that in the subsequent training sessions, time was given to reassuring interviewers that the study was not 'anti-Negro'. They go on to argue that: 'Only by developing a strong identification with the study ... as well as confidence in the authors' fairness' (p. 260) could they overcome the 'dangers' of inaccurate reporting of 'embarrassing' or 'discouraging' responses by interviewers.

The racialized and class relations that were (are) embedded in the organization and the structures of survey research, can also be seen as being played out emotionally and spatially in the disruption of the planned random assignment of geographical 'clusters' of African-American housing units by the 'race' of interviewers in the study. For example, because their study was conducted soon after a 'riot' in Detroit and the murder of Martin Luther King, Schuman and Converse 'decided against sending white interviewers to certain areas because of the possibility of physical danger' (1971: 47). In fact, these 'certain areas' were poor areas, with the majority of sample addresses (65 per cent) earning less than $500 per month. Data on the level of black–white segregation in housing in Detroit between 1970 and 1990 further suggests that Detroit was an area marked by extreme forms of racialized segregation. It is likely therefore that the areas excluded from the study were the 'ghettos' of Detroit – predominantly black and poor, and associated with high levels of recorded crime and violence (Massey and Denton, 2000).

The failure to examine RIE using white interviewers in particular geographical areas because of racialized/class-related fears, was subsequently recognized as a 'doubtful' practice by Schuman and Converse. In a footnote to an article about the study, they state that: 'The need for the exclusion seems doubtful in retrospect: interviewers during the field period reported no instances of personal hostility of any type' (Schuman and Converse, 1971: 47). What is also noteworthy, in relation to class, is that social class was recognized as having an effect upon RIE in the study:

> race-of-interviewer effects are greatest among the lower-income and lower-educated blacks. The difference between extreme class categories is substantial. (Schuman and Converse, 1971: 65)

Schuman and Converse have said that they cannot adequately explain these racialized/class effects. However, such 'effects' do tell us something about the simultaneous, but differential intersections between 'race' and class, and how these intersections can undermine the primary attention given to 'race' in the RIE research. Within much of the survey research on RIE, we can witness the operation and primacy of 'race' as a 'metalanguage' (Higginbotham, 1992, see Chapter 5) that 'masks yet *contains* other axes of difference' (Lewis, G., 2000: 165, emphasis in original). It is only through searching out and making explicit the other social divisions that are carried by 'race' within the studies, that we can begin to understand the processes by which other social differences are produced by (and also sometimes cloaked by) 'race' in RIE.

What we learn from this discussion of the institutional context of the RIE studies is something more about how the predominance of racist and racializing practices in the social sciences have shaped, and been shaped by, the historical formation and constitution of social science organizations, the funding and conduct of research, and the production of knowledge about 'race'. Viewed in this way, the social context of the RIE research can be understood as having two main repercussions for the interpretation of RIE. First, the organization of survey research was itself neither 'neutral' nor 'objective', but was highly racialized, gendered, age-related and classed. These factors were, in turn, connected to the conduct of research, the production of interactions within interviews, and the nature of the knowledge that was/is produced about racialized difference at particular times. These dynamics can be seen as producing a certain interactional order within the interview, in which the racialized differences that are produced are simultaneously a part of wider social, historical and institutional relations, but are also given particular meanings in the micro-interactions within the interviewing process.

Second, in producing and analysing interview data, survey researchers do not simply 'reflect' the data, but construct and reconstruct racialized difference through, from and upon the data. They do this through epistemological assumptions about the research subject, through the design of research studies and through methodological practices. This complex interaction of factors both generates *and* obscures the production and negotiation of a range of social and subjective differences at these various levels. However, at an analytic level, attention is focused upon racialized differences that appear to be produced solely in the interrelations between the research participant, the interviewer and the research topic(s). It is precisely because of these multiple, shifting and complex interrelations in the constitution of 'race' at the social and the interactional levels, that it is misleading to talk about 'race-of-interviewer-effects'. Such a conceptualization not only deflects attention away from the operation of 'race' as a 'metalanguage' (Higginbotham, 1992) that can obscure the intersections of other social divisions with 'race', it also treats 'race' in research as if its effects were limited to interview interactions.

PRODUCING KNOWLEDGE ABOUT 'RACE'

Having discussed and described some of the relations between race, methodology and social contexts that are involved in the RIE studies, I want to return more explicitly to questions of epistemology and how knowledge is produced about racialized difference. What I want to focus upon is how epistemological assumptions about the 'validity' and 'reliability' of survey methodology are undone by racialized difference. In this sense, the RIE literature also gnaws away at the epistemological authority of survey research to know racialized difference through apparently standardized and rational methodological and epistemological practices. In order to examine the epistemological dimensions of this process in more detail, we need to consider more directly the nature of the subjectivity that is assumed in the survey research, and how such assumptions might be different when 'race', ethnicity and other differences are made visible and relevant to research.

Holstein and Gubrium (1998; Gubrium and Holstein, 2002) argue that in survey research, the research subject is assumed to be 'epistemologically passive', and is seen as a 'vessel-of-answers'. Under 'ideal' interview conditions, Holstein and Gubrium suggest that survey researchers assume that research participants should be able to give interviewers 'authentic' reports about their opinions, feelings and behaviours. Hollway and Jefferson, using the example of the British Crime Survey (Mirrlees-Black et al.,1996), have further argued that 'all survey-type research, makes certain assumptions about a research participant' (Hollway and Jefferson, 2000: 11). They characterize some of these assumptions as being based upon a research subject who:

- is knowledgeable about his/her experience (with regard to actions, feelings and perspectives)
- can access the relevant knowledge accurately and comprehensively (i.e., they have a reliable and accurate memory)
- can convey the knowledge to a stranger
- is motivated to tell the truth.

The work of those such as Holstein and Gubrium and Hollway and Jefferson is valuable in that it serves to uncover some of the hidden assumptions about research participants, and has also developed much-needed theory about inter/subjectivity in the interview. However, we also need to look more closely at the generalized claims that survey methodologies (and also some forms of qualitative research) 'fail to problematize the research subject who is seen, in consequence, as either socially constructed and/or rationally driven' (Hollway and Jefferson, 2000: 24).

We can see, for example, that in the case of the RIE literature, research participants in racialized, interracial interviews are indeed problematized. They are positioned as the constitutive 'Other' (see Chapter 1) to the rational, socially constructed research subject that those such as Hollway and Jefferson have seen as being assumed in survey research. Indeed, the research 'subject', when recognized as being racialized, is treated very differently in survey research: as emotional, irrational, uncooperative and deceptive. As such, the assumptions highlighted by those such as Holstein and Gubrium and Hollway and Jefferson reflect assumptions about *particular* research subjects in particular interactional and social contexts. I believe that the epistemological nature of such assumptions (which have been made by both minoritized and 'white' researchers), can be made more visible through attention to the RIE literature.

If we take the points that I have noted from Hollway and Jefferson above, we can see that the RIE literature suggests a somewhat different research subject. The assumptions that Hollway and Jefferson draw attention to and critique become difficult to sustain when we locate these assumptions with regard to 'race', ethnicity and other forms of social difference. For instance, from the research on RIE, we can see that research participants in particular interracial encounters are seen as not sharing meanings with the interviewer. They are seen as not being able to convey their experiences to the (stranger) interviewer, and they are seen as not being motivated to tell the truth. Similar assumptions about the subjectivity of research participants can be found in the literature on researching 'threatening' topics (see Chapter 7). Survey research on sexual behaviour, for example, assumes that research participants who have same-sex relationships and experiences are emotionally defensive and deceptive when talking about these experiences in the interview (see Wellings et al., 1990 for an example).

Taking relationships between social difference and epistemological assumptions into consideration, I would argue that in survey research on 'race' and ethnicity, particularly with minoritized research participants, the focus upon demographic difference is accompanied by more hidden assumptions about the racialized emotions, identifications and un/consciousness of research participants. Such assumptions are based upon a partial acknowledgement of the emotionality of racialized research subjects, who are positioned as being more emotional than those marked as 'non-racial' (i.e., certain white research participants in certain interviews). Racialized research participants are assumed to react to threatening questions on 'racial topics' by disguising or repressing their 'true' feelings and/or opinions. The racialized research subject of survey research is not only assumed to be differently constituted by 'race', but when talking about 'racial topics' with interviewers from another racial group, is also positioned in a stuck state of conscious and/or unconscious defensiveness.

The complexities and the unevenness of processes of racialization at work in these epistemological assumptions can be seen more clearly when we examine studies that have looked at white people being interviewed by black interviewers. Schaeffer (1980) for example, in an examination of national survey data collected in 1972 and 1977 in the US, found large RIE among white people's responses to black interviewers for attitude scale items relating to liberalism on 'race' issues. That is, white research participants gave more liberal responses to four 'racial attitude' scales when the interviewer was black. Although this appears to suggest a white research 'subject' who is also defensive about voicing 'race'-related opinions to a black interviewer, epistemological assumptions about subjectivity operate in different ways when the research participant is white.

These differences in approaches to subjectivity relate to how 'race' is seen as continually structuring the very identity, experiences, emotions and consciousness of minoritized research participants, while 'race' is only seen as sometimes variegating the 'transparency' of whiteness (Winant, 1994) for white research participants. By this I mean the subjectivity and experiences of the white research participant are not primarily treated as racial, *until* they are considered in the context of particular forms of racial-ized difference and racism. For instance, attitudes towards racism can serve to 'race' whiteness to the extent that within certain social contexts being implicated in responsibility for racism can give white people a 'forced awareness' (Lewis and Ramazanoglu, 1999: 50) of their whiteness. Similarly, Winant has suggested that the meanings of whiteness became a matter of real anxiety in the post Civil Rights era, marked by dilemmas of 'the absence of a clear culture and identity ... and the stigma of being perceived as the "oppressors of the nation"' (Winant, 1994: 285).

In a very different way, broad conceptualizations about the defensive-ness of racialized subjectivity can also be found in the writing of minoritized scholars. Clark Hine, for example, has suggested that African-American women's resistance to the material and psychic conditions of slavery entailed emotion management and the development of a concealed 'oppo-sitional consciousness' in 'private identities and inner worlds' (1993: 342). In this interpretive frame, the focus is upon reconfiguring the meaning of the concealing of emotions and opinions among minoritized people in rela-tion to racist social and political structures and interactions. As Brush (2001) has argued, viewing 'race' consciousness as relative to experience within changing social and political contexts produces a non-essentializing and dynamic conception of racialized subjectivity and identity.

This approach to racialized subjectivity is quite different from many of the interpretations that circulate in the RIE literature. The RIE literature var-iously assumes hard, racialized boundaries to the 'inner worlds' of racialized research participants, and these assumptions are far removed from the assumptions that those such as Hollway and Jefferson criticize as being rep-resentative of assumptions about the research subject of survey research. In other words, the literature on RIE acknowledges a racialized twist to the 'telling it like it is' approach criticized by Hollway and Jefferson. It does this through assumptions about the limited nature of a racialized (hyper) emotionality in interracial encounters that is very different from 'tradi-tional' survey approaches to the research subject and approaches to 'race' consciousness in the writings of critical 'race' and feminist scholars.

From this discussion of the survey research, what I want to suggest is that attention to RIE is relevant not only to a variety of contemporary methodological discussions, but also to questions of epistemology. All research is based upon assumptions about the subjectivity of research participants – how the research participant makes sense of the world and how they act – and such notions of subjectivity can appear to be universal. Attention to 'race' reveals how certain epistemological assumptions about research subjects are socially and historically located and can operate to both *symbolize* and to *produce* racial categorizations (Winant, 1994). By this I mean the epistemological processes that assign differently racialized research participants as 'defensive' or 'deceitful' in the methodological literature, are not the stable, objective categorizations they seem or are assumed to be. They are a part of a volatile, relational process through which racial categories can be constructed, secured, resisted and undone in interactional contexts and in the production of knowledge. Furthermore, in relation to racialized difference this process can operate to assign minoritized research participants as particularly defensive and deceptive, and through whiteness and its intersections with positivist assumptions about researchers, can also position and preserve the interviewer as value-free, objective and rational.

How racialized subjectivity is produced and understood through research is thus at once methodological *and* political. Hence, the value of the interrogation of assumptions about the research subject within the construction of RIE lies in uncovering the specific relations between methodology, epistemology and processes of racialization.

CONCLUSIONS

In this chapter, I have focused upon, and examined, constructions of RIE in the US survey literature as an example of the dynamic making of 'race' through the overlapping connections between research methods, epistemology, inter/subjective relations and the social context. To a certain extent this specific focus upon the RIE studies can detract from the recognition that *all* interviews take place within a context of social divisions. In other words, interviews are always characterized by relations of 'race', ethnicity, class, gender, age, sexuality and disability, for example. Yet, the recognition and the relevance of these relations to methodological discussions can vary. They can vary according to how constructions of 'race', ethnicity, class, gender, age, sexuality and disability are given primacy and meaning in the interview, how they are attended to within the analysis and representation of data, and also according to how they are positioned within the wider social and political context. In terms of racialized difference, the question then becomes not whether 'race' and ethnicity affect interviewing relationships, but, rather, *how* and *when* racialized dynamics are produced and negotiated within the interview process, and how they are given meaning in analysis.

In bringing these different points together I want to highlight and reiterate a central theme that has run throughout my argument in this chapter: that race-of-interviewer-effects are not, in fact, race-of-interviewer-effects. The term gives the impression that a complex combination and manifestation of effects can be pinned down to singular and overarching demographic differences in 'race' and ethnicity within the interview encounter. This impression is itself entangled with particular (hidden) assumptions about a racialized research 'subject', a single 'truth', and essentialized and congealed conceptions of 'race' and/or ethnicity. By treating the epistemological, methodological, social and interactional contexts of the interview as a dynamic part of RIE, I hope to have opened out this focus upon the interview.

In order to have made my argument clear in this chapter, I may have given an impression of a clear distinction between these different dynamics in the production of RIE. It is worth stating that in the midst of interview interactions, there are no clear 'cause' and 'effect' relationships between, for example, racializing discourses and practices in social life, inter-subjective relations between racialized research participants and interviewers, and processes of producing knowledge about racialized difference. Rather, what I have suggested is that 'race' connects methodology and culture, and that continual and critical analytic attention is required to understand how these connections are made, re-made and confused within the interview.

SUGGESTED READING

D.W. Davis (1997) The Direction of Race of Interviewer Effects Among African-Americans: Donning the black mask. *American Journal of Political Science*, 41(1): 309–22.

N. Schaeffer (1980) Evaluating Race-of-Interviewer Effects in a National Survey. *Sociological Methods and Research*, 8(4): 400–19.

H. Schuman and J. Converse (1971) The Effects of Black and White Interviewers on Black Responses in 1968. *Public Opinion Quarterly*, 35: 44–68.

A.W. Smith (1993) Survey Research on African Americans: Methodological innovations. In J. Stanfield and M. Dennis (eds), *Race and Ethnicity in Research Methods*. Newbury Park, CA: Sage, pp. 217–29.

NOTES

1. There are a number of different strategies for estimating 'errors' in survey responses to questions about factual information, for examples see Bradburn et al., 1979; Cannell et al., 1977; Sudman and Bradburn, 1982.

2. This discussion also needs to be situated within the wider field of survey research and 'race', where, for example, the 'difficulties' of accessing and enabling the participation of different minoritized groups in survey research (see Elam and Chinouya, 2000 for a discussion of these difficulties), has meant that research often fails to engage with questions of 'race' and ethnicity, and

how 'race' and ethnicity are relevant in interpreting the responses of samples that are categorized as predominantly white.

3. In reading through some of the US literature on research into survey methodology, it is noticeable that there is a large body of research that has examined demographic differences between the interviewer and research participant and the effects these have upon data. These studies have examined differences in 'race' (Hyman et al., 1954; Schaeffer, 1980; Schuman and Converse, 1971), class (Katz, 1942; Lenski and Leggett, 1960), gender (Hyman et al., 1954) and age (Collins and Butcher, 1983; Erlich and Reisman, 1961).

4. *Guardian*, 20 April, 2001.

5. *Guardian*, 20 April, 2001.

6. You should note that for the purposes of this activity, I have chosen specific questions from the Schuman and Converse study that relate to racialized topics and that make reference to the 'riots' in Detroit. The original questionnaire consisted of 130 wide-ranging questions.

7. It is interesting to note that the controlled repetition involved in the generation of survey data is a process that parallels theory about the reproduction of social norms. Butler (1993), for example, discusses gender as performed and secured through repetition.

8. In charting the changes in interest in the opinions of African-American people in survey research, it is interesting how Smith's critique itself produces racialized categorizations of African-American subjectivities through 'logical empiricist assumptions' (Denzin, 1997) about the nature of the relationship between survey research, opinions and behaviour. By 'logical empiricist assumptions' I am referring to the belief in the predictive power of surveys amongst opinion poll and market researchers, and how this relates to assumptions about the subjectivity of African-American research participants (that the attitudes and opinions of African-American people were the cause of the 'riots').

Messy work: qualitative interviewing across difference

SUMMARY

This chapter examines and discusses the methodological literature on interracial interviewing in qualitative research. It interrogates central assumptions about the 'problems' of distance and difference within interracial interviews, and troubles the discursive opposition between racialized 'commonality' and 'difference'. In challenging the binary thinking that sees racialized commonalities as critical to the success of interracial interviewing, I argue for a move from a naturalized commonality to a worked-for connectivity, in which the recognition of points of difference, their meanings and effects are vital.

- The chapter considers ethnic matching strategies and discussions about the advantages and disadvantages of being positioned as an 'insider' and/or 'outsider'.
- A specific focus of discussion is how researchers/interviewers from groups racialized as 'ethnic minorities' have accounted for our own complex social and political locations, and the production and effects of these in interview encounters.

The problems of doing research with minority communities are compounded by the social distance imposed by class and race relations when interviewers are white and middle-class and those being interviewed are not. For white scholars wanting to study race relations … conclusions in the literature are daunting. How can white scholars elicit an understanding of race relations as experienced by racial minorities? How can white scholars study those who have been historically subordinated without further producing sociological accounts distorted by the political economy of race, class and gender? (Anderson, 1993: 41)

Methodological discussions of interracial qualitative interviewing have traditionally been based upon a number of assumptions. By 'assumptions' I mean that the nature and the effects of interracial encounters are pre-judged, taken-for-granted and/or 'known' *before* any research interaction has taken place (see Ahmed, 2000 for an insightful discussion on the already-recognized 'stranger'). The most fundamental assumption in qualitative interracial interviews is that the research encounter is characterized by distance and estrangement between the researcher and the research participant, which the researcher needs to 'overcome' (Marcus, 1998; Shields, 1996). The distance of difference needs to closed or bridged by practices – be they methodological, linguistic and/or imaginative – that bring the researcher closer to the research participant and, through this proximity, can render the difference knowable.

The very nature of qualitative interviews, with their focus upon eliciting meaning, can be very different to survey interviews. While standardization may be the goal of quantitative interviewing, in qualitative research, as Cotterill has observed 'No two interviews are the same' (1992: 601). Questions and language in qualitative interviews are often more negotiable (Rhodes, 1994), and the balance of power between the researcher and research participant may shift according to both the different styles of the interview (Ribbens, 1989), and in relation to the topics that are being discussed. Reed suggests that in the qualitative interview, 'the contextual location of knowledge and the production of knowledge through dialogue ... makes room for a plurality of voices' (2000: para 1.1). The time taken by qualitative interviews – in my experience anything from 30 minutes to 4 hours – and opportunities for repeat interviews, also affects the nature of the interviewing process, research relationships and communication for both research participants and for interviewers (see Thapar-Bjorkert, 1999). The nature and the structuring of communication and research encounters in qualitative interviews can thus have very specific effects in the production of difference in interracial interviews, and this needs to be borne in mind throughout this discussion.

In recent years, methodological strategies based upon matching the ethnicity of the interviewer and research participant have become increasingly popular as a 'solution' to the problems of racialized difference and distance. Yet, matching practices not only assume interviewers from dominant racialized groups as being the 'norm' in interracial research (hence the need for specific matching strategies), they are also based upon ideas of racial identities as being primary, 'pure', mono-cultural and unaffected by differences of gender, class, disability or sexuality. With the rise of post-colonial and black feminist critiques, these dominant, and also 'neat' and hygienic assumptions about interracial interviewing, have been subjected to significant interrogation and debate. Through these debates the messy, complex and dynamic nature of interracial interviewing has been uncovered and examined. This messiness is undoubtedly challenging and problematic for research. However, a central message in this chapter is that we need to value, work through and even enjoy the mess.

What I want to do in this chapter is to make explicit the limitations of existing approaches to interracial interviewing in qualitative research. I also want to suggest better ways of conceptualizing and engaging with difference in the interview. I will do this through three analytic moves that are aimed at identifying and challenging some of the main assumptions about the nature of interracial encounters in qualitative research. The first entails a move away from the clear distinction between the social and the technical in methodological practices. Following the work of Latour (1983; 1987) in his studies of the natural sciences, a theme that weaves in and out of my analysis is how particular methodological practices, such as ethnic matching, can be seen as 'inscription devices' that aim to simplify and codify the complexity and contingency of difference into unambiguous, predictable and apparently manageable processes. This approach builds upon the discussion in Chapter 1 that suggested the importance of recognizing research as a discursive practice which is a part of (rather than separate from) the social construction of the meanings and effects of 'race' and ethnicity.

The second strand in my approach is the analytic move away from the reification of 'race' and ethnicity of freezing and also giving primacy to 'race' and ethnicity within interview dynamics. This point challenges the interpretation and reading of interview dynamics through one category of difference, and it engages with the postcolonial and multicultural realities of hybridity and hyphenated identities (see Song and Parker, 1995). For example, in my hospice research my own 'mixed' identity (Singhalese/Tamil/Indonesian/Scottish) meant that there were no interviews that were ethnically matched, nor is it likely that there will ever be ethnic matching in any interviews in my future research unless parts of my ethnic identity are denied or suppressed. This is a more complex reality of ethnicity and culture than the one constructed in the methodological literature that fails to acknowledge and engage with what Hall has referred to as the 'places of incommensurability' marked by hybridity (2000: 227).

The third related move in challenging the limitations of current approaches to interracial interviewing and in moving discussion forward, involves an interrogation and troubling of the binarism of racial and ethnic categories that operate to produce rigid boundaries between different 'races'/ethnicities. Such binarism serves to obscure differences within racialized/ethnicized groups through discourses of commonality, and can position difference as something that cannot be of value in examining and learning from research encounters.

Using this analytic framework, the discussion in this chapter has been divided into three main parts:

- the first discusses and problematizes ethnic matching strategies as the 'solution' to the distances of racialized and ethnicized difference in interracial interviews
- the second draws upon feminist writing on 'race' and ethnicity in the interview
- the third examines the specific contributions of minoritized researchers to the debates on interracial interviewing.

ETHNIC MATCHING: METHODOLOGICAL AND POLITICAL CHOICES

Discussions about racial and/or ethnic matching, and related concerns about the effects of racialized commonality and difference in interracial qualitative interviews, occupy a central position in the methodological literature on interracial interviewing. They are two sides of the same ideological coin, that confront researchers with a spectrum of epistemological, methodological and political choices. At one end of this spectrum is the choice to subsume the complexities of subjectivity and social positioning under overarching categories (be they racial, ethnic, cultural, religious and/or linguistic); at the other end is the choice to recognize and work through the complexities and contingency of multiple and cross-cutting subjective, biographical and social differences. The range of choices between these two extremes has varying repercussions and implications for the production of knowledge about racialized difference, and for the institutional structuring of racialized relations within the social sciences.

The repercussions and implications of different approaches to interracial interviewing can be made clearer through an engagement with some of the methodological discussions. For instance, in an article on 'culturally competent' research, Papadopoulos and Lees have advocated ethnic matching between researchers and research participants as an example of 'ethnic sensitivity' in research. They suggest that ethnic matching should be practised 'whenever possible', because it:

> encourages a more equal context for interviewing which allows more sensitive and accurate information to be collected. A researcher with the same ethnic background as the participant will possess 'a rich fore understanding' (Ashworth, 1986) and an insider/emic view (Leininger, 1991; Kauffman, 1994), will have more favourable access conditions and the co-operation of a large number of people (Hanson, 1994) and a genuine interest in the health and welfare of their community (Hillier and Rachman, 1996). (Papadopoulos and Lees, 2002: 261)

The discussion advocating ethnic matching strategies by Papadopoulos and Lees encapsulates many of the assumptions that are made about interracial interviewing. Within such approaches, ethnic correspondence between researchers and research participants is constructed as the best all-round solution to the 'problem' of gaining access to the experiences and perspectives of minoritized research participants. What is particularly striking and noteworthy in this example, is that ethnic commonalities are not just seen as a way of addressing cultural and linguistic[1] difference in research interactions – they are also promoted as reducing intersubjective distances between the interviewer and the research participant (see also Bhopal, 2001; Dunbar et al., 2002). Papadopoulos and Lees's assertion that researchers from the same ethnic background as research participants will have a 'genuine interest' in the welfare of 'their community', is illustrative of Bhavnani's (1993) suggestion that matching strategies often fail to take account of power relations between the researcher and research participant, because the rationale of matching can imply that forms of 'unevenness' within the research interaction have been dealt with.

Within matching strategies, 'race' and/or ethnicity are thus approached (and used) as forms of 'methodological capital' (Gallagher, 2000) that can be exploited to build rapport, cooperation and trust, and to gain access to the 'authentic' views and experiences of minoritized research participants. If we look further, there are other dynamics submerged in these epistemological assumptions about the nature of racialized inter/subjectivity in the interview. 'Race' and/or ethnicity, in research with minoritized research participants, are seen as defining the emotional and ethical dimensions of the interview interaction in ways that eclipse differences of gender, class, age, disability and sexuality. Moreover, the eliding of interracial research with the 'problems' of interviewing minoritized research participants, also serves to normalize research involving white interviewers and white research participants (for a critique of this position see Gallagher, 2000). Questions of 'race' and ethnicity in the interview, in the vast majority of research studies, are thus simply not an issue, serving to reproduce whiteness as the undifferentiated norm that is simultaneously naturalized and de-problematized as 'non-racial' (Frankenberg, 1993; Roediger, 1990; Ware, 1992).

The promotion of matching strategies in research has also had an impact upon the numbers and occupational positioning of minoritized researchers and interviewers in academic and social research institutions. Some writers have suggested that methodological considerations have not been the only concern in the promotion of matching strategies. Commenting on the growth in popularity and use of matching practices in the United States, Twine has argued that matching:

> was also invoked as part of a racial justice movement to racially diversify the academy. In other words, 'racial matching' was seized upon by those less

concerned with whether white people could study non-whites than with democratizing the social scientific community by opening it up to scholars of color. (Twine, 2000: 8)

Racialized, gendered and class inequalities and power relations in academic institutions (see Fenton et al., 2000), structure the working experiences of academics and the production of knowledge in different national contexts (Bell and Gordon, 1999; Dyck et al., 1995; Reay, 1999; 2000). Writing with specific reference to class, Reay has pointed to the ways in which academic feminism has failed to challenge the divide between lecturing staff and contract researchers in British institutions:

> The trade in contract researchers is an accepted part of both male and female academic empire-building. To become a female professor, feminist or otherwise, often involves buying into a research marketplace and acquiring contract researchers as so many 'intellectual' possessions ... there is virtually nothing written on the dilemmas of operating as a feminist in an academic industry underpinned by, and shored up through, the appropriation of other, less powerful women's intellectual labour; where despite the best intentions ... hierarchical ways of working remain the norm. (Reay, 1999: 429)

The processes that Reay talks about also affect the employment patterns of minoritized researchers and interviewers and the chains of intellectual labour involved in research. I myself am employed on a temporary research contract, where despite a long history of research, training and writing outside of academia, I started my first full-time, post-PhD appointment earning less than I had done 10 years previously. I have been mistaken in meetings as a white colleague's research assistant, and I have witnessed minoritized, highly skilled, multilingual colleagues go from one short-term contract to another, with no time in between contracts for publication.

Institutionally, in Britain, despite increasing numbers of academics from 'ethnic minorities', our numbers are still relatively small, especially in the social sciences (Fenton et al., 2000). Particular forms of ethnic matching in interviews are thus often achieved through the employment of interviewers on short-term contracts who, despite our skills and knowledge, are marginalized in research teams and in published research outputs. Our professional 'expertise' can become constructed through, and confined to research related to 'race' and ethnicity, creating highly racialized occupational careers and opportunities.

Ann Phoenix (2001) has suggested that matching practices in research can also be exploitative of some minoritized research participants. This is because research participants can believe that the minoritized interviewer has some control over the study, when frequently 'the black interviewer has little control over the trajectory of the research or the analysis of data' (p. 214).[2] The troubling paradox is that apparent concern with enabling the participation of 'ethnic minorities' in research as participants, is frequently achieved through the very compounding, manipulation and exploitation of racialized, gendered and class-related inequalities in academic structures and practices. At another level, interviewing without due regard to social, cultural and linguistic differences in the interview can lead to significant misunderstandings (Riessman, 1987) and/or misrepresentation that can feed into racist practices and the production of knowledge. However, the point is that matching for one social identity fails to take account of the dynamic interplay of social differences and identifications. So even when there is a shared language between researchers and research participants, other differences, such as class, can have a significant effect upon communication and the interpretation of meaning (Edwards, 1998).

The point of identifying the complex epistemological, political and institutional implications and repercussions of matching strategies, is to illuminate the multiple connections and contradictions that are a part of the methodological and epistemological terrain. In straightforward terms, there are no easy 'answers'. Strategies that appear to work well in relation to one site of research interactions, such as fieldwork relations between interviewers and research participants, may produce and reproduce inequalities in employment and intellectual authority relations in research, and vice versa. The specific nature of qualitative interviews is also implicated in the particular and unpredictable configuration of the *meanings* of difference between research participants and interviewers, and how this affects the interview. Despite clear research objectives, plans, interview schedules and topic guides, interactions in both quantitative and qualitative interviews do not always progress according to a controlled and pre-determined logic (see Chapter 7). They take shape through unruly and spontaneous intersubjective, spatial and socially-situated encounters that can undermine the rationalist logic of matching.

In summary, my argument is that the micro-social interactions within interviews should not be interpreted in relation to any one purified category of difference between the research participant and interviewer, because such interactions are never organized or given meaning around a single category of difference (Aitken and Burman, 1999). However, interactions and methodological discourses, such as those relating to matching, are constructed in ways that spotlight the determining effects of one (homogenous) category of difference over another. This can serve to produce and re-produce the apparent dominance – and also manageability – of one category, simultaneously obscuring other forms of difference and power relations. As McClintock writes:

> no social category exists in privileged isolation; each comes into being in social relation to other categories, if in uneven and contradictory ways. But power is seldom adjudicated evenly, different social relations are over-determined for race, for gender, for class, or for each in turn. (McClintock, 1995: 9)

One point that needs to be emphasized and borne in mind throughout this discussion is that although difference is constructed relationally and spontaneously in the micro-interactions of the interview, such configurations are never politically neutral. The nature of the differences that are constructed and manifested within the interview are related to the play of specific power relations within particular interactional and social arenas, which need to be examined, located and attended to within the doing and the analysis of research.

In the remaining parts of the chapter, which examine the specific contributions of feminist and minoritized researchers to the debates on interracial interviewing, we can see how questions of power have been central to these contributions. In this literature, interviewers reflect upon their own experiences of interviewing, social, institutional and interactional power relations, ethics and research practices. Of particular significance in these discussions has been the role of reflexivity, in which researchers' insights into their social location and participation in the research process have been used to examine the relationships between social contexts, research methods and intersubjective relations in research (Anderson, 1993; Dyck et al., 1995). Insightful as many of these accounts are, I will suggest that we cannot take them at face value, and so they also confront us with the problem of how we evaluate and use reflexive accounts and how we connect the 'local' and the 'wider'.

FEMINIST RESEARCH

Many of the debates about the effects of differences between the interviewer and research participant in qualitative interviews have been led and shaped by feminist researchers, who focused attention initially upon the particular advantages and benefits to research of women interviewing women (Finch, 1984; Oakley, 1981). As Warren and Hackney have written, since the work of Oakley and others on feminist interviewing,

> the dyad of a feminist woman interviewing another woman has been valorised, even perhaps romanticized, as the ideal research relationship. (2000: 38)

In many ways, Ann Oakley's (1981) work influenced the agenda for much of feminist writing on the interview in the 1980s (certainly in Britain), through a focus upon how research methods and interviewing practices can construct and reproduce power relations in the interview. Oakley, in a critique of textbook orthodoxy, dismissed 'traditional', highly prescribed interview protocols that promote the clinical detachment of the interviewer, as a 'masculine fiction' that bore little relevance to the reality of interview encounters. For Oakley, such approaches involved the exploitation and manipulation of research participants as mere 'data producing machines'.

Oakley's attack on methodological approaches to interviewing roles and relations was undoubtedly made more powerful by her choice of textbook prescriptions, taken from books written mainly in the 1950s and 1960s. You will find it useful in reading her paper to think about how her choice of texts and their depiction of ideal type models, enables Oakley to caricature, highly effectively, the limitations of rigidly defined and controlled interviews. However, Oakley's analysis fails to make explicit the historical context in which the books were written, in which interviewing was largely grounded in the survey tradition. During this time the promotion of sociologists as 'objective experts' was also a particular historical product of the discipline's struggle to achieve professional recognition and status.

Instead, Oakley argued that the relationship between the interviewer and research participant should be a non-hierarchical, reciprocal one. The interviewer should be prepared to invest herself emotionally in the interview and to answer any personal questions asked by research participants. Drawing upon her experiences of interviewing pregnant women, Oakley claimed that self-disclosure about her own experiences of childbirth and motherhood increased the intimacy and rapport with the women and so improved the quality of interview accounts. According to Duelli-Klein, the benefits of such an approach are both methodological and political, since it 'allows for women studying women in an interactive process without the artificial subject/object split between the researcher and researched' (1983: 95). Some of the ethical implications of self-disclosure by the interviewer are discussed in Box 4.1.

While gender was the primary focus within the early feminist methodological literature on interviewing, things have changed. The growing critique of white feminism from minoritized feminists has played a critical role in highlighting how feminist methods can exclude, pathologize and distort the experiences of people from 'minority' groups (Carby, 1982; Hill-Collins, 1991; Phoenix, 1987). In developing practice and theory that take account of the interrelations between 'race', gender and class in particular, the contributions of minoritized feminists have demanded recognition of the ways in which other social differences can construct and reproduce social inequalities at every stage of the research process (Phoenix, 2001).

While Ann Oakley has suggested that self-disclosure by the interviewer should be an integral part of feminist interviewing practices, other researchers have drawn attention to the problematic nature of the sharing of personal information. Wise (1987) has argued that the interview can never be a non-hierarchical interaction, and that shared gendered experiences are always underwritten by the dominance of the power of the interviewer as researcher. Within the context of such inequalities, in which the ultimate goal of the interviewer is to generate data, Wise suggests that self-disclosure by the interviewer can be used instrumentally to gain information from research participants and can foster the very exploitation that feminists seek to avoid. Drawing upon studies in 'exchange theory', Lee (1993) has also suggested that self-disclosure by the interviewer can be used strategically to ingratiate, so that ethical considerations become displaced. Indeed, the whole area of reciprocity in research is highly problematic. Not only is the social exchange system unstable and ambiguous (Leifer, 1988), but individuals also only ever have intuitive impressions of both what is exchanged and its value. In other words, for both the interviewer and research participant there are no reliable ways of judging when 'enough is enough'.

Box 4.1 Ethical considerations of interviewer disclosures in the interview

'Race', gender and class in feminist approaches to interracial interviewing

Influenced by black feminist writing on the need to pay particular attention to the way racialized and class-related differences are generated through the qualitative interview, Ros Edwards' (1990) work was one of the most high profile in the UK in drawing attention to interracial interviewing in feminist research. In a paper in the *Women's Studies International Forum*, Edwards addressed some of the specific dynamics of white, feminist researchers interviewing 'black' women. Drawing upon her experiences as a white, middle-class woman interviewing African-Caribbean, mainly working-class women returning to full-time education as undergraduates, Edwards challenged assumptions that 'a feminist researcher has some special sort of link with her female interview subjects' (1990: 480). Instead, Edwards argued that 'race' is a fundamental part of social structures, social relations and consciousness that affects how the interviewer and the research participant 'place each other within the social structure' (p. 482).

In contrast to other feminist researchers, who have argued that white women are not 'best placed' to conduct research with minoritized women, particularly when the research is about issues of 'race' (Barrett and McIntosh, 1985; Walton, 1986), Edwards has suggested that what is important is the *process* of research, in which it is vital to recognize that:

> Black women do not talk about all areas of their lives to white, female researchers in the same easy way that white women do, as a result of their structural position and allegiances in society. (Edwards, 1990: 486)

Edwards claimed that the black women in her study were less trusting of her as a white woman (who was also identified with a higher education institution), and that acknowledging differences in 'race' and racialized experiences encouraged the development of rapport and talk about 'private' matters regarding family relationships. Aitken, a white, feminist researcher, who conducted semi-structured interviews with 'black' women, has also suggested that a white woman researcher who is able to share her concerns about racialized difference and possible interactional power differences in interviews, by communicating her uncertainties, might work 'more clearly to subvert whiteness as a powerful category' (Aitken and Burman, 1999: 282). However, Aitken argues that such disclosures might be interpreted by research participants as asking them to assuage white guilt, or to educate researchers about how to develop relationships across racialized differences.

For Edwards, another significant factor that had an effect upon what research participants talked about was the number of interviews. Edwards suggested that multiple interviews gave her the time to establish trust, and to get past the 'yes, no, well' of minimal and tokenistic responses. This approach to interracial interviewing challenges directly some of the interpretations in the survey research on 'race-of-interviewer-effects' (see Chapter 3), where many of the studies have not engaged directly with the need to build up trust throughout the research process. In this respect, Edwards' approach can be seen as establishing a methodological and political process of earning the right to hear accounts of experiences and feelings in the interview (see Briggs, 1986).

Edwards's reflexive approach to interracial interviewing has drawn attention to the significance of research practices, wider social relations and the power of research participants to subvert and/or to resist the interview's intrusions. Within this analytic framework, research participants are recognized as playing an active role in the interview in three main ways: first, in protecting areas of their lives from scrutiny by researchers; second, in questioning the role and motives of the researcher until elements of trust can be established; and third, in exerting powerful control over the interviewing process by withholding information. However, unlike the epistemological assumptions about the research subject in the survey literature (Chapter 3), these intersubjective relations are not predominantly seen in terms of essential, unchanging differences between 'black' and 'white' women[3]. Rather, from Edwards, there is the acknowledgement that meaningful levels of communication in interracial interviews can be achieved through reflexive research practices and an active engagement with the social and interactional effects of difference.

So, although Edwards recognizes that 'race' can affect what 'black' women tell white women interviewers, she does not see a solution to this dynamic as lying with racialized matching between the interviewer and research participant. Rather, the recommendation is that when the interviewer is white, interviews need to be approached in a way that takes account of the racialized meanings of the research topic(s) and how these meanings might change across social spaces, such as in talk about the 'public' and 'private' spheres of life. Interviewers are also asked to address the complexity of power relations within the interviewing process, such as those arising from class differences (see also Ramazanoglu, 1989), and from the institution with which the researcher is affiliated and identified. That is, the interviewer has to continually struggle to make connections between the micro-interactions of the interview and the wider social context in which it is situated, and to develop trust and understanding at several different levels. The lessons that Edwards learned from her research are summarized in Box 4.2 below.

- *Access*: In doing research in/through institutions, white women researchers need to consider how 'black' women may experience the institution, particularly in terms of racialized, gendered and class-related practices, and take these experiences into account in recruiting women into research studies. Assumptions about the status and credibility of institutional associations that can enable access to white research participants cannot be taken for granted. Edwards states: 'When I contacted black women through … educational institutions, I was that institution, defined as white, middle-class, and oppressive' (p. 485, emphasis in original).
- *Trust*: Trust can be engendered through explicit attention to confidentiality and discussion of the researcher's approach to the representation of interview accounts.
- *Rapport*: Rapport can be facilitated by an acknowledgement of racialized difference in terms of both structural power relations and how it can affect the understanding of interview accounts.
- *Talk about 'private' matters*: Discussion of 'private' matters such as family relationships can be enabled through multiple interviews with the same participant, where time is taken to build up rapport within the interviewing relationship.

Box 4.2 White women interviewing black women – Edwards (1990)

Working the hyphen: making connections

Michelle Fine has talked about the struggle for connection across difference, in both more general and more specific terms, as 'working the hyphen' of the self-Other boundary:

By *working the hyphen*, I mean to suggest that researchers probe how we are in relation with the contexts we study and with our informants, understanding that we are all multiple in those relations. I mean to invite researchers to see how these 'relations between' get us 'better' data, limit what we feel free to say, expand our minds and constrict our mouths, engage us in intimacy and seduce us into complicity, make us quick to interpret and hesitant to write. Working the hyphen means creating occasions for researchers and informants to discuss what is, and is not 'happening between', within the negotiated relations of whose story is being told, why, to whom, with what interpretation, and whose story is being shadowed, why, for whom and with what consequence. (Fine, 1998: 132, emphasis in original)

Fine's invitation to qualitative researchers to 'work the hyphen' has direct implications for exploring the interactional, methodological and political implications of interracial interviewing and debates about racialized matching. It unsettles the lurking essentialism behind the rationale of many matching strategies, and pushes us to think through how our methodological practices might be engaged in processes of Othering (see Wilkinson and Kitzinger, 1996 for a detailed discussion of academic writing on Othering). The focus of attention on the 'race' of the research participant then refracts and dissipates, so that analysis is forced to account for the web of power relations and contexts in which difference is produced, represented and has effects.

Working the hyphen raises significant challenges in interracial research, given the complexity of processes of racialization and their intersections with other differences. I will illustrate what I mean by the challenging nature of such complexity by taking an example of what can be seen as 'working the hyphen' from a research account by Anderson (1993). What emerges, in considering actual practices of 'working the hyphen', are the limitations of reflexive practice, which has been seen as a powerful methodological device for attending to, and making explicit, power relations and social and subjective locations within qualitative research.

Anderson, a white-American, feminist researcher, has argued that for white women doing research with women 'of colour', it is vital that reflexivity by the researcher includes specific attention to the production of white privilege in the research process. Such reflexivity should be an integral part of analysis:

Building more inclusive ways of seeing requires scholars to take multiple views of their subjects, abandoning the idea that there is a singular reality that social science can discover ... how, in constructing sociological analyses, can dominant group members examine their own racial identities and challenge the societal system of racial stratification in which what they observe is situated? (Anderson, 1993: 43)

As Anderson's own account goes on to make clear, the work of explicating and attending to the social and interactional constructions of racial privilege in interracial research is by no means straightforward. In her research, involving oral history interviews with white and African-American women, Anderson, like Edwards (1990), made the decision to shun 'conventional', distant and structured interview approaches. She describes how:

> During the interviews, I answered questions about myself, my background, my family, and my ideas ... despite my trepidations about crossing class, race, and age lines, I was surprised by the openness and hospitality with which I was greeted. I am convinced that the sincerity of these women's stories emanated not only from their dignity and honor, but also from my willingness to express how I felt, to share my own race and gender experiences, and to deconstruct the role of expert as I proceeded through this research ... Self-examination of my own privilege as a white scholar facilitated this research project, allowing me to challenge the arrogance that the stand of white privilege creates. (1993: 50–1).

Anderson raises some interesting issues about the dynamics of interracial interviewing, acknowledging how privilege constructed through whiteness, class and professional status can be reproduced in research interactions. Indeed, although many white researchers have discussed the 'problems' of interviewing people from minoritized groups, we only rarely get glimpses of how whiteness is also produced and negotiated through the construction of such 'problems'. Hence, the full range of connections between interracial interview dynamics and processes of racialization and ethnicization often remains unexplored (however, see Watson and Scraton, 2001).

If we return to Anderson's account of her research, we can gain further insights into the methodological and epistemological dimensions of these processes of racialization. For instance, despite Anderson's judgement about the 'sincerity' of the women's stories, it is apparent that her whiteness haunts and disturbs her analysis of her interviews with the African-American women:

> I know that my understanding of these women's lives will always be partial, incomplete, and distorted. I also know that the Black women did not likely report the same things to me as they would have to a Black interviewer, but that does not make their accounts any less true. (1993: 50–1)

This statement is highly significant. It serves to undermine the hard analytic work that Anderson has done in order to make visible the production of racialized and classed power relations in her research, but also through it, Anderson produces whiteness as a uncrossable boundary between the experiences and understanding of white and black women. Such an analysis reproduces epistemological assumptions about racialized difference as an essential, absolute difference that inscribes subjectivities. The possibility of shared understanding across racialized boundaries that was previously opened up, is shut down, and we are left with the apparent intransigence of racialized difference. Such a position serves (inadvertently) to reinforce racial thinking through an interconnected set of essentialist assumptions that fail to recognize the complexity and the ambivalence of racialized subject positions within particular interactional and social contexts (see Lewis, G., 2000 for a critique of these notions in social work practice).

Twine, an African-American anthropologist, has drawn particular attention to differential racialized identifications and positioning amongst 'racial subalterns'. Drawing upon her research in Brazil, Twine has written about the entangled relations between subjectivity, identification and social location, such that the Brazilians of African descent that she interviewed frequently did not express a different political standpoint on issues of racism to white people. Moreover, in relation to interviewing, Twine contends that:

> rather than mistrusting a white researcher, racial subalterns in Brazil may be more likely to identify with them. My experiences suggest that some Brazilians of color do not necessarily feel more comfortable discussing the topic of race and racism with those who resemble them racially ... Moreover, prestige hierarchies and the valorization of whiteness resulted in some Brazilians of color preferring to be interviewed by my white research partner. (Twine, 2000: 16)

Returning to Anderson's evaluation of her understanding of the accounts of African-American women in the light of the points that Twine makes, we might ask how researchers, such as Anderson, make judgements about the effects of racialized difference on interview relations and accounts? How does Anderson *know* that her understanding of the lives of black women will be any more 'partial, incomplete and distorted' than her understanding of the lives of white women? Furthermore, if she is right that her understanding is distorted by racialized difference, we can also ask how she knows that such distortion 'does not make their accounts any less true'?[4]

The line of my argument here serves two main purposes. First, to uncover the epistemological assumptions that are made about the fundamental nature and consequences of racial difference in interracial research. And second, to show the persistence and complexity of the operation of processes of racialization at work in reflexive accounts. Paradoxically, in Anderson's case, these processes of racialization are produced through her very attempts to address white privilege in the research process. In this sense, reflexive accounts of interviewing, such as Anderson's, do not simply examine and uncover racialized interrelations in the interview, they also *construct* them.

REFLEXIVITY

If we compare the accounts of Edwards (1990) and Anderson (1993), we can see both the potential and the limitations of reflexive practices in addressing questions of epistemology, inter/subjectivity and power relations in interracial research. For example, it has long been recognized by feminist researchers that in order to address fully the nature of the inter-relations in the interview, interviewers must also scrutinize their own ideological frameworks, research tools and practices through reflexivity. As Opie has pointed out, researchers' own ideological positions play a critical role in the interpretation of meaning, with such positions taking on specific implications in researching difference:

> Addressing difference would create a much more broken and fissured text and would focus much more attention on the nature of the interpretive processes. It would also have the effect of highlighting the sociological and ideological locations of those involved ... and the implications of location on interpretation. (Opie, 1992: 63)

Gill (1998) has made some important points about the limits of reflexivity with regard to the Sociology of Scientific Knowledge, known as SSK, by questioning why writing has been the main focus of reflexive practice:

> What seems to be missing from discussions of reflexivity within SSK is the sense that it concerns the *entire research process* – not just writing ... there is surely more to reflexivity than how we write ... it is as if the (ethnographic) research process can be left unaltered, and all that needs to change are our (*post-hoc*) textual constructions of it. I suggest that it would be far more destabilizing to empiricism and objectivism if the research process as a whole were interrogated.
>
> [...] the notion of reflexivity proposed by SSK researchers seems to give no space to what Wilkinson (1988) calls 'disciplined self-reflection'. As Paul Rabinow (1986) has argued, despite talk about reflexivity, most academics remain deathly silent about the conditions of their own production. He argues that reflection upon our own social, political, economic and cultural location within the academy is one of the greatest taboos – far greater strictures operate against addressing the significance of 'corridor talk' than operate against the denunciation of objectivism. Until we can bring to the surface and publicly discuss the conditions under which people are hired, given tenure, published, awarded grants and feted, 'real' reflexivity will remain a dream. (Gill, 1998: 37–8, emphasis in original)

However, in my own research I have found that this focus on reflexivity, as making visible the social positioning of the researcher and research participant in relation to processes of interpretation and representation, is not enough to understand and address the complexities of difference. This is particularly so in taking account of emotional dynamics (Hollway and Jefferson, 2000), the ways in which research interactions shape and give meaning to the positioning of the researcher (Hemmings, 2002), and the complicated mediation of experience by language (Ramazanoglu and Holland, 1999). Reflexivity is thus far more layered and problematic than those such as Opie would appear to suggest. As Diane Reay has highlighted, the inherent paradox in reflexive practice is that:

> We explicate the processes and positions we are aware of being caught up in. Some of the influences arising from aspects of social identity remain beyond the reflexive grasp. (1996a: 443)

In the following sections, I will explore the methodological and political use of reflexivity further, by examining discussions of racialized commonality and difference in the accounts of minoritized researchers, whose perspectives and experiences have been marginalized within methodological debates. Through this examination, I want to trouble notions of the interpretive authority of minoritized researchers in research on 'race' and ethnicity. No research is innocent of bias, evasion and selective interpretation (McClintock, 1995). In research where racialized commonalities are identified between researchers and research participants, I will argue that such constructions can pose particular analytic dangers for minoritized researchers, by obscuring differences in power relations and in the nuances of difference.

DIFFERENCE FOR RACIALIZED INTERVIEWERS: COMPLEX POSITIONINGS

There is a surprisingly small literature that explores and theorizes the specific experiences of interviewers from 'minority' groups (Bhavnani, 1993; Bhopal, 2001; Bola, 1996; Dunbar et al., 2002; Marshall et al., 1998; Phoenix, 2001; Ram, 1996; Song and Parker, 1995; Tang, 2002; Thapar-Bjorkert, 1999; Twine, 2000). Many minoritized researchers will, therefore, find that there is little theoretical and methodological knowledge to draw upon to guide the development of interviewing practices. If a study is concerned directly with matters of 'race' and ethnicity, and/or involves interracial interviewing, methodological concerns can become side-tracked into a narrow focus upon 'race', ethnicity, language and, more recently, religion. Several issues can therefore emerge as immediate concerns, and can centre upon how the researcher's 'race', ethnicity, linguistic skills and/or religion may affect the interviewing relationship and interview accounts.

Rhodes has summarized the methodological implications from the literature as ones in which:

> Closeness of identity and, in particular shared racial identity is generally presumed to promote effective communication between researcher and subject and, conversely, disparate identity to inhibit it. (1994: 550)

This approach to interviewing and difference resonates in very loose terms with feminist writing on 'standpoint epistemology', in which lived experiences of difference, and the 'standpoint' that such experiences produce, are seen as critical to the production and development of knowledge (Hill-Collins, 1991; Smith, 1992). There are, however, important differences between the presumptions talked about by Rhodes, which do not engage with the multiple, simultaneous and shifting nature of identifications, and approaches that aim to take into account the active construction and negotiation of situated identities. For example, those such as Avtar Brah (1996), who have criticized the failure of standpoint writing to address the intersections of different identities and power relations in the production of standpoints, have also acknowledged the potential and dynamic links between social positioning and understanding. In relation to autobiographical accounts, Brah has suggested that minoritized 'positionality' can create specific *opportunities* for the understanding of difference:

> diasporic or border positionality does not *in itself* assure a vantage point of privileged insight into and understanding of relations of power, although it does create a space in which experiential mediations may intersect in ways that render such understandings more readily accessible. (Brah, 1996: 207, emphasis in original)

By this I have taken Brah to mean that lived experiences of 'race' and ethnicity do not necessarily mean that all minoritized people will possess a 'natural', politicized understanding of power relations. Therefore, Brah's approach directly challenges epistemological assumptions about the inherent 'race' consciousness of both minoritized research participants and interviewers (see Chapter 5 for a more detailed discussion of these assumptions with regard to research participants). What Brah suggests is that lived experiences of 'race' and ethnicity (with other social differences) may create 'spaces', or possibilities, for people (in relation to this discussion we can think in terms of researchers/interviewers and research participants) from minoritized groups to use our own constructions of 'experience' to develop insights into the connections between social location, power and difference.

It is the dynamic and open nature of the spaces that Brah refers to, that are of particular relevance in considering how the multiple positionings and identifications of minoritized interviewers and research participants may affect interview encounters, and the nature of the accounts that are generated through them. As such, it is not just the potential of such spaces to enable more readily accessible understanding, but also their potential to obscure, skew, contradict and destabilize meanings and identifications that should be recognized.

In order to ground this theoretical discussion in practice, I want to explore representations of the relations between social positioning, identifications and understanding through accounts of interviewing by minoritized researchers. It is here that the value of a move from an emphasis upon 'commonality' to 'connectivity', which I advocated in the introduction to this chapter, can be seen more explicitly. (A more detailed discussion of making connections in research can be found in Chapter 8.)

Commonality and difference

The work of Miri Song and David Parker (1995), provides a valuable starting point in exploring aspects of the distinction between a 'natural' racialized commonality and a politicized move to establish points of connectivity between the interviewer and research participant in interracial interviews. In writing about their own experiences as researchers of 'Chinese and British descent' (David Parker) and of 'Korean-American descent' (Miri Song), Song and Parker have drawn attention to the intricate and unstable nature of identifications of commonality and difference during their qualitative interviews. Miri Song interviewed Chinese young people about their work in Chinese takeaway businesses in Britain. The picture she paints of her interviews is one in which her status and identification as an 'outsider' had evolving and unpredictable effects upon what research participants told her.

> The reporting of research participants' preferences for particular interviewer characteristics (see Bhopal, 2001, for an example) and their relation to interviewing relationships and accounts needs to be viewed with caution, and is also something that is difficult to evaluate empirically in qualitative research. An example quoted by Phoenix (2001), from her involvement in a study of 'Mothers Under Twenty', provides a rare insight into some of the empirical complexities involved in examining the relation between stated preference for interviewer characteristics by research participants and the nature of interview accounts. The example that Phoenix draws upon was taken from the last of three interviews conducted with a 'black' research participant by a black interviewer. Two of the interviews had been with a black interviewer and one with a white interviewer. In this final interview the young woman is quoted as saying to the black interviewer:
>
>> If [white interviewer] had been doing the interview I would have had to tell her that the questions were too nosey because white people don't understand what a typical black family is like ... (Phoenix, 2001: 216)

Phoenix contends that despite the young woman's assertions, the transcript of her interview with the white interviewer did not appear any different in quality to the interviews conducted by the black interviewer. Phoenix does not rule out the possibility that the young woman may have *felt* that the black interviewer may have been more understanding of accounts of black family life, but she suggests that such feelings were not 'analytically discernible' within the different interview transcripts.

In her account of interviewing, Song has suggested that, although being identified as 'different' and an outsider may have inhibited what some individuals told her, her difference and, indeed, distance from Chinese families also encouraged some disclosures:

> I was told by Keryee that she felt more comfortable talking to me about her life in the take-away because I was Korean-American: 'If a Chinese customer comes into the shop, but it's pretty rare, we all panic, like, a relative comes, and we have to be on our best behaviour or something, you know?' Keryee did not worry about me scutinising her family's shop or food because I wasn't Chinese, and I hadn't experienced life in a take-away. Perhaps I was a 'safe' person to talk to because I was neither 'the same' (Chinese) nor totally different (e.g. white). (Song and Parker, 1995: 248)

David Parker has drawn specific attention to the different ways in which he saw his dual heritage as being given meaning during interviews with Chinese young people in Britain about their cultural identity. Parker has argued that his positioning as either 'British' or 'Chinese' was negotiated according to the strength of varying racial identifications, and what he has called 'disidentifications', made by his research participants, that were also related to the nature of the stories that they told him. A further dynamic came into play when Parker interviewed research participants who had one Chinese and one English parent. Of these latter experiences he says:

> The contact that I had with other part-Chinese people in my research profoundly affected my conceptualisations of identity formation. These shared experiences encouraged me to venture more of my *own* experiences in a way that I did not with respondents who were not of dual heritage. The result was a less stilted exchange and telling rememberances of falling outside of the prevalent black/white, Chinese/non-Chinese categorisation systems. A number of Chinese people that I interviewed summarised their sense of identity in terms exactly corresponding to the sort of vocabulary for which I had been struggling. More importantly these connections were not presumed, in the way others had been, which ascribed 'confusion' and 'guilt' to me. (Song and Parker, 1995: 246, emphasis in original)

This extract raises a number of important analytic issues. At one level, Parker's interpretations of his experiences serve to draw attention to the complex and contingent nature of categorizations and representations of 'race' and ethnicity in the interview. According to the dynamics and the stories being told in his interviews, Parker could be positioned as either 'more' or 'less' Chinese or 'more' or 'less' English – or none of these – challenging the literature that assumes neat, bounded and fixed points of racialized commonality in interviews. Furthermore, these shifting and undecided positions are talked about as having both negative and positive repercussions for his interviewing relationships, in terms of what research participants told Parker and his interpretations of points of connection and distance within the interview. For instance, Parker's account of his interviews with research participants of dual heritage, can be seen as producing spaces that positively enabled difficult disclosures about stories of marginalization. However, it can also be read as an indication of the dangers of assumptions of commonality by the researcher (Du Bois, 1983; Hurd and McIntyre, 1996).

A discursive approach[5] is valuable here, because rather than treating accounts as unproblematic and transparent representations of 'experience', the focus is upon the function of language within particular interactional contexts (Potter and Wetherell, 1987). In discourse analysis, there is no reproduction of the duality between 'truth' and falsehood found in the survey literature on 'race-of-interviewer-effects' (Chapter 3). From this analytic perspective, we simply cannot say whether David Parker and the young people of dual Chinese-English heritage in his study shared common experiences. Rather, the extracts that Parker quotes, and his own interpretations of his interviews, can be seen as providing insights into the co-construction of 'race', ethnicity and dual heritage by both Parker and his research participants – within the context of the interviews and within available contemporary discourses of 'race' and ethnicity.

With specific reference to how commonalities and differences are constructed and 'made relevant' in interactions, Frith (1998) suggests that such constructions are better seen as part of a process of co-production. Within this process, commonalities can be made relevant by individuals talking 'as if' they are drawing upon shared knowledge or experience, and differences can be made known when there are explicit indications that knowledge or experience is not shared. In this sense, the stories that individuals told Song and Parker can be seen as serving specific interactional purposes at different times – a point that both Parker and Song draw attention to. Yet, what is more embedded in their analyses are the difficulties and the political risks of interpretations of shared experiences and meanings.

Diane Reay, a white, former working-class feminist who conducted ethnographic research on women's involvement in their children's primary schooling in London, has talked about such difficulties of interpretation in terms of the 'dangers of the proximity' that she felt to the accounts of the working-class women in her study. She has written:

> The affirmation of finding myself at the core of some women's accounts contains enormous power. I can read my centrality where so often there has only been my partiality. However, increasingly, I have come to recognize this centrality as a strength only when it is embedded in an understanding of the weakness associated with being centre stage ... I then had to address the issue of whether I was conflating their many varied experiences with my own. Was I finding in the field the slights, rejections and silencings I had experienced in my own educational career? There is a thin dividing line between the understandings that similar experiences of respondents bring to the research process and the element of exploitation implicit in mixing up one's own personal history with very different working-class experiences. (Reay, 1996b: 65)

Reay's analysis suggests that the interviewer's apparent closeness to particular interview accounts can result in the objectification of both the interviewer and of research participant(s) at the level of interpretation and analysis. Similarly, Hurd and McIntyre (1996), as white, feminist researchers, have written about how the affective pull of sameness can lead to emotional and analytic alignments that leave unexamined particular representations, so that attention to difference can 'silently privilege[d] our similarity'. The issue here is that, although work from feminist researchers and/or minoritized researchers has served to unsettle many of the assumptions about the nature of racialized/ethnicized inter/subjectivity in 'traditional' approaches to interracial interviewing, it has also led to the construction of problematic notions of racialized commonality and difference (see Jaschok and Jingjun, 2000). Such notions can draw attention away from the effects of other social differences (gender, class, age, disability and sexuality, for example) and interactional power relations between the researcher and research participant, and how these can manifest themselves at different stages in the research process (Aitken and Burman, 1999).

During my interviews with migrant hospice service users, narrative accounts of racism were common-place in the interviews. I identified with these accounts, as someone whose family had been subject to racist violence in our early period of settlement in the UK, and through my on-going experiences of racism. So, when research participants told me about their experiences of racism, these experiences were something that I thought I recognized and understood. I presumed shared meanings and common experiences. I did not question my interpretations of these accounts until my interview with Ibrahim, a 46-year-old Ghanaian man with cancer of the kidney. The following extract is taken from the point in our interview when Ibrahim had been talking about the lack of care and information that he had received about his illness in this country:

Yasmin: So did you have a lot of faith in your doctors all during this time?

Ibrahim: When you come here as a foreigner, you tend to think, you don't have that much of choice ... you tend to feel you must accept ... because of your background ... so you go to the hospital and whatever doctor comes up you find it difficult to question the person's activities *like even you guys who's born here* and *you* can question things, *you* can, you know insist on *your rights* and all sorts of things, *we cannot* be able to do that [sighs]. (Emphasis added)

Even though I was not born in the UK, Ibrahim's positioning of me tore to sheds my production of racialized commonalities around experiences of racism. Ibrahim did not see me as a racialized 'Other'. He positioned me as someone 'not-"foreign"', someone who could question and resist authority and someone who had a legitimate claim to 'rights'. This positioning forced me to re-examine and question previous assumptions about shared meanings and experiences, and made me attentive to the detail of differential and biographical constructions of racialized difference in all of my interviews.

In questioning identifications of racialized commonality in reflexive accounts of interviewing, I do not wish to suggest that points of connectivity and identification are not produced in the inter-subjective exchanges that occur in interviews, or that they cannot be examined and addressed at later stages in fieldwork and in analysis. Rather, my point is that we should not take interpretations of such relations at face value. It is also important to recognize that the interviewer/researcher often has some level of vested interest in offering particular representations and interpretations of such processes, and that such interests are linked to social, historical and institutional locations and the construction and reconstruction of experience.

At an analytic level, I would argue that accounts of commonality and difference, and the constructed opposition between these identifications need to be viewed with caution. They are most productively seen as emotional, discursive, interactional and inconclusive movements that test out and push at the boundaries, entanglements and contradictions of the production of identifications in interview encounters. In this sense, interpretations of commonality and difference are simultaneously emotional, political and highly risky. They raise significant questions about how, and at what points the research participant's narrative can come to be identified either as the 'same' or 'different', and demand that researchers account for the effects of such identifications throughout the research process. What I am suggesting is that we must examine critically and carefully how reflexive accounts are produced, and research the many different emotional, discursive and interactional relations and effects that are caught up in the production of such accounts.

Using these insights, my argument is that minoritized researchers need to be just as troubled by our interpretations of racialized commonality as we are by our interpretations of difference. Although commonality can be seen as a form of empathetic identification, it is vital that such empathy is interrogated and grounded in the recognition of the researcher as a separate and interactionally powerful producer, listener and interpreter; a producer, listener and interpreter who needs to interrogate her/his own relationship to the speaker, to the narrative, to the experience that it evokes and to her/his potential audience. Caruth and Keenan trouble any romantic illusion of empathy in their observation that, 'Empathy is about sameness ... Something is not confronted there, when you think you're understanding or empathizing in a certain way' (Caruth and Keenan, 1995: 264–9, quoted in Lather, 2001b).

To confront that which can be avoided in constructions of 'commonality' involves a politics of connection where research practices, interactions, identifications and analysis have to come under rigorous scrutiny. This means that there is a continual accounting for positionality in the whole process of knowledge production (Bhavnani and Haraway, 1994) that cannot be by-passed because of assumptions of commonality along one axis of identity. Ideas about the importance of connectivity to research concerned with questions of 'race' and ethnicity are discussed in Chapter 8. In the context of this discussion on interracial interviewing, what I want to emphasize is the need for methodological approaches to recognize how constructions of commonality and difference, and the 'local' and the 'wider', are always *already* connected and located within research interactions.

Ethical research practices and forms of analysis then become possible only when researchers strive to uncover these connections, and to discover how their own positioning is produced through them. This process of uncovering and discovering could be seen in terms of a 'getting closer to', a position that I critiqued in the introduction to this chapter. What is different about the process that I am advocating here, is that it is not based on a merging with or a swallowing up of difference through imposed and contrived versions of commonality. My worked-for connectivity is based upon a searching out and a recognition of points of disconnection (Probyn, 2000), and a getting closer to others through inhabiting, accounting for and putting to work the distances between us (Ahmed, 2000). In this sense, points of connection in the research interaction are not assumed to be pre-established and guaranteed by levelling commonalities of 'race', ethnicity, religion and/or language; rather, connection is worked for, with and through difference – even when apparent points of commonality are present. Sarah Ahmed's astute analysis of the potentiality for forms of collective politics makes an important point that is relevant to this discussion:

> a politics of encountering gets closer in order to allow the differences between us, as differences that involve power and antagonism, to make a difference to the very encounter itself. (Ahmed, 2000: 180)

CONCLUSIONS

Debates about interracial interviewing and racial and ethnic matching in qualitative research are not only methodological. They express a far greater range of concerns than isolated empirical questions about the consequences of racialized difference – or 'commonality' – in the production of interactions, identifications and knowledge in the interview. In order to gain an insight into these broader questions, we have to address the social contexts in which interview relations are located and, somewhat paradoxically, we also have to de-racialize the dominant discourses of racial difference that circulate within the methodological debates. That is, we have to resist the analytic temptation to see 'race' and ethnicity as being produced from a sole and fundamental difference between 'black' and 'white', or from any racially/ethnically marked characteristics of interviewers and research participants. I have talked about 'temptation' here because there is no doubt that such reified approaches to 'race' and ethnicity have both practical and political pay-offs for all researchers. For minoritized researchers, anxieties about the consequences of racial and ethnic difference in the interview have opened up particular opportunities in the academy, and have enabled us to do research on matters that are of critical significance to our own lives. For many white researchers, matching strategies can be used to avoid some of the analytic and emotional challenges of addressing highly complex and politicized power relations in research.

An underlying argument in this chapter is that decisions about whether to match for 'race' or ethnicity in qualitative interviews cannot be based upon sound empirical foundations or upon assumptions of commonality or difference. I would not argue against the use of broad matching strategies to explore relations between identifications, interactional power relations and the co-production of interview accounts. Indeed, such matching has been a part of research that I have been involved with as a research assistant (VanDyke and Gunaratnam, 2000). However, there is a need to be aware of the risks and dangers when trying to match for any social difference, whilst also questioning what we are aiming to do in the process. If we do believe that 'race' and ethnicity are situated social and political constructions, then matching is far from a 'solution' to the contingent manifestation of difference between the interviewer and research participant. In fact, matching poses its own, very thorny political and methodological questions that can unsettle assumptions about relations of commonality and difference. As Fine has reminded us:

> If poststructuralism has taught us anything, it is to beware the frozen identities and the presumption that the hyphen is real, to suspect the binary, to worry the clear distinctions. (Fine, 1998: 151–2)

Conversely, I think we also need to worry the *lack* of clear distinctions, and think about how hyphens might re-assert themselves and reinflect the apparent smoothness of commonalities in what is, often, only a part of a whole matrix of social and interactional relations within the interview. It is here that attention to connectivity in research is important. Through the pursuit and making of connections, researchers can interrogate points of commonality for the dislocations and differences that they carry. We can also examine difference for how it might position points of alignment and orientation between the researcher and research participant (see Chapter 8) that are a part of the wider contexts and that frame the face-to-face research encounter.

Seeking to recognize how 'race', ethnicity and other social differences are produced and have effects in qualitative interviews is undoubtedly difficult and messy work. Rather than trying to fix this mess with method-ological strategies such as matching, or analyses that erase the complexities of difference and power relations in the interview, there is much to be achieved by distrusting any neatness, and actively searching out and valuing the complexity and richness that comes with the mess.

<hr>

SUGGESTED READING

R. Edwards (1990) Connecting Method and Epistemology: A white woman interviewing black women. *Women's Studies International Forum*, 13(5): 477–90.

M. Fine (1998) Working the Hyphens: Reinventing self and other in qualitative research. In N. Denzin and Y. S. Lincoln (eds), *The Landscape of Qualitative Research: Theories and Issues.* Thousand Oaks, CA: Sage, pp. 130–55.

A. Phoenix (2001) Practising Feminist Research: The intersection of gender and 'race' in the research process. In K.-K. Bhavan: (ed.), *Feminism and Race.* Oxford: Oxford University Press, pp. 203–19.

P. Rhodes (1994) Race of Interviewer Effects in Qualitative Research: A brief comment. *Sociology*, 28(2): 547–58.

M. Song and D. Parker (1995) Commonality, Difference and the Dynamics of Disclosure in In-Depth Interviewing. *Sociology*, 29(2): 241–56.

F.W. Twine (2000) Racial Ideologies and Racial Methodologies. In F.W. Twine and J. Warren (eds), *Racing Research, Researching Race.* New York: New York University Press, pp. 1–34.

<hr>

NOTES

1. I do not deal with differences in language between researchers and research par-ticipants (and issues around interpretation and translation) in any detail in this chapter (see Ryen, 2002 for a discussion of language in cross-cultural interviews

and an overview of some of the literature). However, this is clearly an area that has direct and complicated implications, not only for questions of access, communication and meaning in interracial research, but also for patterns of racialization in employment within the social sciences, and for relationships between differently racialized researchers (see Jaschok and Jingjun, 2000; Marshall et al., 1998; Song and Parker, 1995).

2. This point also touches upon concerns that have been voiced by other minoritized researchers about feelings of accountability and commitment that minoritized researchers might have to 'minority' research participants (Zinn, 1979).

3. I say 'predominantly' here, because there are traces of essentialism in Edwards' account. For example, in her discussion of trust between her and black women in the study, Edwards describes how her whiteness placed her in a negative way, stating that: 'White people are separate, they are not to be trusted, do not engender (!) feelings of safety, unless they prove otherwise' (1990: 486).

4. Thanks to Tom Wengraf for these points.

5. There are many different approaches to discourse analysis, however 'what they share in common is a decisive break with a view of language as a transparent or reflective medium – epi-phenomenal and after the fact' (Wetherell and Edley, 1998: 164). The emphasis upon language thus shifts attention away from the individual to the meanings within discourse and to the power relations such meanings construct and negotiate (Willott, 1998).

The doings and undoings of 'race' – researching
lived experience

Looking for 'race'? analysing racialized meanings and identifications

SUMMARY

In this chapter I discuss the analysis of racialized identifications and their interrelations with other social differences in the interview accounts of minoritized research participants. There are two specific aims within the chapter. First, to build upon themes developed in Chapter 2, about how we might work both with and against racial and ethnic categories in qualitative research – in this instance focusing specifically upon the analysis of interview texts. And second, to explore an under-researched and under-discussed area of research on 'race' and ethnicity: that of the embeddedness and/or elusiveness of racialized identifications within the narrative accounts of minoritized people. What I am referring to is those minoritized research participants who do not express racial and ethnic identifications in explicit ways. In working through case study examples, I will present a combined analytic and theoretical approach that can be used to address the complicated and uneven meanings of 'race' and ethnicity within narrative accounts.

- The chapter will use the analytic technique suggested by Knowles (1999), of 'disassembling' 'race' in accounts of lived experience. This approach advocates the need to breakdown racial categories through reference to the narrative themes that give it meaning in the accounts of research participants.
- A theoretical approach to 'race' as a 'metalanguage' developed by Higginbotham (1992), will provide a theoretical framework for making sense of the connections between the textual hyper-visibility and the invisibility of 'race' and ethnicity in social discourses, practices and narratives.

What is at stake in the 'post' theories (post-structuralism and post-colonialism) that I have drawn upon to inform the discussions of 'race' and ethnicity in this book (see Chapters 1 and 2), is what Schutte has talked about as 'a certain loss of innocence with regard to narratives of identity' (2000: 48). What Schutte is referring to as a 'loss of innocence' is the critical awareness of the regulative power that narratives can have in 'defining who we are, who we are not, and who others are and aren't', bringing relations of power firmly into view, and challenging any simple sense of narratives as transparent representations of the self. However, there is also 'a certain loss of innocence' with regard to methodology and epistemology, as the questions that we ask in researching narratives of racialized identifications are also obliged to shift. Not only do we need to account for the power relations through which identifications are brought into being, but we can also no longer assume singular, bounded and fixed identities or experiences.

By identity, I am referring to a dynamic process of making sense of the self, where the 'instability of subjectivity is signified as having coherence, continuity, stability ... that at any given moment is enunciated as the "I"' (Brah, 1996: 124). In qualitative research on 'race' and ethnicity, questions of identity – how people talk about themselves as an 'I' – are central to the examination of the ways in which racial and ethnic categories are produced and have meaning in individual lives. Yet, this attention to the meanings of 'race' and ethnicity in individual lives is an area of analysis that is under-developed in the field of racial and ethnic studies (Knowles, 1999), and is one that can present significant challenges to researchers.

If we are to take seriously, and also interrogate, ideas about 'race' and ethnicity as socially produced, relational and given particular situated meanings through individual experience, then narratives of identity are of critical importance. Such accounts are important as sites where we can explore analytically the relations between social and subjective processes of 'race'-making, and where we can examine the relations between theory and lived experiences of 'race' and ethnicity. For example, in what ways, when and how are racial and/or ethnic identities claimed and/or resisted by individuals in accounts about their lives? How do these identities relate to wider political processes of the mobilization of collective identifications? How might racialized identifications be formed and mediated through their interactions with other forms of social difference, such as gender, class or sexuality? These are critical questions for a doubled research practice that aims to uncover the dynamism and heterogeneity of the meanings of 'race' and ethnicity, and to challenge forms of oppression based upon the understanding of 'race' and ethnicity as 'natural' categories.

This chapter engages with these important questions through a focus upon the analysis of racialized identifications in the accounts of minoritized research participants. In the first part of the chapter, I examine a critical epistemological assumption about racialized subjectivity, that is, the assumption that 'race' and ethnicity define the identities and being of minoritized people. This discussion will lead into the first interview example, and a demonstration of Knowles's (1999) analytic approach which advocates the need to 'disassemble' 'race' and to examine it through the narrative themes that frame and mingle with it in accounts of lived experience. The second interview-based example will look at accounts where racialized identifications are resisted and are more embedded. I will use Higginbotham's theorizing of 'race' as an encompassing metalanguage that can both mark and mask other social relations, as a way of making sense of some of the unevenness of the manifestations of 'race' and ethnicity in these accounts.

It is important to point out that while Knowles's approach addresses the analysis of 'race' and ethnicity in narrative accounts, and Higginbotham aims to theorize the discursive functioning of 'race' at a social level, my combined use of the work of Knowles and Higginbotham is not something novel. Knowles's methodological concerns assume the functioning of 'race' as a metalanguage that can be examined through varying constructions of 'alterity' (how individuals mark out differences between themselves and Others) in interview accounts. And Higginbotham's theorizing, when applied to methodological concerns, suggests the need to locate and dismantle the totalizing effects of 'race' to 'expose' the ways in which it can operate through a diverse range of 'configurations of difference' (1992: 256) in lived experience. The interrelationships between the approaches, and also their specific levels of focus and concern, should be borne in mind throughout this chapter.

RACIALIZED IDENTIFICATIONS

All research on 'race' and ethnicity is based upon epistemological assumptions about the nature of 'race' and ethnicity and their relation to the racialized/ethnicized research 'subject'. These assumptions relate to two main concerns. First, how 'race' and ethnicity operate in producing and signifying social relations. And second, how individuals make sense of themselves in the world through *subjectivity* and through *identity*, where identity can be understood as a process through which multiple and changing subject positions are given some sense of coherence (Brah, 1996; Hall, 1996). As debates about subjectivity and identity continue to develop and to problematize notions of an ahistorical subject,[1] central assumptions about the critical significance of 'race' and ethnicity to the subjectivity and identities of minoritized people remain unchallenged (Brush, 2001; Stanfield, 1993b). In both quantitative and qualitative research, methodological approaches seek to elicit and tap into the racialized/ethnicized attributes or meanings that are seen as emanating from the racialized subjectivity and experiences of minoritized research participants.

In qualitative research in particular, minoritized research participants are assumed to have some level of a 'race' un/consciousness, which structures how we see ourselves, talk about ourselves and how we live our lives. As Brush has argued in relation to feminist literature:

> By assuming race consciousness – race as a constituent of identity, treated as an issue, and resisted – race takes on the appearance of an essential identity, an identity independent of a particular historical situation. (2001: 175)

In this sense, assumptions about the inherent centrality of 'race' and ethnicity to the identities of minoritized research participants can themselves be seen as the products of racial thinking that can serve to reproduce varying, but nevertheless essentialist ideas about the nature of a racialized subjectivity and identity. It is significant that in the emerging field of 'White Studies', the silences of whiteness as a racialized identity have been seen as critical to social and intersubjective power relations. Simpson (1996), has argued that the silences of whiteness serve the purpose of producing a de-racialized identity, enabling those categorized as white to ignore, deny, avoid or forget their racialized subjective and social positionings. The analytic concern with the evasion and the non-manifestation of 'race' and ethnicity through whiteness has thus led to the mapping of a new methodological and epistemological terrain, concerned with recognizing and uncovering the ways in which whiteness is produced through its silences and invisibility.

I believe that the assumptions that are made about racialized subjectivity do not just have epistemological effects (i.e., they affect how we produce knowledge about 'race' and ethnicity), but can also affect experiences of doing research. In my hospice research, for example, my initial feelings and evaluations of what had been 'good' and 'bad' interviews with minoritized service users, were related to the extent to which questions of 'race', ethnicity and culture had been referred to explicitly within accounts. The interviews that I was initially drawn to (indeed those that I rushed home to transcribe), were those in which I could chart the production and salience of 'race'/ethnicity in narrative accounts. Such accounts articulated a racialized consciousness and included stories about racial/ethnic identifications, racialized difference, and racism and/or migration.

Race consciousness denotes a politicized, oppositional consciousness of race and racism … knowing *that* and *how* the personal is political, that and how the possibilities of one's existence are enmeshed with social conditions (de Lauretis, 1986). It further means that race is understood as a central constituent of identity, that race is, or becomes, recognized as a basis of domination or privilege, and that racism becomes a point of resistance. (Brush, 2001: 171, emphasis in original)

In most of my interviews with minoritized hospice service users, a race consciousness was co-produced in interviews, most often through stories of ethnic and cultural identity, migration, settlement and experiences of racism:

[…] when you're in Africa thinking about Britain and all these big, you know super countries. You always think of, that everything is there for you … when I came to Britain, I thought as soon as I finish, you know my education, I'll get a job. I'll buy a car. I'll buy this. That's not how it is. Things are completely different, um you find yourself really struggling to make ends meet, and you get sometimes caught into … a situation whereby you can't actually, you don't have enough money and yet you can't progress yourself, you, you cannot do anything on progressing yourself because you are trying to make money to survive. So things just stay there.' (James, 46-year-old Kenyan man)

… *you* go into churches … *they* ask you please not to come back, yeah, because if you keep coming there … then *their* people will stop coming. So it was very bad. (Hilda, 63-year-old Jamaican woman, talking about her early experiences of England in the 1950s, emphasis added)

Yesterday … one thing I feel very badly … when we having dinner [at a hospice outing], there was a seat available … so when I was sitting in the other seat next to her [a white service user], she quickly immediately left … and went to somewhere else [laughs] and I did realize that very badly. *Some people are very hostile … towards Asian people.* (Fatima, 39-year-old Pakistani woman, emphasis added)

The interviews that I found myself more distanced from, both emotionally and analytically, were those in which 'race' and ethnicity were not referenced, or where racialized identifications were resisted. At an emotional level, the accounts 'forced' me to question and to examine my own interactional and political responses to research participants within the research. As the research progressed, I became increasingly unhappy with my interpretations of the accounts of these research participants as being a part of an emotional and discursive evasion and negotiation of racialized difference.

Stanfield has discussed assumptions about racialized subjectivity through his recognition that there is very little research that has addressed and examined taken-for-granted, and/or seemingly non-problematic experiences of 'race' in the lives of people from minoritized groups. Writing about American research on 'race' and ethnicity, he observes that:

As much as US social scientists have made interracial interaction into a human dilemma, we rarely develop the methodological tools to probe the countless cases of people who look different phenotypically and yet still get along and live their lives – marrying,[2] having kids, engaging in work relationships, making friends – with no difficulty whatsoever. (1993b: 6, 7)

What's more, and to return more explicitly to questions of epistemology, what I also uncovered through my attempts to interpret such accounts, were the hidden assumptions through which we routinely attempt to understand and read the meanings of 'race' and ethnicity in people's lives. A critical consideration for me was the need to explore how and in what circumstances the non-manifestation of racial and ethnic identifications in the accounts of minoritized research participants could maintain and/or subvert processes of racialization. For example, if the power of whiteness as a social category and an identity is based upon its silence, can the silences of identity in those marked as racial, signal a disruption of racialized binaries (see Chapter 2)? In broad terms, how might we develop forms of analysis that offer sensitive and flexible ways of capturing very different forms of identification, experience and social circumstances?

DISASSEMBLING 'RACE': AN ANALYTIC APPROACH

Caroline Knowles (1999) has discussed similar analytic dynamics and tensions in her experiences of researching 'race' and ethnicity, in her biographical study of 'race' and mental illness. Knowles has suggested that in order to grasp the complexity of the meanings of 'race' in lived experience, researchers need to disassemble 'race' into the smaller concepts that give it meaning, and that are grounded in the co-produced stories of individual lives. Using the case study of 'Dan', a user of mental health services, Knowles argues:

> Deconstructing race into clusters of concepts which compose it make it much easier to deal with analytically. But there is also another reason for disassembling race. Because it is a category of political and social analysis, and not a category of human action and behaviour, it needs to be broken down into concepts which can be applied in the task of making sense of lives. The concept race itself may or may not be used in individual narratives. Whether or not race features *directly* depends on the political culture and the individual's experiences within it. In Britain ... there *are* ready-worked narratives of collective suffering which some people use to make sense of what has happened to them individually ... In [Dan's] case, as in other stories told to us by those to whom racial categories are applied, there are few direct references to race and we have to work much harder to understand its impact on, and significance in, lives. (Knowles, 1999: 123 emphasis in original)

For Knowles, one of the ways in which researchers can begin to examine the filigree of lived experiences of 'race' and ethnicity, is to explore how 'race' operates with, and through, other narrative themes in the making of identities within accounts. Such a locally focused analysis can then be contextualized with reference to the dynamics of the research interaction, to wider available discourses of 'race' and ethnicity and to social contexts. In her analysis of Dan, Knowles does this by focusing upon representations of 'alterity' and mapping these forms of otherness through the concepts of 'mobility' and 'home', charting the ways in which 'race' is acquired and produced in the story of Dan's life. The value of this analytic approach to the development of a doubled research practice can be summarized with regard to four main points:

1. It seeks to put embodied subjects back into the centre of analysis. The work of analysis is then seen in the weaving together of the discursive, the material, the emotional and the interactional in the stories individuals tell about their lives.
2. It theorizes a mutually constitutive relationship between the individual and the social context, in which 'race' is always at play, but can also be 'inaccessible to analysis and commentary' (Knowles, 1999: 115).
3. It allows for, and is sensitive to, the heterogeneity of experiences of 'race' and ethnicity, and therefore challenges essentialism by looking for the ways in which experiences of alterity, such as those relating to gender, class, health status and spatial movements, interact with and inflect racial and ethnic categories.
4. It gives attention to the interview interaction as a site for the negotiation and re-working of identities: 'Performed identities interact with research processes and have multiple possibilities' (1999: 112).

In the following discussion, I will show how productive such an analytic approach can be in my analysis of an interview with James, a black, Kenyan, hospice service user. What I also want to explore in more detail, is Knowles's recognition of the particular challenges of analysing accounts where narrative constructions of 'race' and ethnicity are less marked, and where the very social ubiquity of 'race' can, at times, place it 'beyond investigation'. I will do this through an examination of interviews with Patricia, a black, African-Caribbean hospice service user, in which racialized and ethnicized discourses and identifications were less obvious.

RACIALIZED IDENTIFICATIONS AND CONSCIOUSNESS

One of the most dramatic ways in which 'race' and ethnicity were talked about as alterity/difference in my interviews with hospice service users, was through stories about migration, settlement, belonging and 'home', and racism. Ethnic and racial identifications were articulated most vividly in my interview with James, a Kenyan man of 46 with AIDS, who had migrated to

England in 1972. Central themes in James's construction of his identity in the interview were national, regional and tribal identifications. These identifications were given meaning through discourses of belonging that were replete with talk of embodied, ethnic and cultural essences. James talked about his tribal identity as being 'inside of me', and being characterized by an essential ethnicized 'pride' that was 'carried within'.

James described himself as having been a successful property developer, who had lost his money in foreign investments with 'unscrupulous people'. He had also been active in black community organizations, and his interview was saturated with racialized identifications, marked by the 'we' consciousness (Brush, 2001) of a politicized 'blackness' and references to structural processes of inequality. In the following extract, James describes a specific racist incident in which he was excluded from the opportunity to rent housing in his early period of settlement:

Yasmin: And what was it like when you first came here?

James: Very, very, I'd say we were isolated because we didn't know many people and the, I remember trying to look for accommodation, and one distinctive one is, of one where I went all the way to North London and the woman said that yes, the accommodation is available, and it was raining, horrible winter. The beginning of winter, beginning. I got there, as soon as she saw me, she said to me 'The flat has just been taken five minutes ago'.

Yasmin: And do you think that was because you were African that she said that?

James: I think black ... because on the telephone she couldn't actually work out who I was, and she thought maybe it was some other nationality. But as soon as I got there, the flat had gone.

Yasmin: So how did you feel when that happened?

James: Very, very, very disappointed, and, and that sort of area, because I mean, so long as you get rent, but I mean the people have got reasons for, for doing that sort of thing, but I was upset because of the length of journey I had to make, go from South London to North London.

In addition to this incident, James also speculated about the more insidious effects of racism in structuring his early employment history where, despite a professional qualification in Business Studies, he was unable to find suitable employment:

James: I wanted to get into, um, sales or (...) marketing, sort of, you know advertising. But I found, I found it very, very difficult.

Yasmin: Why was that?

James: Um, I don't know whether it was to do with me, you know at interviews. I tried a number of interviews and I was unsuccessful. The first job I got was in a furniture shop ... As a stock controller, and so that actually gives you a picture that even if you've got qualifications, as a black person, you could end up doing something completely outside your, your qualifications.

What is notable about these extracts is that they can enable us to examine discursive processes in the making of identities within accounts (Wetherell and Edley, 1998). That is, rather than making assumptions about the essential racial/ethnic consciousness of James, we can examine how James 'does' 'race' and ethnicity in the interview. By this I mean, how the co-production of James's account of his experiences with me in the interview, serve to produce him as a black man, living within a particular racialized social context. From the extracts, you can see that my questions are neither 'neutral' nor 'innocent', but do the work of 'calling' (Althusser, 1971; Hall, 1996) James to particular racialized identifications through talk about experiences of racism. In this respect, the interview interaction is one in which both James and I negotiate identifications in ways that are 'intensely located' (Wetherell and Edley, 1998: 171) in biographical histories, interactional relations and differentiated social contexts.

In James's accounts of racism, we can see that there is a strong narrative recognition of himself as 'raced'. James made it clear repeatedly in the interview that different forms of racialization were oppressive and inhibiting. However, his identification with being 'black' is also used politically in the account, in making sense of individual experiences with regard to wider patterns of racist exclusion and marginalization. This articulation of a 'race' consciousness enables James's narrative to engage with, and to transcend, more local identifications based upon nationality and/or culture, and to move backwards and forwards from the idiosyncratic and emotional to the structural and impersonal. Indeed the political potential of such forms of identification can be witnessed in the fact that James went on to become a founding member of a refugee support group, which was set up to provide affordable, good quality housing to African refugees.

By addressing the multi-layering of meanings within the narrative construction of identifications, each of the two extracts can be seen as drawing attention to the practical consequences of racism in James's life, in terms of wasted time, energy and potential, and economic and social hardship. Both accounts are also particularly ambivalent. In the first extract, despite James's 'disappointment' at being refused the accommodation, the economic irrationality of the decision to reject James's rent because of his colour is immediately followed by the suggestion that 'people have got reasons ... for doing that sort of thing'. In the second extract, James suggests that his inability to get a suitable job may have been because of his individual performance at interviews, although the extract ends with the framing of his experiences in terms of the more systematic effects of racism within employment.

Such narrative movements create multiple meanings and locations within the account, in which James's narrativization of identity is simultaneously made vulnerable and made safe by the changing connections, and the autonomy that he constructs from collective, racialized identities. A tension running through both extracts is the simultaneous 'need' to de-personalize *and* to personalize rejection and exclusion. To use racist rhetoric: to know that 'it's nothing personal', whilst also sometimes constructing the possibility that processes of racism are not impossibly systematic, and that exclusion can be attributed to individual failings, rather than seemingly unchangeable and structured racialized relations. There is also a dynamism to the portrayal of identifications and to the consequences of racist incidents within James's story that, although emotionally painful, still need to be managed in order to live and to progress. Later on in the interview, for example, James talked about actively managing his emotional responses to racism, in order to 'slot in':

Yasmin: I just wanted to ask you because you mentioned sort of in your early experiences, and as a black person in this country, finding it quite hard, um, and for a lot of people that would have really affected their self-confidence –

James: It, it does affect you, but you come to a point whereby you virtually, you, you slot in somewhere, and you, you don't care any more whether (…) anybody is standing in your way, but you just want to go and get whatever you want to get. I think it comes to a point when *all black people* feel that way, yeah, that, that you know, they no longer wait by the door to be told to get in. They just open the door and actually go and get what they want. (My emphasis)

MORE THAN THIS: DISRUPTING RACIALIZED IDENTIFICATIONS

From the extracts that I have used from James's interview so far, it is possible to offer some interpretations of the significance of 'race' and ethnicity to the identifications that James and I co-produce in the interview. For example, from the interview account we might conclude that there is a large degree of correspondence between racialized discourses that stress the unity, coherence and homogeneity of ethnic groups and individual identifications. The 'we-consciousness' within James's account is strong, and suggests the importance of racialized identifications in making sense of individual experiences of social exclusion and marginalization. However, if we use Knowles's approach of disassembling 'race' in our analysis of James's account, some of the meanings of 'race' and ethnicity in his life story can be seen to operate in less obvious, and also more contradictory, ways through other narrative themes.

One particular element of ethnicized identity was given complex and ambivalent meaning through James's account of AIDS, and the links he made between the disease, ethnicity and questions of sexuality (questions which were never made clear in the interview).

James's stay within the hospice had been marked by strict procedures of confidentiality about his illness, since he had chosen not to tell his ex-wife, children, relatives and friends about his AIDS. James had lived with the secrecy about his 'taboo illness' for about 18 months before I interviewed him as a hospice in-patient, and during the tape-recorded interview, he avoided naming AIDS, using more general terms such as 'the disease' or 'this illness'. James made it clear that his silence about his AIDS was linked to particular culturalized constructions of shame, and fears of stigmatization within the Kenyan 'community' if it had been known that he had AIDS. He also pointed to the loneliness and isolation engendered by his decision not to tell friends and family about the disease.

The links between James's silence about his AIDS and ethnicity were talked about at a point in the interview when I had asked James about whether he had any contact with Kenyan people in this country:

No. No, and I don't want to have anything to do with the Kenyan community ... with this disease, they tend to actually prey on you ... because as soon as people find ... out that you know, you have actually have contracted this thing, they spread out rumours to the rest of the community, which is quite damaging. So that's why most Kenyans don't want any other Kenyan to know about it.

If we adopt Knowles's suggestion of disassembling 'race' and ethnicity, and examining how they might operate though constructions of alterity in James's account of living with AIDS, we can uncover further, more complex interrelations between ethnicized and racialized identifications and other narrative performances of difference within the account. For example, a part of James's resistance to racism was talked about as being achieved through gendered discourses of 'not caring any more whether anyone is standing in your way ... you just want to go and get whatever you want to get'. However, this racialized-gendered positioning of the strong and emotionally remote man, is undone by the narrative meanings given to AIDS, where the disease and the moral questions it raises position James in a passive, emotional and isolated position of silence. Such a stance disrupts the gendered positioning of 'not-caring' and the 'we-ness' of a politicized consciousness that James had used to articulate both ethnicized and racialized identifications in response to racism.

James's account of his decision to live with the secret of his AIDS thus tells us something more about the negotiation of ethnicized and racialized identifications in the account of his life. It tells us how these racialized .identifications can be contested and mediated in the face of other social differences, and how these processes of mediation can lead to variable configurations of racialized-gendered difference in particular social contexts.

AIDS is a disease that not only involves a brutal assault upon the body, it also carries social and moral meanings that can threaten and assault identities (Lather and Smithies, 1997). In James's account of his AIDS, the meanings of the disease radically disrupt his narrative constructions of ethnic and racial identifications. The narrative meanings given to James's AIDS open up the deep ambivalences, contradictions and precariousness of ethnic and racial identifications as belongingness, where ethnicity can no longer be experienced as the primordial homogeneity of a 'Common People' (Hall, 1993). Through the narrative about AIDS, we are able to see the ruptures and the fracturing of ethnic identifications, in which a fundamental tension arises between the discursive possibility of being both a 'proud Kenyan' and 'living with AIDS'. To draw upon, and to customize an argument made by Stuart Hall (1993), the more ethnic identifications are recognized as being contested, fractured and diverse, the more important analytic and political questions must become of 'which identity?', 'whose identity?' and 'which version?'.

What we achieve by this analytic process of disassembling 'race', is not simply a more nuanced understanding of the construction and the effects of particular ethnicized and racialized identifications in narrative accounts. We are also able to produce more complex analytic questions. We can ask about the types of work that identifications do within particular narrative contexts, and what effects such work has, when and for whom? As researchers we can seek to gain insights into *how* racial and ethnic identifications are situated and relational, being both strategically recognized and resisted in negotiation with the other social identities in narrative accounts.

For example, in James's account we are able to see some of the complexities of the mutual constitution of individual and social contexts through 'race' and ethnicity and their relationships with AIDS. This can be seen in how James points to the social structuring of relationships around AIDS within the Kenyan 'community', while at the same time, his silence about his AIDS is both a product and a producer of these relationships (see Knowles, 1999: 115). We might also see that as researchers, we cannot stand outside the ways in which such a political ordering and negotiation of identifications takes place within the interview. In this way our own social location, and also the interview interaction and how it is embedded with a wider social context, can be made visible and opened to scrutiny.

A particular aspect of how the interview relationship was used in the negotiation of James's identifications with me in the interview, can be witnessed in James's refusal to name AIDS during the tape-recorded interview (although he had named it in the pre-interview discussion). A key dynamic that I want to highlight is that, although James refused to name AIDS within the interview, the whole of his interview narrative was based upon rich evocations of the social and moral consequences of living with AIDS as a Kenyan man in Britian. James used our interview as a place where he could express his anger at what he called the 'ignorance' of the Kenyan community's responses to AIDS, and where he could prescribe the political need for more education to raise levels of awareness and understanding about AIDS. The interview interaction was thus contoured by a simultaneous complicity with and defiance of the moral dimensions of AIDS, in which the interview account was produced as a 'testimony' that challenged the very silencing mechanisms that shaped it:

> Testimony is distinct from other reports because it does not simply affect those who receive it; testimony *implicates* others in what they witness. (Frank, 1995: 143)

James's refusal to name AIDS during the interview was, therefore, much more than an emotional response to the threat (see Chapter 7) of being identified as having AIDS, and served to implicate and locate the interview interaction and the research within the wider social context. It was precisely James's non-naming of AIDS that unhinged neat distinctions between 'safety' and 'threat', 'openness' and 'secrecy', and the 'public' and the 'private' within the interview, reproducing emotional and ethical aspects of his lived experiences of AIDS and challenging the research to do something about this context.

Knowles's approach to disassembling 'race' and ethnicity is thus much more than a technical process of analysis, and also involves attending to how narrative accounts can serve a number of purposes in the production of identifications. With regard to James, these purposes included the ways in which the interview provided opportunities for James to map different versions of himself, through the narrative interrelations of his lived experiences of 'race', ethnicity, gender and AIDS. However, the structuring of these narratives by the non-naming of AIDS also served to situate the interview, and to produce me as a witness to a testimony, politicizing the research and pushing it towards activism.

Having addressed some of the different dimensions that can be involved in the analysis of identifications in narrative accounts, I want to examine further some of the analytic difficulties in recognizing the heterogeneous and context-dependent meanings of 'race' and ethnicity in interview texts. In order to do this, I will introduce a theoretical framework developed by Higginbotham (1992) and will suggest that this framework, together with Knowles's approach of disassembling 'race', can be particularly valuable in examining the narrative elusiveness of 'race' in accounts of lived experience.

THEORIZING 'RACE' AS A 'METALANGUAGE'

All analytic approaches to 'race' and ethnicity require some level of a theoretical understanding of how 'race' might operate in contemporary social life. Here, I will outline a theoretical framework that I have found extremely valuable in examining and accounting for the complexities and nuances of the operation of racial and ethnic categories in interview accounts. In broad terms, this theory, derived from Barthes (1972) and developed by Higginbotham[3] (1992) can be seen as part of 'racial formation theory' (see Omi and Winant, 1994; Winant, 1994). In racial formation theory, 'race' is theorized as a socially constructed and unstable dynamic of meanings that is produced and negotiated at 'macro' social levels and through individual experience. In Higginbotham's approach, 'race' is conceptualized as a mythical, over-determining 'metalanguage' which can function to obscure the meanings of other social differences. In this analysis, Higginbotham suggests that:

> Race serves as a 'global sign', a 'metalanguage', since it speaks about and lends meaning to a host of terms and expressions, to myriad aspects of life that would otherwise fall outside the referential domain of race. By continually expressing overt and covert analogic relationships, race impregnates the simplest meanings we take for granted. It makes hair 'good' or 'bad', speech patterns 'correct' or 'incorrect'. It is, in fact, the apparent overdeterminancy of race in Western culture ... that has permitted it to function as a metalanguage in its discursive representation and construction of social relations. Race not only tends to subsume other sets of social relations, namely gender and class, but it blurs and disguises, suppresses and negates its own complex interplay with the very social relations it envelops. (Higginbotham, 1992: 255).

Within this theoretical frame, 'race' can be both hyper-visible and 'loud', enveloping a plurality of identifications and meanings, and it can be invisible and silent, masking itself and its intersections with other forms of difference. Racialized silences in the lives of 'black' people are particularly ambivalent for Higginbotham, involving the protective need to conceal identifications, alongside localized rhetorical performances that can 'dismantle and deconstruct the dominant society's deployment of race' (1992: 266–7). Within this framework, a refusal to locate identity through 'race' can be seen as a defensive strategy, enabling some individuals to negotiate processes of racialization (see also Clark Hine, 1989). However, it can also be a position that fundamentally threatens the racial order by 'un-locating' identifications from racializing discourses (Ang-Lygate, 1996).

The significant point here is that the political meanings and the repercussions of the refusals of 'race' are open-ended. These refusals can be either progressive or oppressive, depending upon their particular mobilization and effects within the specific contexts in which they are produced and negotiated. This theorization is important in so much as it disturbs the homogenizing, essentializing sweep of processes of racialization that deny diversity and the situated meanings of 'race' and ethnicity.

This theoretical approach to 'race' as a metalanguage is relevant to the wider discussion in this chapter, in that we can read the empirical approach of Knowles into the theoretical framework of Higginbotham. The analytic need to disassemble 'race' in order to examine the other social and subjective relations that produce it in particular ways (Knowles, 1999), recognizes the discursive power of 'race' as an encompassing, obscuring and uneven metalanguage. In this respect, the combined Knowles–Higginbotham approach can enable an understanding and an examination of the intersections between 'race' and other social divisions, *and* the connections between 'race' in its textual hyper-visibility and in its invisibility in narrative accounts.

In many respects Higginbotham's approach resonates with Bourdieu's observations on the multiple dimensions and meanings of class categories in research. Bourdieu has argued that analytic categories always 'smuggle' in and subsume a range of other phenomena that are a vital, but hidden part of the meanings of the explanatory category:

individuals grouped in a class that is constructed in a particular respect ... always bring with them ... properties which are ... smuggled into the explanatory model. This means that a class or class fraction is defined not only by its position in the relations of production, as identified through indices such as occupation, income or even educational level, but also by a certain sex-ratio, a certain distribution in geographical space (which is never socially neutral) and by a whole set of subsidiary characteristics which may function, in the form of tacit requirements, as real principles of selection or exclusion without ever being formally stated. (Bourdieu, 1984: 102)

I will illustrate the value of the combined Knowles–Higginbotham approach in the next sections, where I examine the narrative interviews of Patricia, a Jamaican woman in her early forties, with cancer of the larynx. When I met Patricia she had had her larynx removed and spoke with the aid of a mechanical valve, which gave her a deep, robotic sounding voice.

She was a nurse and a lone parent with a teenage son. I had got to know Patricia in the hospice day centre where I worked as a volunteer during the research, and I interviewed her three times.[4] In all of these research encounters and interviews, Patricia made few direct references to 'race' and/or ethnicity. When Patricia did talk about 'race' or ethnicity, she most often talked about them in individualistic terms and as being a part of her general 'positive' orientation towards life, linked to her family 'background' and Christian beliefs. Indeed, a central theme throughout Patricia's accounts was that of 'being positive'. I have interpreted this theme of positiveness as a form of alterity that was used by Patricia to mark out differences between herself and other people. The important point to note is that alterity need not always be seen in relation to negative forms of difference. Box 5.1 provides a summary of how I have used Knowles's approach of disassembling 'race' to make analytic links in Patricia's accounts between 'race', being positive, and religion.

I was able to make analytic links in Patricia's accounts between 'race', 'being positive' and religion, by searching for how 'race' might be 'smuggled in' – to use Bourdieu's (1984) phrase – through other narrative themes (Knowles, 1999). In the analysis, I examined the narrative connections between themes in Patricia's account and looked at these connections and themes in relation to the wider social and historical context. We know for example, that there are numerous and varied social connections between religion and 'race'. In Britain, and in the United States, the Church has been a central site for the resistance of racism, particularly among people of African descent (Moody, 1997). In a qualitative study of women in America, which explored constructions of self-esteem in women's 'own terms', Chatham-Carpenter and DeFranciso (1998) contend that self-esteem was linked closely to a 'positive outlook', and that there were also racialized differences in the construction of self-esteem.[5] Chatham-Carpenter and DeFranciso suggest that for many of the African-American women in the study, being positive was a 'life survival strategy', which was a part of early socialization within black families and the Church that served to protect them from 'the harmful effects of racism' (p. 473). Research has also made connections between social contexts, the Church and discourses of a common humanity that resist the relevance of racialized difference (Turner, 1997).

Interrelations between religion and 'race' are thus implicated in how we might understand the individualistic language of 'personhood' (Rose, 1996) in Patricia's accounts of being positive, and how this might relate to a refusal or a denial of the relevance of racialized difference in her life story.

Box 5.1   Analytic links between 'race', being positive and religion in Patricia's accounts

I want to begin my account of the analysis of 'race' in Patricia's interview narratives, by examining an extract from my first interview with her, where I had asked Patricia about experiences of racism. I have chosen to begin with this extract because it can be more easily compared and contrasted with James's accounts of racism, and can be used to examine points of similarity and difference in the narrative co-construction of racialized identifications within the accounts. The extract is taken from a point in the interview when Patricia was telling me about how she had migrated to England at the age of 19. At this point, I had asked Patricia about whether she had experienced any 'prejudice' in her early days of settlement:

Yasmin: And did you have any experiences of prejudice Patricia, when you first came?

Patricia: I think subtly, um, but, but I think the thing with prejudice is that it's there but sometimes, maybe you don't see it because you, you're not looking for it, or you rise above it, or people sometimes respond to you because of, who you are and maybe you can overcome their prejudice. I mean, I'm not saying that it changes. It doesn't. I mean the prejudice is there. But I think sometimes people respond to you because of who you are and I'm not saying that lots of other people don't get that, but I think, because of, I've always been a positive person and I sometimes say that, being in the Caribbean, I sometimes see that the youth growing up here would probably experience and feel more prejudice than I do, because I came from such a positive background that those positive things took me on a different plane. Does that make sense?

Yasmin: Yes. So you have a very strong sense of identity and of who you are?

Patricia: Yep, Yep and that, even though the prejudice might be there in the people, because of the way I come over, they then deal with me in a certain way. I think so.

In this extract, Patricia makes narrative connections between being positive, her ethnicity, her (family) 'background' (referenced in an earlier part of the interview) and a psychological capability to refuse to be formed by some of the constraining effects of discourses of racialization and lived experiences of racism.[6] However, unlike James's account, Patricia's narrative refuses to make use of a 'we-consciousness' of racialized identification, even when talking about racism. In this regard, Patricia's narrative complicated my initial analysis of racialized identity (and how I had thought talk about racism could 'call' (Althusser; 1971, Hall, 1996) individuals to racialized identifications), and also 'forced' me to 'deal with' Patricia's accounts 'in a certain way' analytically.

In the extract, Patricia does not use individualistic themes of 'positive-ness' to deny the social pervasiveness or the existence of racism. Instead, her narrative makes a more complex and active connection between social processes, differences in social location, and identifications. By differenti-ating and situating racialized identities (the differences between her and British-born African-Caribbean youth), Patricia suggests how it may be possible for certain individuals from minoritized groups to gain a 'strong' sense of self within a system that is overwhelmingly disempowering. The account therefore dislodges reified and unitary notions of racialized power inequalities, by drawing attention to variable, racialized experiences and subjectivities and the differential possibilities that are available to resist aspects of oppressive power relations.

Class, gender and geographical location can all affect the nature, form and the sites of racist practices and how individuals are able to respond to, or to resist racism. Social class, for example, can shape how we feel about ourselves, where we live, if and where we work, the type of job we do and how we get home from that job. Our class position and the opportunities and limitations that it produces are simultaneously affected by, and affect, the social and subjective meanings of 'race', ethnicity and gender. All of these factors can have effects upon the types of racism that we encounter, our capability to resist racism, and how we make sense of our experiences. Hence, there are social dif-ferences in both types of racism and in responses to it. Yet these differences can be obscured in the way 'race' can operate as a 'metalanguage' within narrative accounts (Higginbotham, 1992). This was apparent in my interviews with minoritized hospice service users. For example, when I had asked Keith and Patricia (both of whom were relatively young and middle class) about their experiences of racism, they acknowledged the existence of racism, while recognizing that their experiences of it had been at a 'sub-tle' level. The forms of racism that Keith and Patricia talked about were more covert and non-violent, in marked contrast to many of the working-class service users who had migrated to this country in the 1950s and early 1960s. In this respect, it is important to note the social embeddedness of the 'positiveness' that Patricia talks about in her abil-ity to overcome 'prejudice' and the ways in which this positiveness is very much related to social class. Patricia's contention that her positiveness can force people to 'respond to you because of who you are' is a discourse about personhood that is most effective in relation to 'subtle', rather than violent physical acts of racism. It is much more difficult to assert 'who you are' in situations of violence. However, Werbner (1997) has suggested that there are ontological connections in racism as violation that span these differences, by the marking of *collective* racial or cultural differences between groups.

By referring to cultural, class, gendered and generational differences between herself and African-Caribbean youth who have grown up in this country, Patricia's account can be seen as recognizing some of the constraining and differential psycho-social effects of racism in inhibiting the development of individual and collective forms of empowerment through 'positiveness'. Her account does not, therefore, deny the significance of racialized relations and structures that can produce particular racialized identifications and experiences. Rather, the text allows for recognition of the *constrained* negotiation and contestation of racialized discourses, identifications and particular power relations. As Knowles suggests, such recognition is important because it can point to individual variation within racialized identifications *and* to the unevenness of racism, serving to disturb existing typologies of 'race':

> Consideration of individual lives ... brings endless variation to racial categories making it possible to take into account important differences between occupants of the same categories. In trying to explain why racism works so unevenly – why are some the targets of racial violence and others excluded from certain jobs – sociologists have been preoccupied with getting their categories 'right' ... without seriously considering the individual lives composing those categories or the conditions in which race is acquired in the living of lives. (Knowles, 1999: 130)

Taking all of these points into consideration within the context of the obfuscation of 'race' within Patricia's broader account, the interview extract can be interpreted as making significant narrative links between three inter-related processes. First, Patricia talks about how, in her case, the accumulation of specific subjective resources through forms of 'positiveness' can mediate racializing social relations (her positiveness 'makes' people deal with her as an individual rather than as a racialized Other). Second, she makes explicit what can get 'done' to these social relations, and how identifications can be simultaneously produced in the process of 'doing' (she is able to both 'overcome' prejudice and through this, to resist definition by 'race'). Third, the narrative is able to come back to issues of social structure and discourse. It does this by addressing the ways in which social relations (where and when you were born and how you are brought up) can serve to distinguish identifications (differences between her and African-Caribbean youth), and therefore the meanings, manifestations and non-manifestations of 'race' and ethnicity, enabling some people and disempowering others. In this sense, Patricia's account can be seen as taking us:

> to the heart of what lies behind the urgent but so often too empty question of our times: 'what is it like for displaced people to become something, someone?' And it reminds us that the question of cultural identity as Michel Foucault so poignantly reminded us, is not in fact 'Who are you?' but 'What can you become?' (Hall, in Alexander, 1996: vi)

What Patricia talked about 'becoming', was an individual who, amid social relations marked by ethnicity, 'race', gender, class, age and disability, was sometimes capable of resisting dominant, racializing discourses by varying specific, racialized identifications and positioning herself within individualistic discourses of positiveness. Box 5.2 provides a short analytic summary of this interpretation.

How I got to this interpretation of the meanings of 'race' in Patricia's accounts was by following initially the narrative traces of 'race' embedded in the way Patricia talked about what being positive meant to her. By examining these meanings in different interview extracts, I was able to identify particular narrative connections between talk about being positive and religious beliefs, Patricia's family background, and 'race'. These connections were most explicit in a narrative extract about experiences of racism. From the propositions of wider research, I could see how the 'thematic field' (see Wengraf, 2001) of being positive could be related to 'race' and to psycho-social defences against racism in particular. However, rather than taking these connections as given, what I did was to look for 'evidence' of their relevance to Patricia's story, by searching for extracts in her interviews where Patricia made links between being positive, 'race', religion, her 'background' and racism. My analysis of the extract about racism, again spoken primarily through discourses of being positive, produced an interpretation in which 'race' as a metalanguage was broken down to reveal differences in its meanings throughout the accounts, its interrelations with subjectivity and with social positioning.

Box 5.2 An analytic summary

AN ABSENT PRESENCE: ANALYSIS AND LIVED EXPERIENCE

So far, it has been possible to map out a combined empirical and theoretical approach that can be used to make sense of accounts in which 'race' and racialized identifications are embedded. In terms of analysis, I have used the approach suggested by Knowles of disassembling 'race' – by examining the ways in which 'race' can be produced with, and through, other narrative themes in interview accounts. In Patricia's case, the theme of being positive was searched for its racialized connections and meanings. This form of analysis has been linked to the theoretical framework elaborated by Higginbotham, who has suggested that 'race' as a metalanguage can serve to superimpose 'a "natural" unity over a plethora of historical, socio-economic, and ideological differences' (1992: 270). I have theorized the hyper-visibility of 'race' and the embeddedness of 'race' in narrative accounts as socially and interactionally located identifications that have a textured significance and complexity in individual life stories.

This combination of approaches has been valuable in exploring the 'slippery' contradictions of 'race' that Winant has referred to as 'an absent presence, a present absence' (1994: 267). However, I also want to push my analysis further. I want to expose some of the incomplete and imperfect relations between analysis and lived experience, or what Bourdieu (1990) has called the differences between analytic and practical 'logic'. By this, I mean how the very dynamic nature of the meanings and the 'doing' of 'race' and ethnicity in accounts of lived experience can often defy analytic description. So, while I have made explicit how researchers might approach the interpretation of accounts in which racialized identifications are embedded, I also want to address the limitations of analysis in attending to what Derrida (1976) has called '*différance*', which refers to both difference and deferral in the construction of meaning.

I will do this initially by drawing upon the insights of narrative-based methods (see Chamberlayne et al., 2000; Hollway and Jefferson, 2000; Wengraf, 2001). These methods suggest that stories based upon events in people's lives (rather than opinions, justifications and generalizations) provide valuable analytic opportunities for understanding the complexity of accounts of lived experience. This is because stories can be less open to conscious rationalization. Stories are theorized as holding an unconscious logic and form (a 'gestalt'), through which meanings, emotions and identifications can be expressed in complicated ways, which can sometimes be beyond the conscious control of research participants.

You may have already noticed that the extracts I have used in this chapter to illustrate ways of interpreting Patricia's accounts are not all narrative accounts (Box 5.3 describes the key components of Western/Northern narrative). They are extracts from my semi-structured interviews, in which the nature of my questions often elicited opinions and generalizations from Patricia about 'being positive'. In order to interrogate the meanings of 'race' in Patricia's life story further, I want to examine a narrative extract from my first interview with Patricia. I have chosen this extract because it is an 'epic narrative' (Wengraf, 2001) featuring a number of episodes and characters, in which the meanings of 'race' are opaque. I have also chosen this extract because it signified a 'turning point' narrative in Patricia's account of her illness, in which her cancer was first diagnosed.

A NARRATIVE ACCOUNT

The extract that I have chosen to examine is part of a much longer and detailed narrative from Patricia's first interview, in which she talked about her experiences of cancer, from what she saw as a 'late' diagnosis, to surgery to remove her larynx, and then chemotherapy. A significant part of Patricia's account of her illness was her belief that initially her symptoms

Drawing upon the work of Linell and Jonsson (1991), Wengraf has summarized the 'classical narrative' as having:

(i)   a kernel of a Central Event Sequence. Prior to this core narration…
(ii)   a description of background in order to orient the listener for the narration to follow and after the completion of the
(iii) central event sequence,
(iv)   a further description of the new situation that has arisen as a result of the narrated action (which might be restoration of the status quo) and, finally,
(v)   then an evaluation or explicit theory of the significance of the events narrated, its 'moral'. (2001: 115)

Box 5.3   What characterizes a narrative?

were not taken seriously by her doctors. Interestingly, Patricia made sense of her late diagnosis by saying that: 'I didn't *fit the category*, in terms of my age, or my history, I didn't smoke and I suppose cancer is one of those things that, that you don't think about unless the picture is right' (emphasis added). In addition to these aetiological factors (she was young and a non-smoker), Patricia also identified professional and social categorizations as impeding her diagnosis: 'It's like health professionals always think there is something wrong with them, um, I was female and I was black.' This passing reference to being 'female' and 'black' was the first time that Patricia had drawn explicitly upon a racialized identification in the interview. This fleeting reference to 'race' is significant in framing, although not explaining, the nature of dynamics within the narrative extract that I will explore.

This extract is taken from the first interview, after Patricia had talked about her symptoms getting worse. Patricia was eventually given an exploratory procedure, a 'laryngoscopy', that revealed and identified the cancer. The cancer was so pervasive that during this procedure, the surgical team had to perform a temporary tracheostomy (a surgical opening in the windpipe), so that when Patrica awoke from the surgery she was without a voice. Patricia talked about this as a 'negative' experience, not simply because of the shock of being unable to speak, but also because she felt that her doctors had not recognized her needs as a person. In this interview extract, she talks about how she dealt with this assault upon her personhood:

Patricia: And dealing with that negative experience, one of the things I did, I wrote a letter, I didn't think I was well enough to um, to er fight them, but what I did, I wrote a letter that went into my case notes … The doctors came on a round [ward round] and I chose the female, one of the female members of the team and said 'I've written a letter. But I don't just want it to go in, I want it read … as if I were able to read it.' And I made her stand up there and read the letter that I had written about listening to people and caring for people and giving … so I dealt with, with the way they treated me and not listening to me and they need to listen to people …

Yasmin: How did they respond to that?

Patricia: Er, I think the older doctors looked sheepish and I think the younger, the younger ones were kind of amazed, um but I think that it would have done something for all of them. Because I needed to say what I said and I did that. And so having, I mean sometimes I think of Ann's [the hospital] and I feel that they made such a balls up of it, that had I gone to the Royal Oak [another hospital] from the beginning could it have been caught before it went to my oesophagus. Because a lot of suffering that I had, is to do with the fact that it had gone to my oesophagus … but then you don't know, and so with time I was just able to let go and I say I don't feel bitter. I mean, I don't, I don't ever want to go to Ann's … I just feel sad that the Consultant should be the way he is and I feel sad that other people, probably who don't have the assertiveness and the training that I've had, and know how, and the links to be able to move on to somewhere else and know that I can say, demand a second opinion and get it. That is sad, but, but I've dealt with it. I'm not bitter. I'm not bitter.

Within this account are a number of identifications that through the alterity of disability and disease also refer to gender, class and cultural capital. Through her account of the letter, Patricia talks about asserting and reinserting herself as an active, embodied and articulate *person* within the interaction. Patricia's 'voice' is talked about as being represented, amplified and identified by her choice of who was to read her letter (a woman doctor), and through talk about the letter's differential impact upon the doctors in relation to their age and status. Within the extract, 'race' is not referenced directly, but it cannot be ignored in making sense of Patricia's attempts to 'make' the doctors 'hear' her voice.

The metaphor of 'voice' is a strong theme in Western/Northern discourses aimed at 'recognizing' (Fraser, 1995) the denied personhood of individuals from a range of different oppressed groups. This discourse has involved the moral imperative for those who are subordinated to 'speak' as 'subjects' in the public and political spheres, and for those in more powerful groups to 'hear' these 'voices' (Alldred, 1998). In this sense, Patricia's story of her experiences of surgery, of being silenced, and her struggle to make herself heard, have both literal and discursive meanings that can be interpreted as embodied experiences and as embodying social location and discourse.

Building upon the previous interpretations of reading 'race' through the narrative theme of positiveness, can enable us to trace racialized connections between Patricia's account of asserting her individuality as part of a resistance to racism and how she talks about the need to reclaim her personhood in this extract. In the extract, Patricia talks about using the letter to 'speak'. As such, the letter has both a symbolic and a literal function within the story. The letter confronts the doctors with Patricia as an embodied, feeling, 'speaking' person, challenging de-humanizing professional defences (Menzies Lyth, 1988) that may have also been a part of Patricia's own experiences as a nurse. In my interpretation, it is the 'Othering' processes of these de-humanizing themes, and Patricia's resistance to them, that produce the discursive and emotional connections that circulate within and across Patricia's accounts of racism, and of hospitalization and surgery.

We know from the earlier interview extract about racism, that the meanings of racism in Patricia's life are narrated in terms of a de-individualizing objectification that Patricia has talked about negotiating and overcoming by her individual positiveness. Patricia's positiveness was talked about as forcing others to see her as an individual, thereby challenging the de-humanizing impulses of racism. So, while 'race' is not directly named as a dynamic in Patricia's accounts of surgery, a focus upon the narrative genealogy of 'being positive', and what this has meant in the story of Patricia's life, has a history suffused with 'race', ethnicity, gender and class. In this example, the analytic uncovering of the relevance of 'race' to the account has taken place by tracing the narrative and discursive meanings around being positive and their connections to forms of alterity (Knowles, 1999). I have been particularly concerned about how these meanings might affect, and be affected by, how Patricia positions herself within wider social discourses (humanism in particular) and how she might use this positioning to talk about defending herself against attacks upon her personhood.

ANALYTIC NEEDS

Despite my claims about the racialized meanings of the themes in Patricia's account of her surgery, I have also been interested in the political process of analysis, and particularly my 'need' to identify 'race' in this part of Patricia's story, and my initial frustration with the textual embeddedness of 'race' in the extract. My 'difficult' experiences of making sense of 'race' in Patricia's interviews also suggest that I need to problematize my own analytic reliance upon the need for ethnic and racial identifications to be made explicit throughout the narratives of minoritized research participants. Narrative accounts inevitably hold elements of a taken-for-granted relationship of familiarity with subjective and social worlds that, by its very nature, is unremarkable and naturalized (Bourdieu, 1977). Rather, the need to identify and explicate racialized identifications in the accounts of minoritized research participants is a more firmly rooted part of the analytic, as opposed to the lived project. The former relies heavily upon the articulation and categorization of identifications in order to represent difference authoritatively.

It would have been useful analytically for me to have been able to identify very specific and explicit representations of ethnic and/or racial identity throughout Patricia's interview accounts. This would have given added empirical 'legitimacy' and 'validity' to the claims that I have made about the racialized meanings and connections between different parts of the interview texts. However, Patricia's story, and stories like hers, demand more complex analytic approaches. The specific textual mechanisms through which Patricia was able to resist the call to racialized identifications in the telling of her story, can be heard as involving the possible suppression, naturalization, contestation, incorporation or the transgression of ethnic and/or racial identifications within particular representations of subjectivity, mainly in the form of ' being positive'.

While it has been possible to trace ethnic and racial identifications in the contexts of Patricia's story and within discourses of positiveness, I have not been able to explore ethnic or racial identifications within the long and detailed story about Patricia's cancer and surgery in specific ways. The highly individualistic themes of positiveness and personhood in Patricia's account mark smooth and often fleeting movements of identification, in which being 'African-Caribbean', 'black' or a 'woman' appear rarely as clear or unitary representations. Rather, in the 'one-is-many mode' (Strathern, 1988), each identification has to be regarded as performing and producing a plurality of discursive subject positions (and interrelations) that can sometimes appear to achieve primacy or visibility. It is here that we can see the value of a doubled research practice which, in seeking to deconstruct the determinism of racial and ethnic categories, can uncover new configurations and meanings of difference and point to ways in which processes of racialization might be interrupted and resisted.

CONCLUSIONS

The combined use of the analytic and theoretical insights of Knowles (1999) and Higginbotham (1992) in this chapter, demonstrate the value of approaches to 'race' and ethnicity that deploy theoretical insights about the operation of processes of racialization to the investigation of accounts of lived experiences. Attention to processes of identity construction within narrative accounts can make important contributions to the understanding of the simultaneous connections and the distinctiveness between subjectivity and the wider racial order, creating new opportunities through which racialized identities and questions of agency may be thought. Just as we need to expose the operation of 'race' as a metalanguage in producing and obscuring social relations and practices, we also need to recognize 'race' and ethnicity as 'providing sites of dialogic exchange and contestation' (Higginbotham, 1992: 252), in which racialized identifications are both socially located and are also in a constant process of individual production and negotiation.

In recognizing these complex and contingent relations between individual experiences of difference and social relations, it is valuable to remind ourselves of Avtar Brah's approach to difference, discussed in Chapter 2. As you will recall, Brah's approach also provides an analytic framework for deconstructing essentialized notions of 'race' and ethnicity, by examining the production of difference across the domains of experience, subjectivity, identity and social relation. Of particular relevance to the discussion here is Brah's suggestion that:

> it is useful to distinguish difference as a marker of the distinctiveness of our collective 'histories' from difference as personal experience inscribing individual biography. These sets of 'differences' constantly articulate, but they cannot be 'read off' from each other ... how a person perceives or conceives an event would vary according to how 'she' is culturally constructed; the myriad of unpredictable ways in which such constructions may configure in the flux of her psyche; and invariably, upon the political repertoire of cultural discourses available to her. Collective 'histories' are also, of course, culturally constructed in the process of assigning meaning to the everyday of social relations ... The same context may produce several different collective 'histories', differentiating as well as linking biographies through *contingent specificities*. In turn, articulating cultural practices of the subjects so constituted mark contingent collective 'histories' with variable new meanings. (Brah, 1996: 117, emphasis in original)

By treating the production of 'race' and ethnicity in individual narratives as a complex, situated co-production that needs to be disassembled through analysis (Knowles, 1999), I think that researchers can begin to deconstruct the discursive power of 'race' as a metalanguage (Higginbotham, 1992). What attention to the situated 'loudness' and the 'silences' of 'race' and ethnicity can do in this respect is to disrupt and reveal the limitations and the binarism of our use of conceptual categories in analysis. Without assuming the monolithic and defining over-determinacy of 'race' and/or ethnicity in the identifications of minoritized research participants, our understanding of discourses and practices of racialization, and also possibilities for resistance and transformation, become so much more complex and interesting.

SUGGESTED READING

P. Brush (2001) Problematizing the Race Consciousness of Women of Colour. *Signs*, 27(1): 171–98.

E. Higginbotham (1992) African-American Women's History and the Metalanguage of Race. *Signs*, 17(21): 251–74.

C. Knowles (1999) Race, Identities and Lives. *Sociological Review*, 47(1): 110–35.

NOTES

1. Ideas about the nature of subjectivity and identity are the site of fierce contestation, particularly in the wake of post-structuralist and psychoanalytic critiques of the subject, which have exposed the historical and political basis of ideas about the nature of the human subject (see Hall, 1996; Yegenoglu, 1998).

2. In critiquing approaches to the analysis of 'race' in this extract, Stanfield also reproduces dominant assumptions about the interrelations between 'race' and sexuality, by constructing a racialized Otherness through a normalized heterosexuality.

3. I am grateful to Gail Lewis for introducing me to Higginbotham's work and for her insistence on its relevance to my analysis here.

4. My second 'interview' with Patricia took place while watching a video she had brought into the hospice for us to watch together. The video featured a TV programme about cancer in which Patricia had appeared, before she had had her larynx removed. She had not seen it since the operation. She told me about the video at the end of our first interview, saying that 'I haven't been brave enough to look at myself, so I might look at it with you.' I asked Patricia if I could record our discussion during the interview, but I had not positioned the microphone well and little could be heard from the recorded tape.

5. The study involved qualitative interviews with 59 women aged between 21 and 94. The sample comprised 37 'Caucasian' women, 21 African-American women and 1 Latina woman. See also Ali and Toner's (2001) research on depression among Caribbean and Caribbean-Canadian women that has suggested that the socially isolating experience of immigration can be related to a greater identification with 'self-nurturant domains' such as religion.

6. Research into 'race', ethnicity and mental illness has also suggested links between 'race', experiences of racism and self-esteem. Fernando has argued that racism is a 'pathogen' that can cause depression by 'promoting blows to self-esteem, inducing experiences of loss, and placing individuals in a position of helplessness' (1988: 132).

'What do you mean?' insecurities of meaning and difference

SUMMARY

This chapter examines the relationships between social identities and meaning, with a specific focus upon the production and analysis of noticeable insecurities of meaning. The need to ascertain meaning in research across racialized and ethnicized boundaries has been seen as critical to the examination and understanding of difference. However, I will argue that we need to question and re-think this perspective if we are going to account for the multifarious and complicated ways in which difference can take shape and have effects in qualitative research encounters.

- The main purpose of this chapter is to elaborate the value of analytic attention to insecurities of meaning in research, and to suggest a form of analysis that can be used to explore what ambiguities of meaning can tell us about social and subjective difference.
- These social and intersubjective dynamics will be examined through an example from a qualitative interview, in which detailed attention is given to the epistemological and ethical challenges of recognizing and working with ambiguities of meaning in a context of shifting interactional, embodied and social power relations.

In Part I of this book, I drew attention to a central tension in qualitative research on 'race' and ethnicity. This tension concerned the theoretical importance of recognizing that the meanings of 'race' and ethnicity are dynamic and contingent, whilst also recognizing that many researchers have to fix these meanings at some points in the process of doing empirical research. In this chapter I want to look at a different aspect of this tension, by examining the production of noticeable insecurities of meaning[1] in researching across difference, and how such areas of ambiguity have been seen as undermining the quality of research interactions and the 'data' generated through them.

I am referring specifically to the field of cross-cultural research here, where there has been a long history of work, particularly in anthropology, on the need to establish meaning across cultural difference (see Ryen, 2002 for an overview). This work has been characterized by 'naturalistic assumptions' (Gubrium and Holstein, 1997), in which some form of pre-established, external reality is taken to be reflected in people's words and actions. As Ryen observes, the 'firm belief in a preexisting cultural reality is the epistemological basis for the demand that the researcher catch or grasp that reality as closely as possible to the way the interviewee does' (2002: 336).

A predominant theme in much of the literature on cross-cultural research has thus been how 'Other' meanings can be accessed and established by the researcher, with the researcher being encouraged to employ a number of different methodological and analytic practices to ensure that meanings are grasped and established. Riessman (1987), for example, urges the detailed transcription of interviews, in which close attention is paid to narrative form. She also suggests the need to include contrasting cases in analyses that 'explicate the diversity of … experiences and the variety of narrative forms used by different cultures' (Riessman, 1987: 189). As such, the 'problem' has been how the researcher can 'overcome' racialized, cultural and linguistic 'barriers' and gain access to the research participant's world of meaning. As Shields has suggested, in a critique of Verstehende's methods in cross-cultural ethnography:

> The actor-subject becomes a medium by which the investigator may fully appreciate foreign events and actions in their social, internal and cognitive context. For this to be possible, a close intersubjective relation must be achieved. There must be a consensus of experience, some sort of a-symptotic merging of two sets of personal and cultural understanding. (Shields, 1996: 279)

For Shields, the overriding goal of shared meaning, accompanied by interactional 'rapport' and 'intimacy', can obscure forms of difference and power relations within the research encounter. In this sense, the striving for 'communication as communion' (p. 276) is seen to objectify the research participant, as the researcher's role is transformed from 'speaking-with' to 'speaking-as'. Shields argues that such methodological practices and aims can themselves be 'a manifestation of ethnocentrism at the epistemological level' (p. 281), that mask how all individuals are 'cultural hybrids', and can also obscure the multi-dimensional and liminal nature of 'truth'.

Rather than using a model of research that privileges one person's understanding over another's, Shields draws upon Bakhtin's (1981) ideas on 'dialogism' to suggest that research should be concerned with the nature of the difference and the dialogue *between* the researcher and the research participant. Dialogue in this sense is linguistic, and also stands for the interaction of ideas and embodied subject positions. The particular value of this Bakhtinian-inspired approach to dialogue is that it is explicitly concerned with difference and multiplicity in communication (see Gurevitch, 2001 for a discussion of different theorizations of dialogue). In relation to research, this emphasis upon the value of difference signifies a significant shift away from the naturalistic assumptions of cross-cultural research, and is not dependent upon the researcher trying to 'forget', or to elide her/his own location with that of the research participant in order to secure shared understanding.

Approaches that stress the value of difference and the co-construction of meaning in research span a range of theoretical perspectives. However, what these varied approaches have in common is that they serve to problematize long-standing methodological practices and epistemological assumptions in cross-cultural research, bringing questions of power and of ethics to the communication process (Schutte, 2000; Spivak, 1992). This attention to power relations in research across racialized and ethnicizied difference, together with the more general move towards approaches that have questioned the inherently representational nature of language (Hollway and Jefferson, 2000; Poland, 2002) have had far-reaching consequences.

It is noteworthy that research involving the use of interpreters is now also questioning the purely technical and linguistic framing of meaning, in favour of more reflexive approaches that seek to explore the effects of the social locations of the interpreter, researcher and research participant upon the construction and interpretation of interview accounts. Edwards (1998) has thus highlighted the ways in which shared ethnicity and language between the interpreter and research participant can be fractured by class difference, which can have effects upon the interpretation of meaning within the interview and in the later analysis stages of research. Spivak, in her provoking analysis of cross-cultural translation as profoundly ethical, rather than purely linguistic, has also suggested that 'simply boning up on the language is not enough; there is also that special relationship to the staging of language as the production of agency that one must attend to' (1992: 187).

In this chapter, I explore the relations between the co-construction of meaning, ethics and difference in more detail. A particular focus of this exploration will be upon how noticeable insecurities of meaning can provide researchers and research participants with valuable indications of how our social identities are made real and can have complex effects in research interactions.

In examining the potential value of attention to ambiguities of meaning in research, the chapter makes three main claims:

- that insecurities of meaning constitute and are constituted by subjective as well as social differences between the researcher and research participant
- that there are particular ethical challenges for the researcher in engaging with and recognizing the embeddedness of ambiguities of meaning within the research interaction and within the wider social context
- that a critical step in the analysis of insecurities of meaning is how such meanings are 're-contextualized' and are connected to inter/subjective and wider social dynamics.

The chapter is organized around these three issues, and begins with an example of an insecurity of meaning from a qualitative interview with Edwin, a hospice service user. This example will be used as a starting point from which to examine the ethical and epistemological challenges of working with ambiguities of meaning in qualitative research concerned with recognizing difference and uncovering and challenging power inequalities. The second section of the chapter introduces an analytic approach that can enhance the ways in which insecurities of meaning can be used to examine the dynamic production of difference within research interactions. The final section returns to ethical considerations, by focusing upon dilemmas in the representation of research 'findings', which bring into view the researcher/research participant/reader triad.

INSECURITIES OF MEANING AND DIFFERENCE

Yasmin: So a lot of the time are you by yourself here?

Edwin: Not 'a lot', most of the time. 'A lot of time?' I'm here all the while on my own.

Yasmin: Right. How does that feel?

Edwin: Well, it's terrible but I have to break my mind to it, init? I have to break my mind to the condition init? From my wife gone, from my wife gone to the [pause] home, I never, one day lay in that bed inside here [indicates bedroom and double bed], and she, the woman, never one day lay in the bed. I stay out here all the while, I don't know why. I don't sleep in the bed.

Yasmin: Not even at night?

Edwin: No.

Yasmin: Really? Since your wife's gone?

Edwin: Yeah, I don't know why. I just, prefer to stay out here.

Yasmin: Yeah, um, so does it remind you of her?

Edwin: Umm.

Yasmin: Umm.

Edwin: [laughs] And um, the reason, er, that is one too, but the reason, most of my reason is because, you know, through these tablets I have, I taking water tablets and I pass my water very often, and um, to get up and walk, to walk to the bed, is a longer movement. But when I sleep out here, I use a pail.

Yasmin: Yes.

Edwin: And I just come off the, this here [indicates couch], easy. I just roll off and have a pee and put it there in the morning and take it out ... And you see, so that's why I don't, that's one of my reasons too for not sleeping in there. And then you know the bed is wide, and when I sleep here, I can make to put me foot up more comfortable ...

This extract is taken from the first of two semi-structured qualitative interviews with Edwin, a working-class black, African-Caribbean man in his late seventies, who, at the time of the interview, had been living with prostate cancer for 11 years. Edwin was a retired cleaner who had worked in the post-office, and was the father of four children – two sons who lived in England, and two daughters who lived in the United States. He had migrated to England from Jamaica in the 1950s, in order to find work.

I have chosen this extract from my interviews with Edwin because it is centred upon *noticeable* insecurities of meaning. By 'insecurity of meaning', I am referring to instances and processes in which the meaning of particular words, phrases or gestures are noticeably unclear and are wide-open to different interpretations and readings – but within certain interactional and social parameters. By examining the co-production of ambiguities of meaning in qualitative research encounters, I will be suggesting that insecurities in meaning are points from which we can begin to examine and make explicit the interrelations between the interactional and social dimensions of meaning that are of critical importance in research concerned with recognizing difference.

My argument is that in noticing insecurities of meaning, the researcher is obliged to ask certain questions, and it is this process of questioning that can be used to challenge essentialism in research. First, there are the questions that relate to the identification of the ambiguity of meaning in the first place. In the interview with Edwin, these questions concern Edwin's references to the bed and its meanings in his life story, identity, and past and present relationships – particularly with his wife, who had been admitted into a residential home following two strokes, 16 months before the interview.

What is Edwin talking about in this part of the extract and why? For example, the phrase 'from my wife *gone*' (emphasis added) evokes feelings of abandonment and loss, emphasized by Edwin's acknowledgement that it is 'terrible' to be alone. There is also another insecurity of meaning in this extract, signified by Edwin's statement that 'she the woman, never one day lay in the bed'. This link made through free association suggests that prior to her admission into residential care, Edwin's wife did not share the bed with Edwin, while the reference to 'lay' is suggestive of sex. The change from 'my wife' to 'she the woman' in this part of the text is objectifying and distant, with the corresponding intonation suggesting feelings of anger and/or resentment. The ambiguity here relates to what Edwin is saying about the marital relationship, his feelings towards his wife, and how these are linked to talk about his illness and choice about where he sleeps.

There are also questions surrounding how the uncertainty of meaning is related to the context of speaking (Burman, 1992), and to the interview interaction itself: why and when I asked certain questions and what I meant by them; how Edwin interpreted and oriented himself to my questions; how he might have resisted the subject positions offered by my questions; and how I interpreted Edwin's responses. Did differences in our ethnicity, gender, class, age and health, as well as our biographical histories affect the production of this insecurity of meaning, and in what ways? What effects did the qualitative semi-structured interview that I was using have upon the nature of the 'interactional order' (Goffman, 1983) of the interview and the meanings that were produced?

Of course these questions raise concerns that are relevant to all researchers. However, when we are concerned with understanding the nature and the effects of social and intersubjective differences between researchers and research participants, and when we are concerned with explicating and attending to the political and historical legacies that these differences carry, uncertainties of meaning have particular implications.

In the following sections, I will make explicit an interpretive process that can be used in working with and recognizing the dynamic and situated nature of ambiguities of meaning. I will then look at this process in relation to my interviews with Edwin, using the interviews to discuss questions relating to the ethics of the interrogation and representation of ambiguities in meaning in research.

ANALYTIC PROCESSES

In discussing relations between insecurities of meaning and difference, I want to introduce a broad process of interpretation that I have identified in recognizing and interpreting noticeable ambiguities of meaning. I have conceptualized this process as characterized by juddering movements of *contextualizing, de-contextualizing* and *re-contextualizing* uncertain meanings. In putting forward this analytic process, I would advise the reader to distrust it as an encompassing and secure methodological prescription or 'model'. It is at once both social and technical and, as an account drawn from my own research experiences, it should be treated as ethnographic data and subjected to cultural analysis (Haraway, 1990). What is particularly significant about this process of recognition and interpretation, is that it is also ethical and involves the researcher in decisions about what is defined as the nature and the extents of 'contexts', and what should be done in representing these contexts. I detail the process here, as a way of elaborating upon a 'doubled' research practice (Chapter 2) which, in working with and valuing ambiguities of meaning, seeks to unsettle the understanding of *all* meanings as fixed and stable.

CONTEXTUALIZING, DE-CONTEXTUALIZING AND RE-CONTEXTUALIZING INSECURITIES OF MEANING

A fundamental dynamic in addressing insecurities of meaning in research encounters, is that the very first stages of identifying an ambiguity inevitably also involves freezing, and then scanning it against our own arenas of experience and understanding. I would argue that this very moment of identification is based upon elements of objectification and disconnection, as the insecurity of meaning is defined, against the context[2] of our own frames of reference.

This contextualization of ambiguities of meaning is, therefore, accompanied by a simultaneous interpretive act of *de-contextualization*. That is, in flagging up the ambiguity/difference of meaning for ourselves, researchers take it out of – even if only fleetingly – the context in which it had psychosocial connections. This de-contextualizing act can serve the purpose of making safe the ambiguity. It can immobilize it, and allow the researcher to view it from the security, and often the defensiveness, of our own perspectives, limiting the danger that the ambiguity could, in fact, lie within, question and/or undermine the researcher's frameworks of meaning (Gurevitch, 1990).

Having outlined these interpretive processes and manoeuvres, and the dangers they pose to a critical and doubled analysis, it is important to describe the ways in which it is possible to use ambiguities of meaning productively, to generate more 'creative understandings' (Bakhtin, 1986). In my interviews, and most importantly in analysis, I found it useful to acknowledge the processes of contextualization and de-contextualization, and then to build upon them by purposefully *re-contextualizing* ambiguous meanings. By re-contextualizing, I mean a process through which I sought to explore the nature of the uncertainty of meaning against a wider context that could shed light upon the ways in which difference can take shape, be expressed in, and constitute the research interaction. I have identified four main areas that this re-contextualization process should address:

1. How the ambiguity of meaning is situated and connected to other narrative themes in the research accounts and/or interviews.
2. How ambiguous meanings might be related to biographical, subjective and social differences between the researcher and research participant.
3. How the research interaction is framed by and located within wider social discourses and social and historical contexts.
4. How and in what ways the subject positions that are constructed, made available or are denied to the research participant and the researcher in the research interaction and analysis might serve to inscribe one or both of the participants into dominant representations (Bhavnani, 1993).

Re-contextualization uses and builds upon the dynamic interplay between subjectivity and processes of objectification in the contextualizing and de-contextualizing movements. These processes can then be used to interpret the insecurity of meaning in relation to a spectrum of analysis (Scheff, 1997; Wengraf, 2000), extending from the tiny detail of the research interaction (the local) to the social and historical context (the global) through which it is formed and takes shape. Analysis, then, has the potential to move away from a focus upon difference as 'defamiliarization' and 'estrangement' (Marcus, 1998), to an engagement with the cross-cutting movement of meanings and identities in the psycho-social spaces of the research interaction. (See Chapter 7 for a discussion of psycho-social space.)

Re-contextualization, in this sense, has particular relevance in research concerned with difference and can enable interpretation to attend to the construction of meaning *and* the positioning of both research participant and researcher. As Bakhtin (1986) has argued, a strong assumption underlying cross-cultural research has been that the researcher needs to relinquish her/his own frameworks of meaning in order to fully enter into the world of the research participant (see also Shields, 1996). In challenging this assumption, Bakhtin suggests that:

if this were the only aspect of understanding it would merely be duplication and would not entail anything new or enriching. *Creative understanding* does not renounce itself, its own place in time, or its own culture; and it forgets nothing. (1986: 7, my emphasis)

The re-contextualization process can thus be of value methodologically and politically in accounting for, and in using in analysis, the subjective and social positionings of the researcher. Where social and interactional dominance come together in the research interaction, they are not 'forgotten', even when de-centred (Schutte, 2000), but they are held accountable and interrogated with regard to history, culture, biography and methods. The ethical implications of such a formulation are particularly valuable in examining more complex power relations during research. For example, for minoritized and 'hyphenated' (Visweswaran, 1997) researchers, there are often several lines of power relations that mediate and complicate experiences and histories of Otherness, which the concept of 'creative understanding' can enable us to explore within the specific context of our role as researchers.

Having described the basic movements within this interpretive process, the following sections will examine how these processes can be used to make sense of my interviews with Edwin.

INTERPRETING EDWIN'S INTERVIEWS

During the first interview, from which the extract is taken, my interpretive processes of contextualization and de-contextualization involved framing and re-creating the change in Edwin's sleeping arrangements (a move from sleeping in the double bed to the settee) as an emotional response to the loss of his wife. Within the extract, Edwin's initial response to my suggestion that the bed might ' ... remind you of her?' is to offer a fleeting, amused and tokenistic acknowledgement 'umm', while elaborating that 'most' of the reason is due to the medication for his prostate cancer, and his need to get up several times during the night to urinate. Looking at the shape of the extract, it is possible to see that Edwin is able to talk to me in length and detail about the range of embodied-practical reasons for the change in his sleeping arrangements. The detail of this description overwhelms both the 'logic' through which Edwin connects talk about sleeping arrangements to talk about his wife, *and* the initial acknowledgement of any emotional component to Edwin's move to sleeping on the settee.

Edwin's willingness to talk about the embodied-practical does not mean that his wife's admission into residential care was without emotional significance, however. In looking at the re-contextualization process of analysis I want to examine this question of emotions as a site for the production *and* the contestation of embodied racialized and gendered identifications in the co-construction of the insecurity of meaning. In attempting to re-contextualize the ambiguity of meaning in Edwin's interview with regard to the 'local' context of the interview interaction, I found it valuable to do a micro-analysis[3] of a segment of the extract with other people (the section 'from my wife gone' to 'I don't sleep in the bed').

The process of micro-analysis that I used was derived from the biographical narrative interpretive method (see Wengraf, 2001), and involved the use of a 'panel' of people, with very small pieces of interview text (sometimes just one or two words) being presented to them in sequence. Based upon the words given to them, the panel suggest possible meanings and formulate hypotheses about the relationships between the meanings of the words, their relation to events and experiences talked about in the interview (for example, what the words might be referring to and what might come next) and the interview interaction (Rosenthal, 1993). Different approaches to micro-analysis can be found in the work of Pittenger et al. (1960), Labov and Fanshel (1977) and Scheff (1997).

Through this analysis, certain interactional and discursive dynamics within the interviews became apparent. The de-contextualizing of the inse-curity of meaning had served to spotlight Edwin in a moment of narrative crisis, caught between recognizing and denying any emotional connec-tions between his account of not wanting to sleep in the 'wide' double bed at night and his wife leaving their home. Yet, this moment of narrative transfixtion contains a more complex interplaying of dynamics and iden-tifications, marked by biographical and racialized, gendered, generational, class, health and research-related forms of difference.

In examining the insecurity of meaning in relation to intersubjective dynamics, it is relevant to acknowledge that a significant period of my adult life was taken up with caring for my father, and a much shorter time caring for my mother. What is relevant in terms of the dialogic production of meaning in the interview, is that I made several attempts both to get Edwin to talk to me about his emotions and to ask him about his family relationships. In presenting my initial analysis of Edwin's interviews to other researchers, I was alerted to the possibility that this line of question-ing, and the generation of insecurities of meaning surrounding emotions, could be reflective of processes of counter-transference (see Hollway, 2001) and to my own anxieties about familial care – and concerns about aban-donment in particular. An alternative interpretation to this psychoanalytic perspective is that my emotion-directed questions were part of the inter-actional order of the research encounter, in which my own biographical experiences were invoked, made 'real' and managed (see Heritage, 1998). Regardless of which interpretive frame is employed, the point that I want to draw attention to is how the researcher's own identity and experiences can be a part of the generation of ambiguous meanings.

By examining the insecurity of meaning in relation to other narrative themes within the two interviews with Edwin, the entanglements of bio-graphy with social differences of 'race' and gender also became apparent. For instance, Edwin's repeated assertions that traumatic events did not bother him, resonate with dominant discourses of masculinity as 'hard' – emotionally invulnerable and distant – and were often accompanied by his repeated use of the phrase 'breaking my mind to the condition'. When I asked Edwin about his feelings when his doctor had told him that he had prostate cancer, for instance, he appeared to deny any emotional response, whilst also representing himself as the passive subject of medical authority and intervention:

Yasmin: So how did you feel when they told you it was malignant?

Edwin: ... No different. I mean, you know me, I just break my mind to the con-
           dition just as he [the doctor] tell me, I said 'Well OK' and I just, just wait-
           ing on them to do what they want to do. It never bothers me.

The phrase, 'breaking my mind to the condition', suggests a forced accep-tance, with the term itself evoking discursive, genealogical links to slavery, where the control of slaves by slave owners was a project of 'breaking' resis-tance, known as 'breaking-in' slaves. This violent expression evokes notions of active, but also forced and protective, situational strategies forged in the context of oppression and trauma, enabling individuals to avoid or to negotiate feelings of fear, pain and powerlessness. In making analytic connections between themes in Edwin's interviews, there were also further links between 'breaking my mind to the condition' and talking about emotions.

Looking at the broader picture in relation to what Edwin said about talking, it appeared that Edwin had a largely instrumental stance towards talking, denying any of the therapeutic or cathartic benefits that researchers have been keen to emphasize (Lee and Renzetti, 1990; Opie, 1992). At several points during the interviews, Edwin questioned the value of talking, the emotional intensity that was often in his voice serving to emphasize a depth of feeling. In relation to a question about whether he had talked with his children about his illness, the response was both angry and clear:

... what need do I have to talk about it? It makes no sense to keep on talking about it.

At one level it is possible to offer a highly gendered interpretation of Edwin's resistance to talking about or acknowledging difficult or painful emotions, through explicit reference to his biography as an older man and, more specifically, to the relation of this biography to popular and academic racialized discourses of masculinity (see Alexander, 2000). Despite a modern growth in emotional reflexivity, particularly among young, white, middle-class people, a key attribute of models of hegemonic masculinity (Carrigan et al., 1985) can still be seen to lie in the devaluing and/or repression of emotional expression. Such constructions of masculinity also intersect with racializing discourses, where specific forms of racial Otherness, particularly in relation to working-class men of African descent, are frequently depicted through blackness being body and not mind (Frosh et al., 2002; St Louis, 2000). As Claire Alexander has argued, popular and academic discourses about 'black' masculinities, in relation to young men, construct them as being 'in crisis':

> At the heart of this 'crisis' is a notion of a masculinity which is inevitably flawed and eternally failing, of a manhood which is at once a biological imperative and a social impossibility. At the same time as 'race' comes to stand for masculinity, it also denies its fulfilment – it becomes a symbol of its own atrophy. More than this, however, the discrepant construction of black masculinity effectively silences alternative interpretations, occupying and espousing a position of 'Truth': black masculinity becomes, then, 'invisible'. (Alexander, 2000: 131)

For Alexander there is a tension between the discursive production of black masculinities as 'discrepant masculinities', constructed as deviant and in opposition to white masculine norms, and the recognition of black masculinities as 'transruptions' that can contest and unsettle dominant discourses. Alexander suggests that what is needed in the discursive move from black masculinities being positioned as 'discrepant' to 'transruptive', is a recognition of a plurality of black male subjectivities:

> it is important to recognize the ways in which black male subjectivities not only enact but also dislocate dominant discourses about the place of the black 'Other'; the debate is thus not only about 'alternatives', but about 'discrepancies' – the performance of alterity which threatens to break through such discourses and translate them. It is also crucial to account for the complex and interwoven layers of black male subjectivities which differentiate, dislocate and transform identifications internal to the imagined collective black male identity. The challenge facing black masculinity then is to move beyond convenient binary categorizations – white/black, male/female, inside/outside, dominant/subaltern, plural/single, straight/gay – to confront a more complex reality. (2000: 136–7)

What I want to suggest, using Alexander's conceptual distinction between 'discrepant' and 'transruptive' black masculinities, is that the ambiguity of meaning in my interview with Edwin can be interpreted as a discrepancy that challenges dominant discourses about the embodied Otherness of black men. It does this by troubling and unsettling the binary between the mind/body. Such an interpretation is important because it highlights the wider discursive void that exists in relation to old and diseased black men, and forces us to question the discursive connections between 'race', gender and age that circulate within dominant discourses of black masculinity.

For example, attention to dominant discourses in the process of re-contextualizing the ambiguity of meaning in Edwin's interview, might suggest that as a 78-year-old, Jamaican, working-class man, the expression of emotions in Edwin's life was shaped by, and shaping of, particular identifications and defences. These dynamics can also be read as being played out interactionally in the interview, creating differences in how Edwin and I positioned ourselves within wider gendered, class-related and racialized discourses of emotionality. Yet, as Jackson has suggested, the differences between men and women's expressiveness should not be seen as indicative of essential differences, but as linked to the possibility that:

> discourses and narratives of emotionality are differentially available to and differentially deployed by women and men ... Growing up as a woman in modern Western societies involves learning a language of the emotions, a sensitivity to cues about others' feelings and a fluency in emotional story-telling. (Jackson, 1998: 60)

By using the re-contextualization process of analysis to address broader social discourses and contexts, it becomes possible to engage more specifically with some of the discursive and interactional dynamics surrounding the particular co-construction of the ambiguity of meaning in Edwin's interview. These dynamics suggest that the racialized and gendered differences in emotional expressiveness that are evoked through the ambiguity of meaning are not essential differences. Edwin, as a black man, is not inherently less emotional than me, a South-Asian woman. Rather, differences in the expression of emotions can be seen as a part of a process of managing and negotiating identities within wider social discourses and in relation to their specific configuration within the research interaction (see Frith and Kitzinger, 1998).

ANALYTIC DANGERS

This recognition of the differential availability, negotiation and deployment of discourses of emotionality, rather than a focus upon essential differences in emotion in my interviews with Edwin, appears to be of tremendous value to the interpretation of the ambiguity of meaning in the interview. However, this approach continues to position Edwin as being 'in crisis'. It is an example of black masculinity as 'discrepant' (Alexander, 2000), but in this instance it also involves the expansion of discursive connections, through old age and disease, to extend the field of pathologization: it is not only young, hyper-physical and hyper-sexual black men who are caught up in the mind/body split, but also older, sick, black men.

Thinking about Edwin as alone and ill and not sleeping in the 'wide' bed at night since his wife's admission into residential care, positions him as being imprisoned by a heightened racialized masculinity, unable to be 'real' even when emasculated by the bodily betrayal of prostate cancer.

Analysis here runs the risk of feeding into dominant constructions of African men that are based upon an epistemological duality between mind and body, which in this case triples to include a splitting between mind, heart (as emotion) and body. Yet, this tripled separation becomes more fraught and blurry, when we take into account old, diseased, black men's bodies, and a form of cancer that strikes at the core of the exoticized 'dick thing' (hooks, 1992) of constructions of phallocentric (but also youthful and able-bodied) black masculinity as hyper-physical and hyper-sexual. In this discursive construction, the black, old and diseased male body is an 'abject body' (Butler, 1993), without a recognizable ontological status within dominant and popular discourses.

In trying to make sense of the ambiguity of meaning in Edwin's interview, the re-contextualization process of analysis has questioned, but not disrupted, the racialized mind/heart/body split. What is particularly dangerous about this process of analysis is that it does not *just* stand to reinscribe Edwin (see Bhavnani, 1993) within dominant representations of black masculinities as 'discrepant'. Precisely because of the discursive void that does not recognize the diverse relationships between 'race', gender, age, class and disease in popular constructions of black masculinity, re-contextualization threatens to begin to fill this void by adding old age and disease to the existing multiple pathologies that are seen as being an essential part of the identity formation of black men.

Furthermore, in the analysis we can see how the mind/heart/body separation can also be read into the interactions in the interview – in the positioning of Edwin as the older, African, man, who will not/cannot talk about emotions, and me, the younger, Asian woman researcher, who is willing to serve emotionally through listening and sympathy. The epistemological assumptions about racialized-gendered subjectivity and bodies that underlie such oppositional constructions, also have effects for the positioning of particular minoritized researchers. As St Louis points out, critiques of the mind/body split by 'black' intellectuals and individuals, can themselves be seen as repeating these epistemological assumptions, where critique becomes possible precisely because:

> We have transcended our bodies, and in developing our minds we have rid ourselves of the taint of our bodies. We have graduated to the seriousness and sagacity of 'mind' and left our bodies behind. (St Louis, 2000: 60)

Of particular relevance to this discussion is how the analysis of insecurities of meaning might be made to recognize and work with/against these very complicated dynamics. What I want to argue is that it is vital that the re-contextualization process takes account of the subject positions that are made available, and that are denied to both research participants and to researchers within dominant discourses. Analysis must then seek to uncover how the subject positions 'offered', contested, negotiated and denied in research interactions and in interpretation, might serve to rein-scribe research participants and researchers within prevailing oppressive relations of representation (see Bhavnani, 1993), *and* obscure experiences that challenge such representations.

Indeed, it is only by taking account of this range of interactional and social dynamics that it becomes possible to see that the generation of the insecurity of meaning in my interview with Edwin cannot simply be reduced to oppositional ethnic, gendered, generational, health and class-based categories of difference. Rather, it is only by situating and contextu-alizing the production of ambiguities of meaning that it becomes possible to see how meanings can become inscribed by social difference, and what effects these processes of inscription have upon research interactions and the production of knowledge.

ANALYTIC AMBIVALENCE

In considering these complicated dynamics, I want to place the exploration of insecurities of meaning, and their relation to social and subjective rela-tions, in the context of previous discussions about the use of racial and ethnic categories in research (see Chapters 1 and 2). I want to examine how analytic attention to insecurities of meaning might challenge the produc-tion of categorical approaches to difference that are based upon the exclu-sions of particular experiences and thought ('the unthinkable'). At the same time, I want to explore two areas of ambivalence in such an approach. First, there are the real difficulties of facing up to the incompleteness, and some would say the 'failures' of methodological practices and analysis. What does it mean to highlight the limitations of our research? To recognize and draw attention to how our methodological and analytic practices are marked by 'breaks and jagged edges' (Lather, 2001a: 477)?

Second, I want to explore ambivalence in terms of a reticent ethics of analysis and representation, in which the researcher is forced to hesitate between the analytic slotting in of a subject to an available subject 'posi-tion' (see Hall, 1996), and the radical disruption of identification, which can reveal the 'breaks and jagged edges' of analysis. To pervert the theore-tical language of identification with the colloquial and dramatized lan-guage of interrogation, the analytic hesitation by the researcher is whether s/he should 'stitch up' the research participant. Whether s/he should render a research participant knowable through some degree of reference to dominant categories of social identity (such as 'race', ethnicity, class or gender), in order to 'close the case'.

This stitching up process has another side. Kamala Visweswaran, in her essays on feminist ethnography, has urged us to be aware of processes of identity formation in research that are characterized by 'the university rescue missions in search of the voiceless' (1997: 69). What Visweswaran is referring to are analytic processes of subjectification based upon the need to capture and 'give voice', and to fully understand subordinated Others. In my mind, and linking with Visweswaran's argument, it is not simply the case that insecurities of meaning in research lead to partial accounts and are therefore 'in-your-face' reminders of the failures of the 'university rescue mission'. It is also that, in the process of interrogating insecurities of meaning in analysis, we can uncover undisclosed and disturbing connections about Others, which, while they make the analysis 'fuller', can betray and jeopardize the research participant.

By betrayal, I do not mean to imply that we need to have some sort of authorization from the research participant in order to legitimize our analysis (how would we ever judge such authorization?). I am referring to an epistemological betrayal that fails to hold itself accountable to the refusals of research participants that are often a part of insecurities of meaning. These refusals, in relation to my interview with Edwin for example, can be located at the crossroads between discursive, emotional and embodied trauma. At this crossroads (that in my interpretation of Edwin's interviews involve dominant discourses about black masculinities, emotions of loss and experiences of terminal illness), the relations between what is 'indescribable'- what cannot be confirmed by external criteria – and what is 'undiscussable' – that is, what can't be said (Bar-On, 1999) – are further mediated by the more ambiguous status of what *won't* be said.

It is important to elaborate upon these distinctions/ambiguities. Bar-On, in a study on 'reconstructing human discourse after trauma' (1999), has examined the difficulties in differentiating between 'genuine' and 'normalized' discourses. In Bar-On's analysis, 'genuine' discourse, while containing certain levels of normalization (suppression, avoidance, deception), is characterized by a 'critical and ethical pragmatism' that enables open questioning and dialogue. 'Normalized' discourse, by contrast, is used to describe an intentional silencing of experience, such as in cases of child sexual abuse or in families where family members were involved or were bystanders in the Nazi holocaust.

What I want to argue is that, while this process of normalization (suppression, avoidance and deception) can constitute and hold the emotional and embodied trauma experienced by individuals, discourses are also affected in the process. The cost to discourse of suppression can be witnessed in the persistence of interrogative discrepancies and contradictions that refuse to be eliminated (see Hesse, 2000: 17). In my line of theorizing, the insecurities of meaning that we can encounter in researching racialized difference, such as that in the interview with Edwin, can embody what is denied in discourse, and can serve to disrupt and to interrogate this denial. The ethical dilemma for the researcher is that the nature of this refusal, which, as I have said earlier, can lie at the crossroads of social discourses, emotions and bodies, when examined in analysis and made explicit, risks pathologization, in a discursive context that is not yet capable of recognizing the complexities and multiplicity of difference. My point is that as researchers, we have to be careful and accountable to what we make explicit in analysis.

For example, in analysing the insecurity of meaning in Edwin's interview in rigorous detail, I came across intimate connections in which the ambiguity of meaning that I have identified 'made sense'. (Did you notice any of the gaps in my analysis? The large parts of the text that have been blocked out and then deleted?) If it is the case that the very intimacy of these connections enabled insights into the contorted relationships between social location, subjectivity and the body, it is also the case that Edwin's refusal of these connections must be considered as a way in which he could resist being 'stitched up/into' oppressive and dominant subject positions. These subject positions are a part of the discursive relations through which 'race' was constructed on the surfaces of the body in nineteenth-century raciology (Gilroy, 2000), and which even today continue to operate to produce men of African descent as body and not mind (St Louis, 2000). Yet, in terms of methodology, particularly in relation to research across racialized difference, Edwin's refusals can be seen primarily as obstacles that need to be overcome and mastered.

Inspired by the pioneering work of Visweswaran (1997), I want to highlight the epistemological and ethical implications of a 'strategized complicity' in the analysis of accounts, which can expose, and yet also evade, the contradictions and ambivalent complications of processes of racialization. Do we (can we?) tell everything in the name of analytic rigour? To whom and to what are we accountable in research? Might silence, in some contexts, be a necessary condition for political progress (Eagleton, 2001)? Or can our silence do discursive damage to the oppositional discourses that can be found in accounts of lived experience?

Visweswaran talks about the shock of seeing herself reflected in the panoptic of ethnography as she tried to unearth an Indian woman's – 'Janaki' – secrets (see Chapter 8). With the realization that Janaki 'was no longer a puzzle for me to solve, but a woman with her reasons, not so unlike me', Visweswaran addresses the ethics of a subversive production of knowledge, based upon complicity between different levels of refusal:

> This strategized complicity between unequal subjects in power unfolds into a
> peculiar form of knowing, one in which the confounding yet tactical junction

of disclosure and exposure is dramatized. In interrupting a Western (sometime feminist) project of subject retrieval, recognition of the partially understood is not simply strategy but accountability to my subjects; partial knowledge is not so much choice as necessity. (Visweswaran, 1997: 50)

By engaging with some of the epistemological and ethical implications of attention to insecurities of meaning in research, I think we also need to consider how we can begin to produce ways of knowing and *not-knowing* that are responsive and accountable to the challenges of researching difference. Patti Lather, in a beautifully crafted account of the 'ruins' of ethnography in the wake of post-structuralist critiques, has referred to the need to 'think against' the certainties of method as a resource in getting through 'stuck places'. She writes:

> This might be termed a 'praxis of stuck places' (Lather, 1998), a praxis of not being so sure, in excess of binary and dialectical logic that disrupts the horizon of already prescribed intelligibility. (2001a: 482)

In relation to the politics of methodology, I would argue that insecurities of meaning should be seen as both an analytic and an ethical resource for recognizing and attending to the 'stuck places' of researching difference. Knowledge in this context is approached as both situated and uncertain, generated through analytic processes and practices that are 'always histori-cally specific mediations through which we and everybody else must know the world' (Haraway, 1988: 577). An underlying theme in my argument has been that engaging with how these mediations are problematic, contradic-tory, ambiguous and lacking is not only valuable methodologically, but can also help us to disturb and question what has been seen as more straight-forward and/or unproblematic.

At an ethical level, insecurities of meaning can produce and underline ambiguous political and moral positions for the researcher and the reader. They can force us to confront and question the ethical dimensions of representation. The partiality of knowledge production in this sense is both imposed and produced, as we make difficult judgements about what is rep-resented and how our 'findings' might be read in relation to historical, social and textual power relations.

CONCLUSIONS

In this chapter I have used a discussion of noticeable ambiguities of mean-ing in research as a way of examining some of the methodological, episte-mological and ethical challenges that can confront us in researching difference. A key issue to consider in this discussion is the relationship between immediate methodological tactics, and more long-term analytic goals. In particular, I have tried to show the methodological benefits of working with insecurities of meaning in order to gain a different – more complex, but also self-consciously uncertain – understanding of the dynamic and situated nature of difference within research encounters. In the immediate context of this chapter this has meant highlighting the analytic value of insecurities of meaning by tracing the insufficiencies of method, epistemology and ethics.

A general analytic goal has been to unsettle and question scientific and rationalistic notions of intelligibility. In this regard, I have used the discussion of noticeable insecurities of meaning to make visible the uncertain and intersubjective qualities of all forms of knowledge in social research. My argument has been that if researchers interrogate and work the play of differences that generate insecurities of meaning, through the process of analysis we can begin to produce ways of knowing and not-knowing that are accountable to the challenges and the limitations of researching difference.

In using Edwin's interview to examine some of these challenges and limitations, my interpretations of Edwin must also be questioned. I have produced interpretations that have allowed me to identify and cast possibilities *into* and *onto* Edwin's life story. Some of these possibilities have served to make visible and to problematize my own social and subjective positionings in the interactional and interpretive process, whilst also examining alternative ways of experiencing and of knowing. This has been both risky and difficult. And it is important that I give recognition to how my interpretations of my interview with Edwin risk the objectification and the setting in stone of the very aspects of our identities and experiences that constituted the differences between us at particular times and in particular places – this 'freezing' serving to solidify, rather than to show, the instability, dynamism and on-going productivity of the interrelations between difference and the construction of meaning.

As a researcher, my interpretations build upon and sustain some of my own authoritative positionings in the research process, in a way that appears contrary to Bakhtin's (1986) dialogic, 'creative understanding'. Yet, it is important to recognize that Edwin was an active participant in our interviewing relationship, challenging my interpretations and subverting some of the interactional power relations of the interview itself. Indeed, although I am able to occupy the powerful position of offering interpretations of my interviews with Edwin, it was Edwin, rather than myself, who problematized and questioned radically the role of research and interviewing relationships. At the end of our final interview, in response to a 'routine' closing question about whether Edwin had any questions he would like to ask me, he addressed both the interview and my role. I will not dismiss the possible gendered and generational power relations underpinning his comments, however, they offer us an insight into the challenges of dialogical approaches to analysis that, in refusing to marginalize the Other's voice, must also serve to question what we do, how we do it and why. Indeed, through this process, it was Edwin himself, who performed a radical re-contextualization:

Yasmin: Ok. Are there any questions that you want to ask me before I go at all?

Edwin: Well [pause] what should I ask you about? [pause] There's no questions that I have to ask you because you're just an interviewer, and um, I don't see why I should ask much questions, well, you can't really help me.

Yasmin: [pause] Yeah, that's true.

Edwin: Umm.

In closing this chapter by re-centring the analytic focus upon the co-construction of meaning, I want to leave the ambiguities in Edwin's statement to stand in the hope that they will spark a dialogue with readers that will be relevant in reflecting upon and questioning their own research practices.

SUGGESTED READING

R. Shields (1996) Meeting or Mis-meeting? The Dialogical Challenge to Verstehen. *British Journal of Sociology*, 47(2): 275–94.

K. Visweswaran (1997) *Fictions of Feminist Ethnography*. Minneapolis: University of Minnesota Press (Chapter 3).

NOTES

1. Of course the very concept of 'insecurity of meaning' can be read as setting up yet another form of dualistic thinking with clear distinctions being implied between 'insecure' and 'secure' meanings, and this is something that I wish to avoid. Assumptions about the certainty of meaning are being challenged and interrogated in both the social and the natural sciences (see Zadeh, 1965 for an account of 'fuzzy logic' in computer science), and some social theorists would argue that all meanings are, indeed, insecure (Derrida, 1976). In general terms I would not argue with this, but what I wish to flag up in this chapter is the examination of *identified* and, in many senses *obvious* ambiguities of meaning. Those instances, such as in the extract from Edwin's interview detailed here, that make us sit up and question 'what was that about?', 'what did they mean?' and 'what did I mean?'

2. I use the term 'context' in a general sense in this chapter, to refer to wider social and interactional circumstances. It is important to point out that the term has

very specific meanings within Conversation Analysis (CA). In relation to the study of institutions, Heritage (1998) has made explicit some of the analytic assumptions about the relations between 'context' and interactions in CA:

> The assumption is that it is fundamentally through interaction that context is built, invoked and managed, and that it is through interaction that institutional imperatives originating from outside the interaction are evidenced and made real and enforceable for the participants. We want to find out how that works. Empirically, this means showing that the participants build the context of their talk *in* and *through* their talk. (Heritage, 1998: 163, emphasis in original)

3. Scheff (1997) has suggested that micro-analysis, in its focus upon the minute detail of interactions, can be interwoven with the analysis of systems and structures to illuminate part/whole relations. Scheff argues that insecurities of meaning can be understood if part/whole, 'morphological' methods are used.

Threatening topics and difference: encounters in psycho-social space

SUMMARY

Talking about particular topics in certain places and times, can be difficult, or can be avoided or resisted by both research participants and researchers alike. Such relations have been conceptualized in terms of 'topic threat' in the methodological literature. In this chapter, I will argue that attention to the co-production of topic threat and its effects within research interactions can provide a valuable opportunity for examining the spatial dimensions of difference in research encounters. A theoretical framework is put forward that conceptualizes research interactions as being produced by, and producing, specific *psycho-social spaces*, in which locations of 'safety' and 'danger', *and* power relations, can be multiple and shifting.

- The conceptualization of psycho-social space used in the chapter draws upon and adapts ideas from cultural geography on the production of social space (Lefebvre, 1991). This conceptualization will be used to examine the possibilities and the tensions in the dual concern with emotions and with politics in qualitative research.
- A focus upon the co-constituted nature of psycho-social space will examine how individuals and space produce each other.

Concerns with, and experiences of space, occupy a significant position in the methodological literature on racialized difference. By space, I am not simply referring to geographical space, although this is clearly a critical point of analysis, particularly in relation to postcolonial theory (see Ahmed, 2000). I am also referring to space with regard to psycho-social relations and with regard to epistemology. For example, debates about ethnic matching (see Chapters 3 and 4), cross-cultural communication

(Chapter 6) and topic threat (see Lee, 1993), all assume some notion of psycho-social space between the researcher and research participant, which the researcher has to manage, negotiate or cross in order to access 'the truth'. In relation to epistemology, recognition of complicated postcolonial relations and globalizing processes, and also the sexual and gendered nature of space, have led to the development of cartographic forms of analysis (see Brah, 1996; Fortier, 1999; Hemmings, 2002; Marcus, 1998). Such analyses involve the mapping of research relations across diverse geographical and cultural spaces (see Chapter 8), and epistemological commitments that set out to create new spaces of knowledge production. Such commitments include analytic practices based upon making critical juxtapositions that pursue and legitimize subordinated knowledges, and that generate models of experience as partial and transitory (Hemmings, 2002).

In this chapter I will use methodological debates and an empirical example to theorize the production of psycho-social space in qualitative research interactions, and to examine how attention to spatial dynamics in research can expand our ability to recognize and respond to difference. A point of focus in this discussion will be the methodological literature on researching 'sensitive topics', which examines topic threat in research. My approach to understanding the complexity of relations between social difference and the production of threatening topics is marked by an exploration of the ways in which topic threat is produced by, and within, the psycho-social spaces of research encounters. In this sense, I do not see the production of topic threat as relating in any predictable way to stable asymmetries of power and positioning between racialized, gendered, illness-related or methodologically structured relations in research. My contention is that topic threat is located, negotiated and 'moves' within the knotty connections between the embodied, the social, the material and the methodological.

In making sense of these complex relations, I will draw upon work in cultural geography to explore the much-neglected subject of space in research interactions. What I want to theorize and examine is the on-going production *and* effects of psycho-social space in research interactions. By 'interaction' I am referring to four main qualities of research encounters:

1. *Subjective processes* – that is, situated thoughts and feelings that include inter-subjective relations *between* the researcher and research participant.
2. *Embodied activities* – the overt forms of embodied interaction such as those marked by verbal expression, silence, touch and movement, and the more hidden aspects of body language such as gestures, eye movements and posture.[1]
3. *The social context of the research interaction* – the historical, cultural and political structures and discourses that frame the meanings and experiences of researchers and research participants within the research

interaction, and that include the researcher's epistemological assumptions about subjectivity.

4. *The physical research environment* – where research interactions take place, including the sensory environment of the sounds, sights, smells and 'feel' of the research setting.

In order to examine relations between these four qualities of research interactions and how they might relate to the production of threatening topics, I will draw upon the work of the French social theorist and cultural geographer Henri Lefebvre (1991 [1974]).[2] I will use the work of Lefebvre to look at the production of psycho-social spaces in research interactions and the operation of power within them. Exploring these different issues further, in the following sections I will:

- examine approaches to topic threat in the methodological literature.
- discuss in further detail the qualities of psycho-social space in research.
- describe the basic analytic themes in Lefebvre's conceptualization of the production of social space, and detail how I have used these themes to formulate an analytic approach to psycho-social space.
- apply this analytic framework to a case study that will examine relations between topic threat and psycho-social space, and explore how such relations might be recognized in research.

TOPIC THREAT

Avoidance and difficulty in talking about topics at particular times in research has been addressed in the methodological literature in terms of the threatening or 'sensitive' nature of research topics (Brannen, 1988; Lee, 1993). More specifically, the threat of particular topics has been seen as leading to defensive emotional responses in the research participant and in the researcher (although threat to the researcher is under-explored in the literature), that can have negative consequences upon the quality of the research accounts that are generated. In this respect, topic threat has been seen as having distinct and significant methodological and ethical implications for how we approach research interactions and the methods that we use. Brannen has identified several distinguishing features of research on 'sensitive topics':

> First, respondents can be easily identified in written reports both by themselves and by others because of the personal and unique nature of the data. Second identification carries with it the associated risk of sanctions and stigma. Third, respondents are likely to find confronting and telling their stories a stressful experience. This is a problem for researchers as well as

respondents. The researcher therefore has some responsibility for protecting the respondent. Protection is required both with respect to the confidences disclosed and the emotions which may be aroused and expressed. (1988: 552–3)

What is particularly significant about the methodological discussions of topic threat in the context of the concerns in this chapter, is that the discussions assume research interactions as being variously constituted by psycho-social space that needs to be monitored and managed by the researcher, both methodologically and ethically. That is, there is some account taken of research interactions as taking place *somewhere* and/or as involving moving experiential activities and states.

In methodological terms, the need for the researcher to manage the psycho-social spaces of the research interaction can be seen in concerns about how to reduce levels of topic threat, through attention to the types and the structuring of questions within interviews (see Lee, 1993), the number of interviews (Oakley, 1981), and where the research interaction takes place (Brannen, 1988). In relation to ethics there are concerns about confidentiality, anonymity and informed consent for research participants, and the need for the researcher to 'ensure that the physical, social and psychological well-being of research participants is not adversely affected by the research' (British Sociological Association, 2002: 3).

Despite varied and on-going methodological work on topic threat, a central problem in both the quantitative and qualitative literature lies in its inability to address the complex psycho-social dynamics involved in the situated meanings and co-produced nature of threatening topics. Different researchers have used varying descriptions of topics as being 'embarrassing' (Barton, 1958), 'demeaning' (Sudman and Bradburn, 1982), 'sensitive' (Lee and Renzetti, 1990) or 'dangerous' (Lee-Treweek and Linkogle, 2000) to convey notions of threat. Such descriptions are evocative, and researchers have attempted to give us a clear idea of what topic threat involves and how it might be linked to the wider social and historical context (Lee, 1993). Nevertheless, we have far less insight into its dynamic, discursive and intersubjective qualities.

Renzetti and Lee's definition of 'sensitive topics', which draws heavily upon notions of 'threat', illustrates some of the analytic difficulties in conceptualizing the dynamic and co-constructed nature of topic threat:

sensitive topics seem to involve particular kinds of costs ... these may take the form of psychic costs, such as guilt, shame or embarrassment. Alternatively, sensitive topics are threatening because participation in research can have unwelcome consequences ... As a result the relationship between the researcher and the researched may become hedged with mistrust, concealment and dissimulation ... a sensitive topic is one that potentially poses for those involved a substantial threat, the emergence of which renders

problematic the collection, holding, and/or dissemination of research data ...
Experience suggests ... that there are a number of areas in which research is
more likely to be threatening ... These include (a) where research intrudes
into the private sphere or delves into some deeply personal experience,
(b) where the study is concerned with deviance and social control, (c) where
it impinges on the vested interests of powerful persons or the exercise of coer-
cion or domination, and (d) where it deals with things sacred to those being
studied that they do not wish to be profaned. (Renzetti and Lee, 1993: 5–6)

Contained within this description is reference to the subjective and social
dimensions of topic threat, and we are also given indications of the types
of topics that are most likely to be perceived as 'threatening' for research
participants. However, what is less clear is how we should approach and
theorize the range of subjective, embodied, interactional, material and
social dynamics that are subsumed under the general category of 'topic
threat', and that are likely to be constituted and to operate in very different ways within different research encounters. As Foddy argues in relation
to interviewing, topic threat might be generated by a number of different
factors:

some that are idiosyncratic to the particular respondent; some that arise out
of characteristics of the questions *per se*, and some that arise out of the relationship between the researcher and the respondent. At the same time it
seems unreasonable to assume that the kinds of threats associated with each
of these factors are necessarily the same. (1993: 119)

This focus upon the idiosyncrasies, and the different types of topic threat,
challenges the emphasis given in the survey literature to social difference
in explaining responses to threat. Box 7.1 provides a summary of
approaches to topic threat in survey research, and gives examples of
'de-sensitizing' and 'de-jeopdardizing' techniques that have been used to
'manage' threat in research encounters. There are two points to note here.
First, as Hollway and Jefferson (2000) have suggested, assumptions about a
'socially constructed subject', i.e., 'a subject largely determined by demographic factors', fail to fully account for the 'individual-social paradox' –
that is, those individuals who act 'outside' the norm. An example of the
'individual-social paradox' might be those minoritized research participants who do not moderate their 'radical' views on issues of 'race' when
interviewed by a white person (see Shosteck's (1977) research on 'respondent militancy').

This brings us to the second point, which involves a recognition that
responses to topic threat can vary considerably, and can manifest themselves in many different ways in relation to the nature of the research interaction. For instance, it is possible that experiences such as discomfort, pain,
anxiety, fear, enthusiasm and exhilaration[3] can all be produced in relation

Survey research on 'threatening' topics has been based around the need to develop techniques in asking questions that can either 'de-sensitize' (Sudman and Bradburn, 1974; 1982) or 'de-jeopardize' (Tracy and Fox, 1981; Warner, 1965) threatening topics. The rationale behind such techniques is that purposeful changes in the design and administration of interviews can be used to reduce threat and therefore maximize disclosures. In other words, *the reduction of topic threat in the interview has been seen as leading to more valid and reliable accounts*. Hence, there is great wealth of technical research that has examined such issues as question format (Barton, 1958; Sudman and Bradburn, 1982), the use of familiar words (Bradburn et al., 1979) and the mode of administration of interviews (Bradburn and Sudman, 1979; DeLamater and MacCorquodale, 1975).

De-sensitizing techniques have sought to reduce the level of perceived threat of questions and have been primarily concerned with question content, form, context and the mode of the administration of questionnaires. A fundamental concern has been the extent to which 'social desirability response sets' lead to either the over-reporting or under-reporting of particular behaviours, or to the concealment of attitudes. In a meta-analysis of the literature, Sudman and Bradburn (1974; 1982) have identified a number of general factors that they claim can facilitate the reporting of sensitive information. They suggest that open, long questions, using familiar words, are better for obtaining information on the frequencies of socially undesirable behaviour, and that embedding the threatening question in a list of more or less threatening questions can reduce question threat. However, such findings have been contested in practice. For example, Johnson et al. (1994), in their survey of sexual attitudes and lifestyles, found in developmental qualitative research that research participants favoured the use of formal language. In using formal terms to describe sexual behaviour in the survey, the researchers have also argued that because the survey was going to be used to generate data to understand the spread of HIV infection, it was necessary to be clear about the description of behaviours.

De-jeopardizing techniques, as summarized by Lee, aim 'to minimize the respondent's feelings of jeopardy when asked to admit to behaviour which is stigmatizing or incriminating in some way' (1993: 83). An example of a de-jeopardizing technique is 'randomized response', which uses indeterminate questions (i.e., the question answered by the research participant is unknown to the researcher) to maintain the anonymity of responses (for an example see Orton and Samuels, 1987). Research has suggested that individuals are more likely to admit to socially undesirable behaviours with randomized response techniques than with an anonymous questionnaire (Bradburn and Sudman, 1979). Lee (1993) has made an important point in his observation, however, that while the individual is protected by the use of de-jeopardizing techniques, this does not preclude the possibility of collective jeopardy in research involving particular, identified social groups.

Box 7.1   De-sensitizing and de-jeopardizing techniques in survey research to threatening topics, yet they can have very different consequences for research interactions and for the stories and actions of research participants. I have found in my own research that the co-construction of topic threat means that we cannot understand relations of threat as existing independently from the research interaction. The nature and the meanings of threatening topics are not rigid and stable, but can change as research relationships develop over time, and also according to where research interactions take place. That is to say, what people tell us or show us, or do not tell us or show us, is sensitive to the psycho-social organization, structuring and physical context of research relations.

TAKING ACCOUNT OF PSYCHO-SOCIAL DYNAMICS: A THEORY OF PSYCHO-SOCIAL SPACE

Taking account of the complex and dynamic nature of topic threat is particularly important in research that is concerned with the operation and effects of power relations and how such relations are produced and negotiated within research interactions. In exploring how we might theorize this matrix of subjective, material, social and embodied interrelations in qualitative research, I want to draw upon work in cultural geography that has challenged ideas about space as being a passive and inert background surface upon which social and interactional relations are played out. In emphasizing space as a co-constituted product of 'relations/interactions', the geographer Doreen Massey urges us to recognize that 'You are not just travelling across space; you are altering it a little, moving it on, producing it' (2000: 226).

Massey's point is important in thinking about the co-constituted nature of the psycho-social spaces of research interactions. How might we address the ways in which research participants and researchers are 'altering, moving and producing' research spaces through their interactions with each other and with the wider material environment? What this question uncovers in relation to the preceding discussion of the methodological literature on researching 'sensitive' topics, is that there are significant limitations in the ways the literature fails to examine threat as a dynamic co-construction, involving a multiplicity of histories, experiences and contexts that collide in and with research spaces, producing and changing them in the process. With regard to social difference, we can also see that this failure to engage with these complex inter-relations and with multiplicity, can have the effect of freezing difference in ways that are ill equipped to deal with complexity and with changing relations of power.

In order to produce a conceptualiztion of psycho-social space in research interactions that is equipped to recognize the co-constituted nature and the power dynamics of space, I will draw upon themes in Lefebvre's (1991 [1974]) theory about the production of social space. For the sake of clarity, in laying out my ideas about psycho-social space, I will provide a brief overview of Lefebvre's theory, followed by an example taken from my research that I will use to examine the application of Lefebvre's ideas.

LEFEBVRE AND SOCIAL SPACE

In very broad terms, Lefebvre's work has theorized social space as being produced through the tensions and interrelations between three spatial registers, often designated as 'conceived', 'perceived' and 'lived' spaces. This triad of spatial categories can be summarized as:

- dominant *conceptions of space* ('Representations of Space') that attempt to prescribe the use of space
- *perceptions of space* derived from the actual use and imagined use of space ('Spaces of Representation')
- *spatial practices*, which underlie and secure both of the other forms of space through *lived* practices that serve to signify what is appropriate and what is 'out of place'

The application of Lefebvre's approach to social space can be seen in the work of Allen and Pryke (1994), who have examined the service spaces of the City of London. Allen and Pryke use the example of the 'abstract' space of finance to demonstrate how a particular dominant coding of space has been achieved through the routine spatial practices and global networks of those who work in the financial markets. What is particularly interesting in Allen and Pryke's analysis, is how their focus upon the spatial practices of an invisible, largely migrant contract workforce, 'those who clean, secure and cater' (p. 467), shows how the dominant coding of financial space can be subverted and 'appropriated'. For example, in relation to cleaning staff, Allen and Pryke draw attention to the spaces within buildings that are used by cleaners to meet their own needs. These are 'a place to put up posters, read newspapers, listen to the radio and the like' and which 'represent a rejection of all that is signified by a particular dominant space' (p. 471). By examining the use of the same space by different workforces, Lefebvre's emphasis upon power relations is used to explore how power is practised, achieved and maintained through spatial practices, and how such power is also constantly open to challenge and subversion.

My notion of psycho-social space, derived loosely from Lefebvre, sees psycho-social space as an actively constituted and constituting quality of research interactions produced through social, embodied and material dynamics *and* the tensions between elements of dominance, compliance, cooperative negotiation, contestation and transgression. This means that power relations are also an integral part of my conceptualization of the psycho-social spaces of research interactions.

> Lefebvre's conceptualization of the three forms of space was highly influenced by the work of Karl Marx. In particular, Lefebvre was concerned to explore the links between dominant 'modes of production' in capitalist social systems and the production of space. Lefebvre saw the rise of capitalism as being characterized by forms of power that served to produce 'abstract', commodified spaces or 'representations of space', which deny difference but that can also be resisted and 'contradicted' by the everyday use of space. In contrast, Lefebvre's 'spaces of representations' were theorized as being shaped by how they are perceived 'through associated images and symbols' (Lefebvre, 1991 [1974]: 39) and their everyday use: 'Such spaces may be public or private, they may overlay or disrupt the dominant spaces, or indeed they may take shape alongside them' (Allen and Pryke, 1994: 454). Spatial practices in linking the other two types of space, evoke 'a specific level of performance' (Lefebvre, 1991 [1974]: 33), that in ensuring degrees of continuity and cohesion, can also constrain alternative interpretations and uses of space.

In the next sections I will discuss my research relationship with Frank, a hospice service user, to look at how my notion of psycho-social space can be applied to understand the co-construction of topic threat in research encounters marked by social difference.

FRANK: TOPIC THREAT AND PSYCHO-SOCIAL SPACE

I was made most aware of the contingent and 'moving' nature of topic threat, and its connections to the production of psycho-social space, in my research relationship with Frank. Frank was a softly spoken, black, African-Caribbean man of 76, a practising Catholic who had prostate cancer that had spread to his bones. I first met Frank through my participant observation as a volunteer helper in the hospice day centre, in the early stages of my research. Frank lived with his son and often complained that his son was rarely in the home and that loneliness was a real problem for him since his illness.

I had known Frank in the day centre for about two months before my first, 'formal' interview with him in his small council house in a deprived inner-city area. Frank, like all of the other day centre users, had been told about my research, and while in the hospice I wore a name badge with 'Researcher' printed on it. Despite this, and frequent reminders to service users about my research role, I often felt that my research role could be forgotten, and my relationship with service users in the day centre was qualitatively different from when I interviewed some of them, most often in their homes. In my day centre role, I was one of many, predominantly female, and overwhelmingly white, volunteer helpers who made and served tea and coffee, cleaned up, and helped with various craft classes. Within this highly gendered role, service users could exert more control and choice over the nature of their interactions with me.

It was during my work in the day centre, when I was greeting and giving service users a morning drink, that I had a conversation with Frank that proved to be highly significant in my research relationship with him. This conversation unfolded when Frank asked me about my parents and I told him that they were both dead. At this point in the conversation, because of Frank's difficulties with hearing, and also because of the personal nature of what we were discussing, I sat down in an armchair beside Frank. My disclosure about my parents being dead was of great significance in the development of this interaction with Frank. He was visibly moved and interactionally engaged. Frank leaned forward and towards me in his chair, offering his condolences and expressing regret that I should be without both parents at a 'young' age.[4] My notes of this interaction in my field work diary describe how Frank then:

> told me that his father had died when he was a child and that his mother had brought him up single-handedly. He then told me that his older sister had died when he was a teenager. He couldn't remember any details about the illness that caused her death. He then went on to talk about the poverty he had lived in, in the Caribbean, and this was an issue that was clearly traumatic for him to recall. He said that in his opinion 'poverty is a crime'.

What was remarkable about this discussion for me was Frank's revelation about the deaths of his mother, father and sister, and also the emotional and political expressiveness of Frank's views on poverty, in which he repeatedly and forcefully denounced 'poverty as a crime'. This expressiveness was in marked contrast to the impression that I had about Frank through my work in the hospice day centre. In the day centre, Frank was a remarkably quiet and reserved man, who despite telling me about how lonely he felt in both of our interviews, had strong feelings about the expediency of keeping 'himself to himself'. Frank chose to spend most of his time in the day centre alone, because of the perceived threat that social interactions could cause 'trouble' between individuals if there were differences in opinion.

This tension between feelings of loneliness and 'choosing' to be alone was a recurring theme in how Frank talked about his life in both of our interviews. For example, in our first interview he told me:

I'm a person, I'm a very quiet person. I don't like too many friends, so much company, 'cause they put you in trouble. And I stay in my own place, even I been up there [hospice day centre] I could be in one place, I just relax until I feel alright. I don't like too much talking and sometimes, you know I talk and say, you know you might say something that go against you that you shouldn't say. You don't know, also before that I kept myself to myself. I never liked, even when I was a boy … always used to be on my own, so I used to that.

In our second interview, Frank described himself as 'a loner', and again talked about the dangerousness of expressing his opinions. In this account, the dangers that Frank talked about were described through generalized images of saying or doing 'the slightest thing, or mostly nothing at all, can get your death'. This dramatic portrayal of the lurking, unpredictable dangers of social interaction, heralded a more personal, local narrative that drew attention to the racialized dimensions of such danger, in a story about Frank's previous experiences in a pensioners' lunch club:

when I was in that pension club, before I took sick, I had a few friends there, white chaps, sitting on the same table and I said to one of them about God and this and that and they used to get very, very annoyed and say there is no such thing.

Frank's conversation with me in the day centre and/in particular, his political denouncement of poverty as a crime, was thus extraordinary, appearing in contrast to the quiet and guarded Frank that I had come to know over a period of months in the day centre. This was also the first indication that I had had from Frank, despite a previous interview, about the biographical, emotional and political significance of his early life in the Caribbean. Yet, this conversation was taking place in the 'public' space of the day centre, in the midst of other service users and at a time when I also needed to carry on with my work. Because it had felt inappropriate to carry on this discussion, particularly in front of others, I told Frank that I would like to talk to him some more about his experiences during our next interview and Frank agreed to this. However, when I raised the topics of the conversation again, in the middle of our second interview,[5] at his home, Frank was clearly uncomfortable and told me very assertively that he did not want to talk about it:

Yasmin: So in the day centre before you were talking to me about when you were young, and you said it, was it your mother who died very, was it your mother or –?

Frank: Aye, my Mum. Ehh. My mother died pretty young age, as, at 40 she died.

Yasmin: And how old were you when she died?

Frank: I can't remember now. Mind you I was a big young man.

Yasmin: So did your father die when you were quite young?

Frank: Yes, my father died when I was very, very young, see and although they wasn't together, I was brought up with one parent, which is my Mum, but, as I said, as I told, anyway, let me get that question you asked me, at the centre, every Wednesday. You see *I don't want to bring that thing back here.* Now as I told you that, I'm sorry to tell you, (Y: Umm) but think I should stop you there because um, it brings back memories (Y: Sure) and, and I don't want it, it's poverty, poverty, I pass a lot. Well they say poverty is not a crime, but at times I say poverty is a crime really, so I don't like to talk about that anyway (Y: Yeah) *I don't want to bring back sore.*

Yasmin: Don't want to bring back?

Frank: Sore. You got sore on your body and so on, and that's what we say.

Yasmin: Oh right. I've never heard of that before.

Frank: Ah, so you're never too old to learn.

Yasmin: Is, is that a Caribbean expression?

Frank: Well yes, I don't know if it's, but that where I learned it from anyway.

Yasmin: Yeah.

Frank: And, very, very, very hard. It was very hard on me when I was a young boy growing up through poverty. My mother was on her own. I was small, couldn't work. [Pause] But now this passed already and I don't want to talk about it. (Y: Sure) You know, I have to look for the future, um, although, I doesn't really expects a future. Not really, mind you [five taps of walking stick on floor, loud breath out] we don't know I mean even another two years, three years, four years, five years or I may die at one time you cannot tell because only God knows.

Yasmin: Umm. So, do you have any brothers or sisters at all?

(Emphasis added)

USING MY CONCEPT OF PSYCHO-SOCIAL SPACE

Drawing upon my conceptualization of psycho-social space, it is possible to see a number of different dynamics in operation in this extract. Most striking for me is my lack of recognition of the difficulties for Frank of talking about traumatic experiences in an interview. My questions at the beginning of the exchange were direct and specific, orientated to inducing factual information rather than narrative. In response to this style of questioning, Frank responds with some basic reporting of general information about the deaths of his mother and father. Beyond this, an emotional and spatial language of movement, resistance and withdrawal marks this part of the exchange. The phrases 'I don't want to bring that thing back here', and 'I don't want to bring back sore' evoke a mixture of embodied-emotional, temporal and environmental dimensions to Frank's refusal or inability to talk about this part of his life in the interview.

With regard to the context of Frank's previous disclosures in the day centre, it is also possible to see how changes in Frank's ability to talk about the same topics could be related to differences between our spontaneous interactions in the day centre and to our more structured and contrived interactions in the interview. Using my concept of psycho-social space I want to suggest that in some ways, the interview in Frank's home produced a different, more distant and threatening psycho-social research space between Frank and myself than our interaction within the day centre. In other words, interviewing Frank at home may have served to interrupt some of the power relations across our roles in the day centre of 'service provider'/'service user' and across the sites of 'home' and 'away'. What I also want to suggest is that it is important to consider how such differences were performed and had effects in these spaces, and how they might have played a part in Frank's resistance to talking about the deaths in his family and their links to his experiences of poverty.

LEFEBVRE'S THEORY, PSYCHO-SOCIAL SPACE AND TOPIC THREAT IN RESEARCH

This broad interpretation of how the threat of topics may have been produced and negotiated by Frank and me in our different research inter-actions, can be developed further by a more detailed engagement with Lefebvre's theorizing on the production of social space, which I have summarized previously as involving three spatial moments, i.e.:

- dominant *conceptions of space* that attempt to encode space
- lived *perceptions of space* derived from the use and imagined use of space, and
- *spatial practices*, which underlie and secure both of the other forms of space by signifying what is appropriate and what is 'out of place'

My argument is that research encounters, such as those described between Frank and me, constitute particular forms of psycho-social space that are inhabited, experienced and struggled over, consciously and unconsciously, by researchers and research participants. In research interactions, it is the research plans and designs of the researcher that, in general, attempt to prescribe and regulate the use, meaning and nature of the spaces of research interactions. I have conceptualized these formalities as encapsulating the characteristics of Lefebvre's dominant conceptions of space or, as he calls them, 'representations of space'. Such formalities can be seen in the often abstract and standardizing nature of research protocols, ethical procedures and topic guides that are now often a required part of research proposals. I see the formal organization of the psycho-social spaces of research interactions as assuming compliant and 'manageable' research participants. It assumes that research participants are both self-knowledgeable and cooperative (however, see Chapter 3 about the somewhat different assumptions that are made about racialized research participants), and will tell us or show us what we need to know (if we practise research skilfully and ethically). Within my analytic approach, I see the effects of topic threat as sometimes serving to challenge the intrusive dominance of the formal prescriptions of research, through the power of research participants to consciously or unconsciously refuse information and/or conceal areas of their lives.

I have theorized these latter interactions in terms of Lefebvre's 'spaces of representation' that are simultaneously subject to, but also challenging of the potentially dominating research plans, procedures and practices. As such, my argument is that the production and negotiation of threatening topics in research interactions can be understood in terms of the perceived 'spaces of representation' that can serve to reveal, disrupt and question attempts to regulate interactions and power relations in research. I have theorized the link between the dominant *conceptions* of research and how research is *perceived* as relating to Lefebvre's 'spatial practices', which evoke *performance* and doing. An analytically useful aspect of Lefebvre's theory is that it draws attention to how dominant spatial practices can serve to secure a coding of space, 'although never with utter success' (Allen and Pryke, 1994: 455). There is always a possibility that the spatial practices of those with less power can 'contradict' the dominant coding of space. Examples of dominant spatial practices in research are how interviewers, armed with a tape-recorder and pre-planned topic guide, signify to research participants what is expected to take place within the psycho-social space of the interview.

The spatial practices (especially the initiatives) of research participants in the interview can be seen in relation to encouraged, allowed, or produced interruptions in the interview or through the subversion of the tape recording of interviews. Such spatial practices, like those of the contract workforces in Allen and Pryke's study of the City of London, can contradict what is signified by the dominant coding of the spaces of research. My own experiences of the tape-recording of interviews have shown on numerous occasions how research participants can actively subvert dominant spatial practices. For example, in my tape-recorded interview with James (see Chapter 5) – a man with AIDS, who had not told his friends and family about his AIDS – he refused to name AIDS within the tape-recorded interview, although he named it when our discussion was not being recorded. Other research participants have left their mobile phones, or in the case of health care professionals their 'bleeps', switched on, so that interviews were opened to constant interruption.

Such spatial practices are under the varied control of research participants. However in other instances, the very ontological nature of difference can function to contradict dominant spatial practices. For example, in discussing power imbalances in her interviews with women, Cotterill (1992) has discussed some of her dilemmas of trying to adapt to some of the 'poor interview conditions' when interviewing women with pre-school age children. Bemoaning the fact that such experiences 'are rarely addressed in methodological textbooks or on methods courses', Cotterill describes how:

> Three of the single parents had pre-school children, and a problem that I never fully resolved was how to interview whilst entertaining a 3 year-old … I have in the space of an hour, been amused, frustrated, and exhausted, emotions which came flooding back later during the transcription of the tapes when the respondent's voice was inaudible, completely drowned out by a vociferous child. (1992: 602)

Cotterill's experiences provide an example of spatial practices that can be out of the control of research participants, but are an integral part of lived experiences of difference, which are not accounted for by research plans and methods, and which pose significant 'difficulties' for the control of the research space and interaction by the researcher.

POWER RELATIONS AND TOPIC THREAT

In referring back to Lefebvre's concern with power and social space, we can see how Frank's 'resistance' to my questions reveals something about the nature of power relations between us. For me, these power relations were related to relationships between the different spaces of the research interactions, my changing research role, and gendered, racialized and class difference.

My research role as a volunteer in the day centre was gendered not simply in terms of the fact that volunteer work in the hospice was largely done by women, but also in terms of the cultural coding of the qualities of the work. The work that I did in the day centre was about serving individuals both emotionally and physically, work that is generally seen as unskilled and of low status, and which characterizes 'women's work' in the private realm of the home (James, 1989; 1992). This role, with diminished status and power, was in some contrast to my interviewer role, and also to my implicit assumptions about the psycho-social spaces of the interview and how I thought I could use this space.

For me, my second interview with Frank, in a private place and where the discussion could be tape-recorded, was where I as a researcher could have greater control in the research interaction. I could ask Frank more about his experiences, without interruptions and without anxieties about other people over-hearing what was being said. The tape-recording of the interview also relieved my anxiety about 'missing' or 'losing' the detail of Frank's narrative.

What is important here is how I felt I could use the spaces of the interview, and how these assumptions – and, to use Lefebvre's term, 'spatial practices' – functioned to try and prescribe what should happen in the interview interaction. In short, I had begun the second interview with the expectation that the interview conditions would provide a more suitable space (what Lefebvre would call a dominant 'representation of space') for Frank to tell the story of his childhood and his early life in the Caribbean.

However, the public nature of the day centre may have felt more like a 'safe' place/space for Frank, because of the real possibility that our conversation could not go much further (in the light of interruptions from other service users and the fact that I had work to do). There is also the possibility that the very nature of the communal spaces of the day centre, in which Frank would be surrounded by people for the rest of the day, had an effect in reducing the threat of the topics. Frank's statement that he didn't want to 'bring that thing back here' can be read in the wider context of Frank's anxieties about being alone in his home for long periods of time and in the context of the emotional meanings of 'home'. For instance, Van Manen has suggested that basic human experiences are wrapped up in the concept of home:

> In the concept of home or dwelling, there is a strong sense of watching over something, preserving a space in which the human being can feel sheltered, protected, and what is thus preserved in the idea of a house with its walls and fences is a safekeeping, holding, or bearing of something that needs to be watched over. (1990: 60)

It is possible that Frank was able to avoid the emotional danger of the memories of his early life 'invading' the protective spaces of his home, where he was often alone, by splitting our interactions in the day centre and his home through projected distinctions between the safety and danger of the different interactions and spaces. As such, Frank's 'refusal' to talk about his experiences within the interview can be seen as involving responses to changing levels of difficulty in talking about past experiences, whilst also being a political expression of our relationship within a particular psycho-social context (Burkett, 1997). Disclosure and 'resistance' to disclosure can then be understood as a powerful means through which the emotional and political context of our interrelations could be expressed.

Within the context of our day centre interactions it is possible that emotional identifications between Frank and myself (as bereaved children) and the public space of the day centre changed the nature of topic threat for Frank in ways that were both valorizing and creative. This change may have enabled Frank to talk about himself and to be expressive in a way that departed from how he 'usually' managed social interactions. However, such relations had changed within the interview situation, where my relationship with Frank was more contoured by the structured formality and activity of the interview. In this sense, the interview situation could have produced an increase in topic threat and interactional difference that inhibited disclosures, and also evoked Frank's coping strategies of personal censure and diffidence. The power relations between us and their connections to the different psycho-social spaces of the research were extremely complex, however.

For example, although I may have been in a more dominant position in my interviewing role, it could also have been the case that the interview on Frank's 'home-ground' enabled Frank to resist my research interest in ways that were not possible in the hospice day centre, where he was receiving a service. At another level, my serving role within the day centre, and my postioning beside Frank both physically in the armchair, and subjectively as a bereaved child, may have produced a psycho-social space that contained and engaged (Bion, 1984) with Frank's emotional pain, rather than diverting and converting it into interview material. So, while Frank may have found it difficult to talk about his family and his experiences of poverty, the nature and consequences of this difficulty were neither essential nor stable, but were responsive to subjective, interactional and spatial changes in our research interactions over time. As Crang has pointed out, Lefebvre's conceptualization of space offers valuable insights in thinking about the interactions between the different types of space, where it is 'not just multiple permutations of "scapes" but qualitatively different senses and types of space that are interacting' (1999: 176).

THE CHALLENGE TO LEARN

From this discussion it is possible to offer interpretations of the differences in how Frank and I produced and made sense of the 'safety' and the 'danger' of the psycho-social spaces of the interview. In my interpretation, our face-to-face-interaction across Frank's small table in his home, the tape-recorder, and the visible topic guide served to generate an atmosphere of distant formality to our interaction in the interview. Not only was I in a more interactionally powerful role as an interviewer than I had been as a volunteer in the hospice day centre, I was also in a more *active* role in trying to elicit an account of Frank's experiences. I did not 'stand-by' Frank emotionally in the interview as I had done in the day centre. Rather, what I now feel is that I avoided the pain and the political implications of engaging with Frank's experiences of poverty, and the difficulties of talking about this in his home, by doing the work of asking questions. Waddell (1989), in an article on social work, has suggested that the activity of 'doing the work' in many social care organizations is about a defensive reaction against the difficulties of thinking about, and tolerating the psychic pain of 'clients'. Similarly, I would argue that preoccupations with the work of interviewing, can serve as a defence against the anxiety of witnessing and holding emotional pain in the interview.

Such an interpretation is made more complex in considering interactional and social power relations in research. The formal 'work' of an interviewer is to elicit 'data', and the form of the interview can often produce and reproduce complicated and contradictory inequalities in power. For instance, while I may have been in a more powerful research role in my interviews with Frank, he was able to challenge these potentially authoritative forms of power by 'refusing' to talk about his experiences. I believe that Frank's comment to me that 'you're never too old to learn', invokes, resists and inflects elements of the differences in power between us in the interview interaction. The effect of this comment was not simply patronizing or ironic (in terms of the over 40 years' age difference between Frank and myself). It can also be interpreted as an expression of Frank's authority and power in the interview, within the context of talk about his wounding experiences of poverty in the Caribbean, in which as a South-Asian woman and middle-class researcher, I was positioned as having something to learn.

By not talking to me about his experiences (by not 'teaching' me, in effect), Frank was able to resist an 'easy', detached appropriation of his experiences through the research and was able to confirm me in a position of 'not knowing'. This ignorance about Frank's experiences of poverty in the story about his life can also be re-contextualized further (see Chapter 6), by reference to wider social relations. Systems of privilege and oppression are based upon socially structured forms of ignorance, in which unspeakable levels of emotional and physical trauma (Bar-On, 1999; Sedgwick, 1993) are concealed and/or are not taken responsibility for by those in positions of power.

What I want to suggest is that the technical and discursive machinery of research can facilitate and legitimize this ignorance, and the toleration of the pain and suffering of research participants. This happens when the silences, resistance and/or refusals of research participants are (mis)constructed as technical matters that can be addressed primarily through methodological procedures and practices. By linking the micro-interactions of my interview with Frank to wider social processes, we can see that what I am talking about here is not simply a gap between experiences, but Frank's challenge to me to learn.

Of relevance to the point I am making is Elspeth Probyn's (2000) essay on reconciliation, in which she has talked about the need for feminists to think through, rather than to shy away from disconnection, and to begin to interrogate the production and topography of ignorance. In the context of my interviews with Frank, what I have taken from Probyn is the need for researchers to address and connect the dynamics between knowing and ignorance at the interpersonal and social levels. For me, this has meant recognizing and thinking about the subjective and social production of emotional pain that is often a hidden part of the meanings of the threat of certain topics.

CONCLUSIONS

Through an exploration of my research interactions with Frank, I have aimed to demonstrate the relevance of my conceptualization of psycho-social space for thinking about the dynamic production and meanings of threatening topics in research. In the example used, I have been concerned to show how specific topics might come to be constructed as threatening, but also how this constructed experience might change and be mediated by what is happening both within and around the research interaction at particular points in time. What I have also wanted to do in this chapter is to question and trouble the implicit division between 'threatening' and 'non-threatening' topics. The assumption in the literature – that there are clear differences in the nature of threatening topics and non-threatening topics – takes for granted the stable existence of 'safe' topics.

As I have shown, this assumed distinction can operate to obscure the ways in which the nature of the relations between the 'threat' and/or 'safety' of a topic are not stable, but can change and move in relation to the co-construction of the psycho-social spaces of the research interaction. In this regard, my approach to topic threat does not assume its pre-determined existence and unchanging nature outside the research encounter. Rather, it seeks to encourage examination and exploration of how the many boundaries around threatening topics are produced, defended and crossed in research interactions. In this sense, recognition of a relationship between the co-constitution of topic threat and psycho-social space in research interactions is not enough. We also need to interrogate how the safety or threat of a topic can move, and how it might be forced to move through particular configurations of psycho-social space *both* in research interactions and in analysis. Through such an approach, we can see how the negative meanings attached to 'threat' are based upon the normalization of implicit, positive assumptions about the safety of topics and research interactions, in which the research participant is positioned as comfortable, open and disclosing. Within such a scenario, interactional relations, particularly power relations, can escape detailed analytic attention, as we become focused upon why research participants do not talk about certain subjects, rather than examining why and when they talk about others.

Here, my own constituting of the links between subjectivity and politics in the production of topic threat and responses to it, needs to be examined closely in its application to different research interactions. Of particular importance is the need to blur the distinctions between subjectivity and politics, while at the same time acknowledging that the nature of the relationships between the two might be constituted in different ways as psycho-social events in different research encounters. What can be particularly hard to recognize is how researchers can be active in producing these very relationships. What is at stake in recognizing the permeable connections between points of 'safety' and 'danger' for the researcher in the doing of research and in analysis, is what we can avoid, deny or miss in research encounters. There are two main points of 'safety' and/or 'danger' for us here. First, how an excessive concern with subjective and intersubjective dynamics in research can obscure the construction, operation and effects of social power relations throughout a research encounter (see Seu, 1998). Second, how the 'activities' of methodological preoccupations, and also of attending to and making explicit power relations in research, can act as defences which can enable us to avoid the painful experiences of research participants.

In recognizing these complicated relations, what I am suggesting is that we need to re-think approaches to threatening topics in ways that attend to the fine detail and dynamism of how threatening and 'safe' topics are produced and experienced in the psycho-social spaces of research. In addition, we also need to question how our focus upon threatening topics can itself serve particular defensive and political purposes at particular times in research.

SUGGESTED READING

J. Brannen (1988) The Study of Sensitive Subjects. *Sociological Review*, 36(3): 552–63.

R. Lee (1993) *Doing Research on Sensitive Topics*. London: Sage (Chapter 5).

G. Lee-Treweek, and S. Linkogle (eds) (2000) *Danger in the Field: Risk And Ethics In Social Research*. London: Routledge (Chapters 5, 6 and 7).

E. Young, and R. Lee (1996) Fieldworker Feelings as Data: 'Emotion work' and 'feeling rules' in first person accounts of sociological fieldwork. In V. James and J. Gabe (eds), *Health and the Sociology of Emotions*. Oxford: Blackwell, pp. 97–113.

| NOTES

1. I have been able to address some of non-verbal interactions in the case study used in this chapter, through re-transcription of the original interviews and through my fieldwork notes. However, the detail of the non-verbal inter-actional components of psycho-social space in the case study is inadequate for demonstrating how valuable attention to these components can be. The use of video in social research has been seen as providing opportunities to examine the nature of these interactions in far greater detail (see Heath, 1998), but this carries with it its own epistemological and political challenges.

2. My approach to psycho-social space has developed out of work with Gail Lewis on the production of space within welfare agencies (Lewis and Gunaratnam, 2000).

3. Drawing upon her experiences of qualitative research on 'sensitive' topics, Brannen (1988) has argued that it is possible that the very risks of being involved in research on threatening issues are also precisely what can make it attractive to some research participants.

4. Lankshear (2000), in talking about her experiences of doing research in a hospital delivery suite, describes the emotional threat she felt of appearing 'a loser' to the hospital staff if she told them about her own traumatic experiences of child birth and the fact that she had had a child who had been labelled 'a slow learner'. What is relevant to my discussion of Frank, is Lankshear's sug-gestion that her perceived emotional vulnerability may have had a negative effect upon her professional image. She writes of the possibility that the staff might have felt 'sorry for me which would damage both my self-image and my professional image' (2000: 87). 'Professional image' here connotes a traditional, gendered notion of professionalism marked by emotional distance and invul-nerability (Davies, 1995). In my interactions with Frank at the day centre it is possible that it was identifications of emotional vulnerability, through my bereavements, and their mediation of my researcher role that enabled Frank to talk to me about his experiences.

5. There were problems with the recording of this second interview with Frank, and parts of the interview were untranscribable due to both 'white noise' and because Frank was softly spoken.

Towards multi-sited research: connection, juxtapositioning and complicity

SUMMARY

In this final chapter, I engage with ideas generated in ethnography about 'multi-sited' research – an approach that advocates the need for researchers to trace both the local and the wider connections of research interactions, across different cultural and discursive spaces. These ideas provide a reflexive analytic framework for discovering and making links between the micro-interactions of research encounters and broader contexts. Multi-sited research involves a politics of connection that is particularly relevant to research concerned with 'race' and ethnicity, where many different sites of experience and knowledge/power can come together, unravel and have unique effects within research interactions.

The preceding chapters have been concerned with addressing key debates, dilemmas and practices in research concerned with questions of 'race', ethnicity and social difference. In this final chapter, I want to engage more specifically with ideas about the need to develop 'multi-sited' research (Marcus, 1998), in which analysis is used to trace and connect research relations across social, cultural and epistemological spaces, to wider outside contexts. What multi-sited strategies have to offer research concerned with questions of 'race' and ethnicity, is an innovative and comparative framework where attention to 'the local' can be used to probe and complicate understandings of dominant discourses and their links to wider sites of social relations. This non-reductive approach to the relationships between local and wider contexts is achieved by the problematizing of key spatial, interactional and ethical parameters through which research interactions have been understood. Research sites, as bounded and discrete entities, are problematized. Research interactions, as characterized by the crossing of outsider/insider boundaries and the movement of knowledge, are problematized. And the power relations of research are problematized, as difference is recognized but common predicaments and orientations between the researcher and research participant are also searched for and learned from.

A multi-sited approach to methodology is necessarily spatial and involves practices of movement, connection and juxtapositioning (see Brah, 1996; Foucault, 1986;[1] and Hemmings, 2002). These 'cartographic' approaches to analysis are, in many respects, particularly suited to examining how racialized experiences are produced and have effects across space and time (I will come on to the difficulties later). They also complement the theoretical approaches that I have used throughout the book, which stress the socially constructed, situated and relational nature of 'race' and ethnicity. The value of thinking about research interactions in terms of where they are, how they are, and how they might relate to other social spaces, is that our multi-sited concerns can enable us to uncover previously hidden or excluded meanings and experiences.

Clare Hemmings, in her critical examination of bisexuality, has suggested that cartographic strategies are vital for researchers who want to challenge unitary notions of identity and who are concerned with the specific, rather than the abstract effects of difference in local, national and international contexts. Hemmings contends that for ethical research that is concerned with subjects whose knowledges are produced from diverse, multiple and often marginalized social locations, an engagement with space and embodied movement is critical. Key research questions then become:

> How do sexual, gendered and raced subjects 'take up space'? What is the relationship between dominant and subcultural locations? How are queer subjects produced in both discursive and actual spaces? What imaginative as well as actual geographical spaces do the disenfranchised create and occupy? (Hemmings, 2002: 46)

These questions are clearly relevant to all research, and in relation to research concerned with 'race' and ethnicity, can serve to challenge dominant and reified assumptions about the meanings of racial and ethnic categories and racialized difference. This is because the questions focus attention upon the production of difference and its effects, within and through specific cultural formations, rather than taking the meanings of difference to be pre-given. Of course, the tracing and mapping of research relations, and the meanings that they generate, are particularly important in the context of postcolonialism and contemporary global environments, where there can be a complex interweaving of processes of social connection and processes of fragmentation and differentiation (Eade, 1997b; Hall, 1992).

Marcus (1998) makes the point that in relation to anthropological research, the multiple and diverse sites of cultural formation have challenged traditional approaches to research. Anthropologists, Marcus argues, can no longer do research with 'the sense that the cultural object of study is fully accessible within a particular site, or without the sense that a site of fieldwork anywhere is integrally and intimately tied to sites of possible fieldwork elsewhere' (1998: 117).

Approaches to multi-sited research, which seek to reconnect research with regard to history, cultural contexts and the social locations and experiences of the researcher and research participant, can be found in the work of a range of different writers such as Haraway (1988), Scheff (1997) and Visweswaran (1997). I have chosen to focus upon Marcus's (1998) ideas of multi-sited research because he has produced an extended and concentrated discussion of various facets of a multi-sited research agenda. This discussion is both relevant to the different concerns raised in this chapter and will also provide a convenient resource for readers to explore in greater depth.

This analytic concern with the complex and uneven meanings of 'the globe' in individual lives is critical in qualitative research. In my hospice research, it was clear that the social and emotional meanings of local and global connections were highly significant in the production of racialized difference. From my interviews with minoritized service users (Gunaratnam, 1999) I could see that talk about 'home', in the context of where individuals wanted to die, or wanted their bodies to be buried, was much more than a geographical location, and involved embodied and imagined negotiations of space, time and relationships (Ahmed, 2000). As Stuart Hall (1997) has pointed out, the grasping and resurgence of narratives that appeal to a localized homeland, need not always be seen in terms of the construction of purified and exclusive identities, but can constitute an important point of challenge to discourses that stress the encompassing and homogenizing nature of globalization. Hall's careful analysis seeks to make clear how these more dynamic notions of the local, are not based upon essentialism:

The homeland is not waiting back there for the new ethnics to rediscover it. There is a past to be learned about, but the past is now seen, and has to be grasped as a history, as something that has to be told. It is narrated. It is grasped through memory. It is grasped through desire. It is grasped through reconstruction. It is is not just a fact that has been waiting to ground our identities. (1997: 38)

Uncovering how research interactions are situated and can connect very different social, spatial and emotional relations can be problematic and difficult. How, for example, can we distinguish between the reactionary essentialism and the creative dynamism of racialized identifications and meanings within research encounters? To a certain extent this is where the cartographic imagery can start to fall apart – where the lines of the relationships between discourses can be discontinuous, ambiguous and choppy (Marcus, 1998). What is challenging for the researcher in this respect is how to use and interrogate reflexively the 'internal' dynamics of the research relationship in ways that can push the analysis outwards, and towards the tracing of connections which can contextualize and situate meanings. In the context of dealing with fragments and partiality in her research on bisexuality, Hemmings has argued that reflexivity is less about making visible the researcher's positioning and more about 'being open to the ways in which collision, collusion, and conflict with one's research bodies shape one's own position and give it meaning' (2002: 51). With specific regard to racialized social relations, Clifford suggests that it is a positioning in 'the uncomfortable site' between moving and contradictory cultural processes and the generation of racialized and ethnicized identifications that can be critical for researchers:

> it is here that we can cultivate a kind of historical 'negative capability', aware of our own partial access to other historical experiences, tracking interference patterns and sites of emergence, piecing together more-than-local patterns, big-enough stories of the 'global', of intersecting 'historical' trajectories. (Clifford, 2000: 97)

My focus upon multi-sited research in this final chapter, is intended to examine the relationships and interfaces between local and wider sites, and to build upon the political process of joining up the methodological, epistemological and ethical concerns examined in the previous discussions, to consider in more detail the doing of research that is concerned with critical juxtapositions. It is important to point out that by 'local' I am not referring only to geographical space, but to differentiation and to 'a status of marginalization within broader discursive realms' (Wuthnow, 2002: 195). What might a multi-sited research project – that engages with such discursive and spatial relations – look like in practice? What knowledge about social difference is it capable of producing? What different understandings might it bring to how we examine, experience and represent research encounters and relationships? What ethical dilemmas will confront us?

In examining these questions, the chapter will focus upon Marcus's conceptualization of multi-sited research and complicity in ethnography. It will then move on to examine examples of multi-sited research, looking both at the analytic process and at practices of representation.

MULTI-SITED RESEARCH

For Marcus, multi-sited research is not simply, as its name might suggest, about doing research in many different sites. It is about a necessary engagement with circulation and mobility, as a part of 'new' and simultaneous cultural formations in the absence of singular and 'reliable holistic models of macroprocess ... such as "the world system," "capitalism," "the state," "the nation," etc' (1998: 87).

In Marcus's approach, previous notions of the ethnographer moving from 'outsider' to 'insider', as s/he becomes immersed in understanding and describing the life of 'Other' bounded cultural systems, is no longer possible (if it ever was) or desirable in the present-day context. So, although multi-sited ethnography can be based on research in one 'site', the focus of research is broadened through 'a multi-sited research imaginary', so that connections are investigated and made between previously unconnected sites – as in places, systems, experiences and discourses – bringing 'macro-structures' into view:

> The idea is that any cultural identity or activity is constructed by multiple agents in varying contexts or places, and that ethnography must be strategically conceived to represent this sort of multiplicity, and to specify both intended and unintended consequences in the network of complex connections within a system of places. (1998: 52)

This approach to research is seen as having direct implications for the type of knowledge that researchers can generate:

> I would argue that the particular kind of local knowledge or culture that this kind of ethnography does probe is the register of critical consciousness in any domain of discourse and action as the expression of counter-discourses. In other words, and in Raymond Williams's terms (1977), the ethnographer is particularly after what is emergent in discourse and action aside from what is obviously dominant. (1998: 53)

The 'aside from what is obviously dominant' is a point that I want to emphasize. My interpretation of this point is that the researcher is urged to seek out and to trouble any apparent coherence of discourse, through attention to moments of 'critical consciousness' and fragmentation that might contradict and/or subvert the dominant discourse. I have drawn particular attention to this point because it offers a way of exploring a variety of contemporary racializing discourses and practices that can be ambivalent, partial and/or suppressed within the accounts generated in research.

Ien Ang is one social theorist who has suggested that it is important to explore how processes of racialization and ethnic Othering have been transformed in the multicultural era, giving rise to more complex and also more ambivalent forms of power (Ang, 1996). Ang's main argument is that if we are to grasp the intricacies of contemporary racialized social relations, then we need to be concerned with the dynamic nature of lived experience that 'cannot be sufficiently understood in terms of the secure binary oppositions of racism/anti-racism and tolerance/intolerance and to a certain extent dominant/subordinate' (1996: 41).

As Ang has suggested, processes of racialization can be frustratingly subtle and elusive, rendering them difficult to uncover, analyse and challenge. In fact, it was precisely this frustration with the embedded nature of 'race' and ethnicity in parts of my ethnographic research in a hospice, that led me to use cartographic strategies to examine the production of difference in its movements across different sites of service relations, and between and within the spaces of different interview accounts. One way I did this was to create an imagined dialogue between staff and service users, using extracts from separate interview accounts where they had talked about the same topic (see Gunaratnam, 1999).

For example, in a dialogue constructed about food, I used the computer programme Nud.ist to search across all of the interview accounts and to identify any narrative extracts that referred to food and eating (Gunaratnam, 2001b). At a very basic level, this involved the cutting and pasting of commentaries from and between the interviews. The selection and bringing together of these different 'voices' in a highly choreographed conversation, was used to amplify and dramatize the 'varivoicedness' (Bakhtin, 1973) of the accounts, where various discourses and positions could mingle, contradict and question each other about the relationships between 'race', ethnicity, culture, ill-health and food, and how these relationships might be connected to the production, distribution and consumption of food within the hospice.

In constructing this conversation, I was interested in examining how different locations across sites of service provision, and particularly in relation to racialized, gendered, classed and health-related social positions, related to each other and produced particular effects. Although this form of analysis enabled me to uncover and map the multi-sitedness of particular racialized service relations within the hospice, my own role and movements within the production of the accounts was more hidden. This limited the potential of the approach to examine how my presence in the research constituted a significant 'elsewhere' for research participants, and how the conversation I produced might have been oriented towards this elsewhere.

Marcus's reformulation of complicity as the bridge between local and wider contexts (the 'elsewhere') in research is most relevant in this regard, in bringing the researcher and his/her social and interactional locations into analytic view.

COMPLICITY

Attention to a politicized complicity in research is what charaterizes a multi-sited research agenda, and transforms it from being 'just' about the spatial mapping of research relations. For Marcus, complicity in research is what is needed to displace the 'regulative ideal' of rapport that is based upon the need to gain access to the worlds of experience of research participants. Complicity, Marcus argues, begins from the same insider/outsider positioning as rapport, but does not presume to be able to move 'inside' in order to obtain local knowledge. Rather, complicity is about a reflexive positioning at the inside/outside boundary, and is characterized by how the researcher can use this position to understand how the research relationship is situated within a broader social context (see also Quayson and Goldberg, 2002). In this sense, the researcher and research participant are not required to 'forget' who they are (and where they otherwise would be), to produce a rapport-filled research relationship. Instead, 'affinity' comes from the recognition of:

> their mutual curiosity and anxiety about their relationship to a third – not so much the abstract contextualising world system but the specific sites elsewhere that affect their interactions and make them complicit (in relation to the influence of that 'third') in creating the bond that makes their fieldwork relationship effective … Complicity here rests in the acknowledged fascination between anthropologist and informant regarding the outside 'world' that the anthropologist is specifically materialising through the travels and trajectory of her multi-sited agenda. This is the OED sense of complicity that goes beyond the sense of 'partnership in an evil action' to the sense of being 'complex or involved,' primarily through the complex relationships to a third. (Marcus, 1998: 122)

This shared, troubling 'curiosity and anxiety' between the researcher and research participant(s) to an outside, 'elsewhere' is what needs to be recognized, explicated and interrogated within the topography of the research relationship as a part of broader contexts, which are themselves subject to dynamic and on-going changes. The tension between complicity as 'complex or involved' and as 'partnership in an evil action' produces a morally charged and ethically complicated terrain, in which the researcher 'is always on the verge of activism, of negotiating some kind of involvement beyond the distanced role of ethnographer' (Marcus, 1998: 122).

Having laid out some of the quite 'heavy' conceptual scaffolding of multi-sited research and complicity, I feel that it is important to provide some examples of how researchers concerned with multi-sited strategies have negotiated their way through the complicated ethical economies of multi-sited research. In the following sections I do this by looking at questions of representation in the work of Visweswaran (1997) and Lather and

Smithies (1997). I then move on to a more detailed examination of what a multi-sited analysis has to offer qualitative research on 'race', ethnicity and difference, using an example from my hospice ethnography.

EXAMPLES OF COMPLICITY IN ANALYSIS AND REPRESENTATION: VISWESWARAN AND LATHER AND SMITHIES

Visweswaran (1997), in an essay on betrayal portrayed through a theatrical analysis of her fieldwork experiences with women who were active in the Indian nationalist movement, offers us a challenging example of what complicity might look like and what demands it can make upon the researcher. Visweswaran's 'strategized complicity' is one that reaches for an 'accountable positioning' (Haraway, 1988) amid intermeshing power relations between three women and herself, in which her own activism can be witnessed, and felt, in what is revealed and what is withheld in analysis. In this analysis, Visweswaran uses her own conspiratorial entanglement with a series of fieldwork 'betrayals', revolving around a woman's ('Janaki') silence about her marriage, to suggest that relations of betrayal are very much implicated in the ethnographic need to know.

In her account, Visweswaran leads us through the chains of betrayal between the women. Differential class and caste positioning, marriage, the subject positions offered by nationalist ideology and by the research relationship are all sites that are investigated as sources of 'evidence' in a political and ethnographic 'whodunit?' However, ultimately, interpretation of 'the truth' is refused by Visweswaran, and instead 'temporality, silence and the multiple identities set into play by silence' (1997: 42) are used to point to numerous 'suspects', including the feminist ethnographer and the reader's appetite for convenient portions of subjectified difference. Visweswaran reminds us that, in her account:

> there is a complicity between different kinds of refusals: Janaki's in refusing to tell me what I wanted to know, and my own as ethnographer, in refusing to tell my audience all it wants to know about Janaki. (1997: 50)

What this example from Visweswaran speaks to, is how complicity, when addressed in relation to both the micro-interactions of research and broader social and disciplinary contexts, is not 'simply' about how we do research or about producing 'fuller' knowledge. In engaging specifically with the positioning of minoritized researchers *vis-à-vis* minoritized, but differently positioned research participants, complicity for Visweswaran becomes conspicuously ethical *and* epistemological. At the same time, the tensions between ethics and epistemology are seen as leading to struggles 'with the demands of identity and community' against the dominant representational practices of social "science"' (p. 15). In relation to Visweswaran's research relationships, it is clear that a broader context that she makes 'felt' within research interactions, is an invasive, colonial social science. In relation to analysis and representation, Visweswaran's 'circumstantial activism' (Marcus, 1998) is to place herself between the women and the interrogative impulses of feminism and ethnography:

> Suspicious of feminist and ethnographic desires to 'know' the other, I rendered a subject who resists any single positioning for very long. My attempt was to describe how a woman emerged out of a series of performances and positionings, and not render the category 'woman' intelligible through recourse to sociological variables as abstract descriptions of reality. (1997: 76)

The concerns in multi-sited research with space, movement, connection and juxtapositioning thus have critical implications for the representation of research. How can we represent identities and subjective positions in process, multiple and cross-cutting sites of power/knowledge and spatial slippage, discontinuities and interconnections in research?

Troubling the Angels, the title of a book written by Lather and Smithies (1997), which draws upon qualitative interviews and support group meetings with 25 white, African-American and Hispanic women living with HIV/AIDS in four cities in Ohio, provides an example of how researchers have addressed such questions of representation in multi-sited projects. According to Lather, the book was written to be accessible to a general audience, whilst also being a 'messy text' (Marcus, 1994), 'denying the "comfort text" that maps easily onto our usual way of making sense' and reflecting 'back at its readers the problems of inquiry at the same time an inquiry is conducted' (Lather, 2001b: 205).[2] The multi-sitedness of the research can be witnessed in the ways the book traces accounts through a series of spaces between individual lives and wider national and international contexts, and across the researcher–research participant relation. What is particularly interesting about *Troubling the Angels* is how the authors have tried to convey this interweaving of sites and experiences in the text. Thus, Lather describes how in the book:

> Interspersed among the interviews, there are [angel] inter-texts, which serve as 'breathers' between the themes and emotions of the women's stories; a running subtext where the authors spin out their tales of doing research; factoid boxes on various aspects of the disease; and a scattering of the women's writing in the form of poems, letters, speeches and emails. (2001b: 206)

The preface to the book tells us that:

> Efforts were made to not 'sanitize' each woman's way of speaking and each thematic grouping of chapters includes some of the women's own writing.

> Each story series is followed by an intertext on angels which chronicles the social and cultural issues raised by the AIDS pandemic. The angels of the intertexts are intended to serve as both bridges and breathers as they take the reader on a journey that troubles any easy sense of what AIDS means. Across the bottom of much of the book is a continuously running commentary by us ... the co-researchers, regarding our experiences in telling the women's stories that moves between autobiography and academic 'Big Talk' about research methods and theoretical frameworks. Occasionally, the subtext opens out to include one of the women, as she narrates her recent changes, providing a counter-story to her earlier story at the top of the page. (Lather and Smithies, 1997: xvii)

Through these textual practices, particularly the split pages, with the women's accounts at the top of the page in larger font, and the researchers' narratives at the bottom, something of the complicity between the researchers and the women who participated in the research can be glimpsed. The points of alignment in the research relationships appear at first to be about the joint concern of making known the complicated stories of living with HIV/AIDS. Yet, as the book unfolds it becomes apparent that what also connects the women and the researchers is the negotiation of differential relationships to illness, suffering, death and loss, which for me at least, is the wider 'elsewhere' materialized through the research. The different sites of these relationships and connected anxieties are represented by Lather and Smithies through the layering of different texts such as interview accounts, diary entries, emails, poems, demographic and medical information about HIV/AIDS, social theory and autobiography.

An example of this textual staging of anxieties can be seen in one part of the book where a group discussion about the 'double-life' of living with AIDS is underwritten by an entry from Lather's research diary, where she describes a hospital visit to Louisa:

> I think of myself frozen like a deer in Louisa's glare in the hospital room ... What was this research project in the face of her story of eight months without eating, a baby dead of AIDS ... hair fallen out from chemotherapy, surrounded by the women in a family she felt she had to protect from her despair and anger? What was her twitching that I carried with me for days afterward, a restlessness, as Chris and I finally named it, to be much about our lives? Was it some horror at turning the tragedy of this 24 year old Puerto Rican woman's life into part of the spectacle of the research? (Lather and Smithies, 1997: 154)

Through this textual juxtapositioning of sites of experience, another dimension is added to Marcus's conceptualization of complicity. This dimension concerns the triangulation of the relationships between the researcher, researcher participant and the reader/audience, and how the representation of research might disrupt an easy consumption of the Other by the reader (see Chapter 6) and so open up new possibilities of thinking through and against dominant discourses. (For further examples and discussion on representation see O'Neill et al., 2002 and Skeggs, 2001.)

Practices of representation are clearly a critical area of concern in relation to multi-sited research and complicity; however, I want to examine further and in more detail what attention to complicity might mean for how we do and understand our research. In the next sections, I will discuss an example from my hospice research, in which its multi-sitedness across service experiences and spaces served to produce fraught and challenging relations of complicity. In this instance, I explore a different dynamic of complicity to that of Visweswaran, and to that discussed in Chapter 6 – here, I focus upon complicity between the minoritized researcher and white, racist research participants.

WORLDS APART?

In my hospice research, I spent time with staff as a volunteer in the hospice day centre and in accompanying hospice 'home-care' nurses on visits to service users. I also facilitated interviews with different groups of hospice professionals (nurses, doctors, social workers and members of the chaplaincy team). As I have pointed out elsewhere (Gunaratnam and Lewis, 2001), my participation in these interviews often involved the management of my own emotions in relation to identifications with, and distancing from accounts. A central mode for the construction of racialized difference in staff accounts was talk about the dilemmas of intercultural care (Gunaratnam, 2001a). These dilemmas were framed within a context of multicultural and anti-discriminatory discourses that were developing as key areas of concern in the hospice movement in the 1990s (see Hill and Penso, 1995).

In facilitating the group discussions with the (mainly white) hospice staff, I was especially disturbed and challenged by those accounts that involved racist and racializing discourses about the 'difficulties' that some white staff said that they experienced in responding to the needs of minoritized service users. How might a minoritized researcher engage with such discourses in research through attention to complicity? What could be the possible affinities and alignments that can be traced between the minoritized researcher and a white professional with specific organizational powers *and* responsibilities to minoritized service users? What could be happening in the dynamics and the tensions of such research encounters that are tied to events and processes elsewhere, through the intersections between locality and 'globality' (Kraidy, 2002: 187)? For me, one way of addressing these questions is through attention to how my uncomfortable positioning within research encounters can be used to search for any 'oppositional spaces' (Marcus, 1998) within dominant discourses, and to figure out how such spaces might be connected to my own positionings in researching 'race' and ethnicity.

The example that I am going to use is from a group interview with four white, British hospice nurses. The extract focuses on an account from 'Gill', of caring for an Ugandan woman with AIDS:

Gill: I was just thinking about this one lady in particular. I found it extremely hard to get alongside her. I would say because of the cultural differences I would think, um, but I'm not sure, there was a lot to her case in particular, but, I feel that with, here, we do get alongside patients, and, and we're very good at that. Very good at getting to know them ... and caring for them, but this, er, I found it with Ugandan women in particular actually, that I find it very difficult to, to I suppose read them. You know, I suppose I go a lot on people's non-verbals as well as what they say, and when the language is different you go a lot on people's non-verbals. And when you're faced with somebody who's Ugandan, who their very culture, you know, er sort of suppresses facial features, you know and they've got a very flat face, um –

Yasmin: A non-expressive face?

Gill: Yes. Yeah. I'm trying to think of the right word, but yes that's what I mean. But that was coupled with slowed mental processes from dementia. So it was very difficult, but I found we never really got alongside her ... I suppose I view that as a failure of care in a way ... but then can you, can we ever, as somebody from a completely different culture, you know, that's what I find interesting, is can I, could I ever have done that you know, given more time? Because there was you know, there, it's in-bred in, it was in-bred in her not to er, divulge much information, which you know, she didn't want us to get to know her. So you know I don't know really [laughs].

This extract is just one vivid example of the production of numerous dilemmas that I listened to, as staff spoke about different aspects of caring for minoritized hospice service users. In this dilemma, the racializing themes that operate to produce an essentialized embodied, 'in-bred' Otherness in the Ugandan woman, and that simultaneously normalize whiteness, are stark, but are also ambivalent and confused.

When we look more closely at the extract, we can see that this dilemma carries the hallmark of inherently contradictory themes (Billig et al., 1988). In this instance, the contradictions are played out between the tensions surrounding the cross-cutting meanings of 'in-bred' difference. On one axis, biological and cultural notions of difference are called up and are centred upon 'race'.[3] On the other, gendered connections between Gill and the Ugandan woman are displaced, but are also refracted through 'race' and its slippage with AIDS, to produce Otherness through a dis-eased configuration of 'race', ethnicity, culture and gender.

The idea that all Ugandan women are emotionally remote and self-censoring evokes and resonates with ethnographic discourses of cross-cultural translation, interpretation and of knowing others. Gill's interpretation of gendered 'Ugandaness' as an essentialized subjectivity, embodied and observed in the 'flat face' of Otherness that confronts her, is given added authority by reference to her experiences of all the Ugandan women she has nursed. Yet, this interpretation sits right alongside a radical uncertainty about how the black, diseased, female body is able to represent and hold the boundary that marks such absolute difference. How real is the 'race' seen and felt in the construction of the distances between Gill and the Ugandan woman in this English hospice ward? Could things have been different given more time? Is this 'simply' a failure of cross-cultural communication and care, or an inevitable result of an un-negotiable alterity, complicated by language differences and AIDS dementia?

Gill's uncertainties about the nature of racialized difference and the explanatory power of 'race' as a category of identification, are points of weakness and contradiction in her racializing discourse that are instantly recognizable. These contradictions and tensions pervade local and national policies on race equality and approaches to the training of health professionals in 'cultural competence' and 'cultural sensitivity' (Gunaratnam, 1997). However, they also mark critical epistemological and political dilemmas in the social sciences. And they mark my own experiences of researching and writing about 'race' and ethnicity. In Marcus's terms, Gill and I are aligned in complex and unexpected ways in the research encounter, through our complicity with different sites of power/knowledge relating to the negotiation of uncertainties, tensions and ambivalence in how to work with racial categories. These are the lived dynamics and the entanglements of the 'treacherous bind' (Radhakrishnan, 1996) of 'race' discussed in Chapter 2.

There are numerous connections between the racializing dilemmas constructed by Gill as a hospice nurse, and the dilemmas produced in epistemological discussions about cross-cultural research. It is not simply that Gill's problematic positioning as a cultural interpreter within the extract, re-enacts and speaks to the 'crisis of representation' (Marcus and Fischer, 1986) in ethnographic claims to know and to represent the Other (see also Stacey, 1988). It is also that the practitioner–'patient' relationship, within models of holistic, 'new nursing' (Porter, 1996), map almost too readily onto aspects of the researcher–research participant relationship, particularly with the increasing use of psychoanalytic frames in research (see Obeyesekere, 1990). Gill's dilemma thus evokes particular postcolonial complicities between hospice practitioners and social scientists in their claims to know racialized difference. The position that I find myself in, as a minoritized, feminist researcher, in confronting these complicities is particularly uncomfortable and disconcerting. As Chow (1992) has already recognized:

> The task that faces Third World feminists is not simply that of animating the oppressed women of their cultures, but of making the automatized and animated condition of their own voices the conscious part of departure in their interventions. This does not simply mean they are, as they must be, speaking across cultures and boundaries; it also means that they speak of the awareness of 'cross-cultural' speech as a limit, and that their very own use of the victimhood of women and Third World cultures is both symptomatic of and inevitably complicitous with the First World. (p. 112, quoted in Visweswaran, 1997: 93)

UNEASY ALIGNMENTS

Having identified relations of complicity in the research encounter, Marcus suggests that researchers need to trace and establish:

> intersecting genealogies of shared concepts and concerns ... through a sort of ethnographically sensitive translation between 'worlds apart' power/knowledge arenas, such that mutually relevant discussions might occur between scholars and experts who might never have thought that they had much in common. (1998: 206)

In tracing the linking genealogies around uncertainty and ambivalence in the use of racial categories, I have 're-contextualized' (see Chapter 6) my research encounter with Gill in relation to two main sites (Gunaratnam, in progress): the socio-economic and the epistemological. In relation to the former, a multi-sited analysis enabled me to trace connections between the local context of multicultural service provision in an English hospice ward, and the wider global context of AIDS and bio-politics in which there are significant and growing disparities between the North/West and those in 'Third World' countries, particularly in Africa.

In relation to the epistemological, I have looked for the ways in which Gill's ambivalence and uncertainty in using racial categories might connect fields of power/knowledge for her, as a white hospice nurse, and me, as a minoritized social scientist. For example, as far as Gill's narrative reflects and constructs dominant discourses on 'race', we can see that the 'oppositional space' (Marcus, 1998) within this, discourse lies not simply in the tensions spotlighted between 'race' and 'humanness', but also with whether to use racial categories or to abandon them. These significant, yet marginalized tensions run across anti-racist political projects and activism, the academic study of 'race' and ethnicity, and indicate a site for dialogue between academics and health care professionals.

The identifying and tracking of the many social relations, experiences and sites that converged in my research interaction with Gill, included the following points of analysis:

- How the tensions in Gill's account about the usefulness of 'race' as a concept resonate with academic, 'de-racination' debates. At the time of the research, Paul Gilroy, a leading figure in the debates, was calling for researchers in the social sciences to (once again) engage with the prospect that 'the time of "race" may be coming to a close' (Gilroy, 1998: 840). Gilroy called for the renunciation of 'race' as a concept.
- The links between the de-racination debates and the technological 'scape' of AIDS health care. Here I have addressed Gilroy's contention that developments in microbiology and body imaging technology[4] in moving beyond the surfaces of the skin, hold new challenges for racial thinking. The imaging technology that Gilroy discusses is used in the diagnosis of AIDS related cerebral infections. In addition to this, Gill is also someone who, through a wide range of experiences of nursing and familiarity with different levels of bio-technology, 'knows' about the biological meaningless of 'race' in the deep structures of the body and in matters of death and dying.
- The juxtapositioning of the epistemological dimensions of technology alongside the ontological dimensions of lived, felt *experiences* of technology (Quayson and Goldberg, 2002). In order to examine these lived experiences, I drew upon an interview with Hilda, a black, Jamaican, retired hospital 'domestic' with cancer, in which she talked about the experience of her body being scanned in order to diagnose the cancer. This attention to Hilda's experience pointed to the contradictions and discrepancies of socio-economic, post-colonial relations, where as a cancer 'patient', the total cost of Hilda's 30–40 minute scan (not including the cost of the scanner itself) was more than she would have earned in a month as a hospital domestic at the bottom of the National Health Service.
- Socio-economic discrepancies were also traced between local multi-cultural commitments to the inclusion of ethnic 'Others' in English hospice care, and global bio-political relations, in which Third World countries have been excluded from access to affordable AIDS drugs and from being able to provide adequate health care.

In this analysis, it is possible to see how a concern with linking the research interaction to wider contexts, pulls several non-local connections into view, at the same time serving to challenge any sense of the global as an encompassing totality. However, we would have been able to trace several of these connections without an engagement with relations of complicity. By examining the different sites evoked in Gill's account, for instance, we would have been able to situate the account within the vast inequalities of postcolonial relations surrounding AIDS and bio-political forms of power at a global level. This is, of course, an important dynamic to recognize and to examine in the interpretation of the account. Likewise, attention to power relations within research would have enabled me to locate my research encounter with Gill within a more complicated ethical framework, in which the inequalities of the researcher–research participant relationship were mediated by differences in 'race' and ethnicity, and by my positioning as a minoritized researcher.

In order to make clear what the idea of complicity has to offer, over and above these analytic insights, I want to return to Marcus's assertion that complicity forces us, as researchers, to recognize two main dynamics within the research interaction. First, we are propelled to recognize the researcher as an ever-present and travelling marker of 'outsideness', who makes that outside present and felt within the research encounter. And second, we must also recognize research participants as being concerned with and affected by the outside that is signified and embodied in the researcher's presence. What researchers are after then, is not the solid authenticity of the insider account, but the doubled-sided local 'knowledge' of both the research participant and the researcher 'that arises from the anxieties of knowing that one is tied into what is happening elsewhere, but … without those connections being clear or precisely articulated' (Marcus, 1998: 119). It is a commitment to this version of complicity, in which the researcher and research participant are seen as being curious and anxious about how local narratives might be related to 'great and little events happening elsewhere' (p. 118), that can transform analysis and interpretation.

With regard to my research interaction with Gill, we can see how this notion of complicity, where there is a search for moments of shared orientation, does not allow me to distance myself from Gill by categorizing and essentializing her discourse as racist (see also Blee, 1991). Complicity in this instance, pushed me to try and piece together how, in the co-production of Gill's account, there are points of discourse that connect different sites of the research, not simply in relation to staff and service user relations within the hospice, but also in relation to how Gill's positioning might overlap with mine. This movement is quite different from traditional approaches to 'fieldwork', and involves what Ahmed has referred to (in a discussion of transnational feminism) as a 'getting closer to others in order to occupy or inhabit the distance between us' (2000: 179). This is what moved the analysis in the direction of the de-racination debates in academia at the time of the research, and through these debates brought me to the epistemological and experiential dimensions of body imaging, to the contradictions of racializing imaginaries, and to the weaknesses and deficits of knowledge production on 'race' and ethnicity.

The finding and recognizing of points of distance, alignment and collision in the local research interaction is what drives the analysis in different directions in multi-sited research, and serves to broaden ethical and reflexive concerns in research. Sites of power become more diverse and ambivalent, and reflexivity has to take account of how both the researcher's position is produced through the embodied collisions within the research encounter (Hemmings, 2002), and how these collisions are connected to what is happening elsewhere. Drawing these different points together for the purposes of clarity, multi-sited research can be summarized as involving: an intensive investigation and inhabitation of a research site; the use of this investigation to imagine, juxtapose and describe relationships between two or more sites 'previously thought to be incommensurate (Marcus, 1998: 14); and the interrogation and tracing of complicity within the micro-interactions of research to broader, outside socio-cultural dynamics.

Ultimately, then, multi-sited research is about an attempt to understand and trace the dynamic criss-crossing of bodies, narratives and social processes within and across the spaces of research interactions.

IS MULTI-SITED RESEARCH REALLY THAT MUCH OF AN OPTION?

The purpose of this discussion has been to show the profound challenges *and* the potential that multi-sited research and attention to complicity holds for research concerned with and informed by questions of 'race' and difference. Multi-sited research goes against the grain of much that I have been taught about what research should be, what research encounters might mean, and how analysis should proceed. The research topic that we try so carefully to make specific, bounded and coherent in our research proposals and in projects, is a topic whose boundaries will be systematically dismantled in multi-sited research, as attention to broader concerns and connections demands that we move across topics, frameworks, experiences and spaces.

I can understand how many teachers and students might feel unnerved by a multi-sited research agenda. Doesn't it make research much more difficult and confusing, particularly for new researchers? Isn't it too ambitious? My own experience is that I have felt much more lost and confused without such conceptual frameworks that legitimize many of the experiences and interrelations that researchers encounter in fieldwork and in analysis, but which are rarely named and addressed in the methodological literature or in teaching. We can all have some appreciation from our own experiences that 'race' does not operate in singular, neat, coherent and visible ways. It is 'At once evanescent and ferocious, ephemeral and intense, conspicuous and unspecifiable' (Winant, 1994: 267).

Unruly racialized power dynamics and meanings that are constituted through transnational connections, movement and multiplicity, mark all groups and individuals. Such entanglements are reflected in encounters with research participants, who not only act and talk in ways that reference intersecting and multiple identifications, but are also able to be more demanding and refusing of research encounters at many different levels (see Chapters 6 and 7). In this regard, it is important to underline what is perhaps obvious: the racial order is itself multi-sited, and its multi-sitedness is being proclaimed and claimed by research participants and growing numbers of researchers, who are refusing the narrowness of focus and the constraints of 'traditional' methodological approaches.

So, in many senses I do not think that we really have that much of a choice when it comes to multi-sited research. But I also recognize that there is need for dialogue within, between and outside our disciplines about what a multi-sited research agenda means for our research practices, for our understanding of ethics, the types of knowledge that we produce and how we might judge and represent this knowledge.

INCOMPLETIONS

Multi-sited research is about a methodological and epistemological politics of connection and juxtaposition that lends itself to the examination of 'race' and ethnicity, and to the uncovering and challenging of racism and oppression. What wide-ranging discussions of multi-sited research have made clear (Marcus, 1998; Visweswaran, 1997) is that experimentation and uncertainty (Lather, 2001b) are part and parcel of the experience of pursuing genealogies of social and cultural phenomena across experiences, meaning frameworks and spaces. The idea that uncertainty is methodologically valuable may provide some comfort to those of us who are struggling with some of the dilemmas, challenges, contradictions and difficulties of researching 'race' and ethnicity that I have highlighted throughout this book. However, I am also aware of how frustrating, undermining and painful such uncertainty can be, particularly within contexts where many of us work with teachers, supervisors, peers and in disciplinary arenas where the significance of 'race' and racism are simultaneously demonstrated and denied on a daily basis. My hope is that this book might speak to and engage with some of these experiences, in an uncertain move towards multi-sitedness that invites critical dialogue with its own partiality and incompleteness.

SUGGESTED READING

P. Lather (2001b) Postbook: Working the ruins of feminist ethnography. *Signs*, 27(1): 199–227.
G. Marcus (1998) *Ethnography Through Thick and Thin*. Princeton: Princeton University Press (Chapters 3 and 4).
K. Visweswaran (1997) *Fictions of Feminist Ethnography*. Minneapolis: University of Minnesota Press (Chapter 3).

NOTES

1. Foucault has argued that:

   We are in an epoch of simultaneity: we are in an epoch of juxtaposition, the epoch of the near and far, of the side-by-side, of the dispersed. We are at a moment, I believe, when our experience of the world is less that of a long life developing through time than that of a network that connects points and intersects with its own skein ... the anxiety of our era has to do fundamentally with space, no doubt a good deal more than time. (1986: 22–3)

2. The 'messy' textual format of Lather and Smithies book in conveying something of the multi-sitedness of experiences of living with HIV/AIDS provides a direct engagement with the 'crisis of representation' in ethnography, encapsulated by what has come to be known as the 'Writing Culture' debates of the 1980s (Clifford and Marcus, 1986; Marcus and Fischer, 1986). These debates took their name from an edited collection by Clifford and Marcus (1986), that was subtitled 'The politics and poetics of ethnography' (see Denzin, 1997 and Atkinson et al., 2001 for more about the debates). The tenor of the critique of ethnographic representation in the debates was marked by a number of different influences, including postcolonial theory (Said, 1985 [1978]), feminism (Skeggs, 2001) and post-Marxist and post-structuralist enquiry (Spencer, 2001).

3. Stuart Hall has referred to the interdependence of biological racism and cultural differentialism as 'racism's two registers' (Hall, 2000).

4. For Gilroy, developments in microbiology and in the imaging of bodies have superseded the eighteenth-century 'perceptual regimes' through which 'race' was given meaning:

   Nuclear magnetic resonance spectroscopy [NMR/MRI], positron emission tomography [PET] and several other innovations in multidimensional body imaging have remade the relationship between the seeable and the unseen. By imaging the body in new ways, they impact upon the ways that embod-. ied humanity is imagined and upon the status of bio-racial differences that vanish at these levels of resolution ... Our questions should be this: where do these changes leave racial difference, particularly where it cannot readily be correlated with simple genetic variation? (1998: 846)

References

Agnew, J. (1999) *Geopolitics: Re-visioning World Politics*. New York: Routledge.

Ahmad, W.I.U. and Sheldon, T. (1991) 'Race' and Statistics. *Radical Statistics Newsletter*, 48 (Spring): 27–33.

Ahmad, W.I.U. and Sheldon, T. (1993) 'Race' and Statistics. In M. Hammersley (ed.), *Social Research: Philosophy, Politics and Practice*. London: Sage, pp. 124–3.

Ahmed, S. (2000) *Strange Encounters, Embodied Others in Post-Coloniality*. London: Routledge.

Aitken, G. and Burman, E. (1999) Keeping and Crossing Professional and Racialized Boundaries: Implications for Feminist Practice. *Psychology of Women Quarterly*, 23: 277–97.

Alexander, C. (1996) *The Art of Being Black: The Creation of Black British Youth Identities*. Oxford: Clarendon Press.

Alexander, C. (2000) (Dis)Entangling the 'Asian Gang': Ethnicity, identity, masculinity. In B. Hesse (ed.), *Un/settled Multiculturalisms: Diasporas, Entanglements, Transruptions*. London: Zed Books, pp. 123–47.

Alexander, J. and Mohanty, C. (eds) (1997) *Feminist Genealogies, Colonial Legacies, Democratic Futures*. New York and London: Routledge.

Ali, A. and Toner, B. (2001) Symptoms of Depression Among Caribbean Women and Caribbean-Canadian Women: An investigation of self-silencing and domains of meaning. *Psychology of Women Quarterly*, 25: 175–80.

Alldred, P. (1998) Ethnography and Discourse Analysis: Dilemmas in representing the voices of children. In J. Ribbens and R. Edwards (eds), *Feminist Dilemmas in Qualitative Research: Public Knowledge and Private Lives*. London: Sage, pp. 147–70.

Allen, J. and Pryke, M. (1994) The Production of Service Space. *Society and Space*, 12: 453–75.

Althusser, L. (1971) *Lenin and Philosophy*. London: New Left Books.

Anderson, M. (1993) Studying Across Difference: Race, class and gender in qualitative research. In J. Stanfield and R. Dennis (eds), *Race and Ethnicity in Research Methods*. Newbury Park, CA: Sage, pp. 39–52.

Ang, I. (1996) The Curse of the Smile: Ambivalence and the 'Asian' woman in Australian multiculturalism. *Feminist Review*, 52: 36–49.

Ang, I. (2000) Identity Blues. In P. Gilroy, L. Grossberg and A. McRobbie (eds), *Without Guarantees: In Honour of Stuart Hall*. London: Verso, pp. 1–13.

Ang-Lyngate, M. (1996) Everywhere To Go But Home: On (re)(dis)(un)location. *Journal of Gender Studies*, 5(3): 375–88.

Ashworth, P. (1986) (ed.) *Qualitative Research in Psychology*. Pennsylvania: Duquesne University Press.

Aspinall, P. (2000) Should a Question on 'Religion' be Asked in the 2001 British Census? A public policy case in favour. *Social Policy and Administration*, 34(5): 584–600.

Aspinall, P. (2001) Operationalising the Collection of Ethnicity Data in Studies of the Sociology of Health and Illness. *Sociology of Health and Illness*, 23(6): 828–62.

Atkinson, P., Coffey, A., Delamont, S., Lofland, J. and Lofland. L. (eds) (2001) *Handbook of Ethnography*. London: Sage.

Axelrod, M., Matthews, D. and Prothro, J. (1962) Recruitment for Survey Research on Race Problems in The South. *Public Opinion Quarterly*, 2: 254–62.

Bakhtin, M. (1973) *Problems of Dostoevsky's Poetics*, trans. R. Rotsel. Michigan: Ardis Press.

Bakhtin, M. (1981) *The Dialogical Imagination*, trans. C. Emerson and A. Holquist. Austin, TX: University of Texas Press.

Bakhtin, M. (1986) *Speech Genres and Other Late Essays*, edited by C. Emerson and A. Holquist. Austin: University of Texas Press.

Barker, F., Hulme, P. and Iversen, M. (eds) (1994) *Colonial Discourse/Postcolonial Theory*. Manchester: Manchester University Press.

Bar-On, D. (1999) *The Indescribable and the Undiscussable: Reconstructing Human Discourse after Trauma*. Budapest: Central European University Press.

Barrett, M. and McIntosh, M. (1985) Ethnocentrism and Socialist Feminism. *Feminist Review*, 20: 23–45.

Barthes, R. (1972) *Mythologies*, trans. A. Lavers. New York: Hill and Wang.

Barton, A. (1958) Asking the Embarassing Questions. *Public Opinion Quarterly*, 22: 67–8.

Bashi, V. (1998) Racial Categories Matter Because Racial Hierarchies Matter: A commentary. *Ethnic and Racial Studies*, 21(5): 959–68.

Bell, S. and Gordon, J. (1999) Scholarship – The New Dimension to Equity Issues for Academic Women. *Women's Studies International Forum*, 22(6): 645–58.

Bengston, V., Grigsby, E., Corry, E. and Hurby, M. (1977) Relating Academic Research to Community Concerns: A case study in collaborative effort. *Journal of Social Issues*, 33(4): 74–92.

Bhabha, H. (1996) Culture's In-Between. In S. Hall and P. du Gay (eds), *Questions of Cultural Identity*. London: Sage, pp. 53–60.

Bhabha, H. and Comaroff, J. (2002) Speaking of Postcoloniality, In the Continuous Present. In D. Goldberg and A. Quayson (eds), *Relocating Postcolonialism*. Oxford: Blackwell, pp. 15–46.

Bhattacharyya, G., Gabriel, J. and Small, S. (2002) *Race and Power: Global Racism in the Twenty-First Century*. London: Routledge.

Bhavnani, K.-K. (1993) Tracing the Contours of Feminist Research and Feminist Objectivity. *Women's Studies International Forum*, 6(2): 95–104.

Bhavnani, K.-K. and Haraway, D. (1994) Shifting the Subject: A conversation between Kum-Kum Bhavnani and Donna Haraway on 12 April, 1993, Santa Cruz, California. In K.-K. Bhavnani and A. Phoenix (eds), *Shifting Identities, Shifting Racisms: A Feminism and Psychology Reader*. London: Sage, pp. 19–39.

Bhopal, K. (2001) Researching South Asian Women: Issues of sameness and difference in the research process. *Journal of Gender Studies*, 10(3): 279–86.

Billig, M., Condor, S., Edwards, D., Gane, M., Middleton, D. and Radley, A. (1988) *Ideological Dilemmas: A Social Psychology of Every Day Thinking*. London: Sage.

Bion, W. (1984) *Learning from Experience*, 2nd edn. London: Maresfield (1st edn 1962).

Blee, K.M. (1991) *Women of the Klan: Racism and Gender in the 1920s*. Berkeley, CA: University of California Press.

Bola, M. (1996) Questions of Legitimacy? The fit between researcher and researched. In S. Wilkinson and C. Kitzinger (eds), *Representing the Other*. London: Sage, pp. 125–8.

Bonnett, A. (1996) Anti-racism and the Citique of 'White' Identities. *New Community*, 22(1): 97–110.

Bonnett, A. (1998) Who was white? The disappearance of non-European white identities and the formation of European racial whiteness. *Ethnic and Racial Studies*, 21(6): 1029–55.

Bourdieu, P. (1977) *An Outline of a Theory of Practice*. Cambridge: Cambridge University Press.

Bourdieu, P. (1984) *Distinction: A Social Critique of the Judgement of Taste*. Cambridge, MA: Harvard University Press.

Bourdieu, P. (1990) *The Logic of Practice*. Cambridge: Polity Press.

Bradburn, N. and Sudman, S. (1979) *Improving Interview Method and Questionnaire Design: Response Effects to Threatening Questions in Survey Research*. San Franciso: Jossey-Bass.

Bradburn, N., Sudman, S., Blair, E., Locander, W., Miles, C., Singer, E. and Stocking, C. (1979) *Improving Interview Method and Questionnaire Design*. San Francisco: Jossey-Bass.

Brah, A. (1996) *Cartographies of Diaspora: Contesting Identities*. London: Routledge.

Brah, A., Hickman, M. and Mac an Ghaill, M. (1999) Thinking Identities: Ethnicity, Racism and Culture. In A. Brah, M. Hickman and M. Mac an Ghaill (eds), *Thinking Identities: Ethnicity, Racism and Culture*. Basingstoke: Macmillan, pp. 1–21.

Brannen, J. (1988) The Study of Sensitive Subjects. *Sociological Review*, 36(3): 552–63.

Briggs, C. (1986) *Learning How to Ask: A Socio-linguistic Appraisal of the Role of the Interview in Social Science Research*. Cambridge: Cambridge University Press.

British Sociological Association (2002) *Proposed New Statement of Ethical Practices for The British Sociological Association*. Durham: British Sociological Association.

Brush, P. (2001) Problematizing the Race Consciousness of Women of Colour. *Signs*, 27(1): 171–98.

Bulmer, M. and Solomos, J. (1996) Introduction: Race, ethnicity and the curriculum. *Ethnic and Racial Studies*, 19(4): 777–88.

Burkett, I. (1997) Social Relationships and Emotions. *Sociology*, 31(1): 37–55.

Burman, E. (1992) Feminism and Discourse in Developmental Psychology: Power, subjectivity and interpretation. *Feminism and Psychology*, 2(1): 45–59.

Butler, J. (1993) *Bodies That Matter: On the Discursive Limits of 'Sex'*. London: Routledge.

Calhoun, C. (1994) Social Theory and Politics of Identity. In C. Calhoun (ed.), *Social Theory and Politics of Identity*. Oxford: Blackwell, pp. 1–26.

Campbell, B. (1981) Race of Interviewer Effects Among Southern Adolescents. *Public Opinion Quarterly*, 45(2): 231–44.

Cannell, C.K., Marquis, K.H. and Laurent, A. (1977) A Summary of Studies. *Vital and Health Statistics*, Series 2 (106). Washington, DC: U.S. Government Printing Office.

Carby, H. (1982) White Women Listen! Black feminism and the boundaries of sisterhood. In Centre for Contemporary Cultural Studies, *The Empire Strikes Back: Race and Racism in 70s Britain*. London: Hutchinson, pp. 212–35.

Carrigan,T., Connell, B. and Lee, J. (1985) Towards a New Sociology of Masculinity. *Theory and Society*, 14(5): 551–603.

Caruth, C. and Keenan, T. (1995) The AIDS Crisis is Not Over: A conversation with Gregg Bordowitz, Douglas Crimp, and Laura Insky. In C. Caruth (ed.), *Trauma: Explorations in Memory*. Baltimore: Johns Hopkins University Press, pp. 256–72.

Chamberlayne, P., Bornat, J. and Wengraf, T. (eds) (2000) *The Turn to Biographical Methods in Social Science: Comparative Issues and Examples*. London: Routledge.

Chatham-Carpenter, A. and DeFranciso,V. (1998) Women Construct Self-Esteem in Their Own Terms: A feminist qualitative study. *Feminism and Psychology*, 8(4): 467–89.

Chow, R. (1992) Postmodern Automatons. In J. Butler and J. Scott (eds), *Feminists Theorize the Political*. London: Routledge, pp. 93–116.

Clark Hine, D. (1989) Rape and the Inner Lives of Black Women in the Middle West: Preliminary thoughts on the culture of dissemblance. *Signs*, 14(4): 915–20.

Clark Hine, D. (1993) 'In the Kingdom of Culture': Black women and the intersection of race, gender and class. In G. Early (ed.), *Lure and Loathing: Essays on Race, Identity and the Ambivalence of Assimilation*. New York: Allen Lane, pp. 337–51.

Clifford, J. (2000) Taking Identity Politics Seriously: 'The Contradictory, Stony Ground ...'. In P. Gilroy, L. Grossberg and A. McRobbie (eds), *Without Guarantees: In Honour of Stuart Hall*. London: Verso, pp. 94–112.

Clifford, J. and Marcus, G. (eds) (1986) *Writing Culture: The Politics and Poetics of Ethnography*. Berkeley, CA: University of California Press.

Collins, P. and Butcher, B. (1983) Interviewer and Clustering Effects in an Attitude Survey. *Journal of the Market Research Society*, 25 (January): 278–86.

Cotterill, P. (1992) Interviewing Women: Issues of friendship, vulnerability and power. *Women's Studies International Forum*, 15(5/6): 593–606.

Crang, M. (1999) Globalization as Conceived, Perceived and Lived Spaces. *Theory, Culture and Society*, 16(1): 167–77.

Daniel, W.W. (1969) *Racial Discrimination in England: Based on the PEP Report*. Harmondsworth: Penguin.

Davies, C. (1995) *Gender and The Professional Predicament of Nursing*. Buckingham: Open University Press.

Davis, D.W. (1997) The Direction of Race of Interviewer Effects Among African-Americans: Donning the Black mask. *American Journal of Political Science*, 41(1): 309–22.

DeLamater, J. and MacCorquodale, P. (1975) The Effects of Interview Schedule Variations on Reported Sexual Behaviour. *Sociological Methods and Research*, 4: 215–36.

De Lauretis, T. (1986) *Feminist Studies/Critical Studies*. Bloomington: Indiana University Press.

Denzin, N. (1997) *Interpretive Ethnography*. Thousand Oaks, CA: Sage.

Derrida, J. (1976) *On Grammatology*, trans. G. Chakravorty Spivak. Baltimore: Johns Hopkins University Press.

Derrida, J. (1981) *Positions*. Chicago: University of Chicago Press.

Du Bois, B. (1983) Passionate Scholarship: Notes on values, knowing and method in feminist social science. In G. Bowles and R. Deulli-Klein (eds), *Theories of Women's Studies*. London: Routledge and Kegan Paul, pp. 105–16.

Du Bois, W.E.B. (1899) *The Philadelphia Negro*. Philadelphia: University of Pennsylvania Press.

Du Bois, W.E.B. (1969 [1903]) *The Souls of Black Folk*. New York: Signet.

Dubow, S. (1995) *Scientific Racism in Modern South Africa*. Cambridge: Cambridge University Press.

Duelli-Klein, R. (1983) How To Do What We Want To Do: Thoughts about feminist methodology. In G. Bowles and R. Duelli-Klein (eds), *Theories of Women's Studies*. London: Routledge and Kegan Paul, pp. 84–104.

Dunbar, C. Jr., Rodriguez, D. and Parker, L. (2002). Race, Subjectivity and the Interview Process. In J. Gubrium and J. Holstein (eds), *Handbook of Interview Research: Context and Method*. Thousand Oaks: Sage, pp. 279–98.

Dyck, I., Lynam, J. and Anderson, J. (1995) Women Talking: Creating knowledge through difference in cross-cultural research. *Women's Studies International Forum*, 18(5/6): 611–26.

Dyson, S. (2001) Midwives and Screening for Haemoglobin Disorders. In L. Culley and S. Dyson (eds), *Ethnicity and Nursing Practice*. London: Palgrave, pp. 149–68.

Eade, J. (1997a) Identity, Nation and Religion: Educated young Bangladeshis in London's East End. In J. Eade (ed.), *Living the Global City: Globalization as Local Process*. London and New York: Routledge, pp. 146–62.

Eade, J. (ed.) (1997b) *Living the Global City: Globalization as Local Process*. London and New York: Routledge.

Eagleton, M. (2001) The Problem of Alice Walker's 'Advancing Luna' – and Ida B. Wells' and J.M. Coetzee's Disgrace. *Feminist Theory*, 2(2):189–203.

Early, G. (ed.) (1993) *Lure and Loathing: Essays on Race, Identity and the Ambivalence of Assimilation*. New York: Allen Lane.

Edwards, R. (1990) Connecting Method and Epistemology: A white woman interviewing black women. *Women's Studies International Forum*, 13(5): 477–90.

Edwards, R. (1998) A Critical Examination of the Use of Interpreters in the Qualitative Research Process. *Journal of Ethnic and Migration Studies*, 24(1): 197–208.

Elam, G. and Chinouya, M. (2000) *Feasibility Study for Health Surveys among Black African Populations Living in the UK: Stage 2 – Diversity among Black African Communities*. London: National Centre for Social Research.

Erasmus, Z. (2000) Some Kind of White, Some Kind of Black: Living the moments of entanglement in South Africa and its academy. In B. Hesse (ed.), *Un/settled Multiculturalisms: Diasporas, Entanglements, Transruptions*. London: Zed Books, pp. 185–207.

Erlich, J. and Reisman, D. (1961) Age and Authority with Interviewing. *Public Opinion Quarterly*, 25: 39–56.

Fenton, S., Carter, J. and Modood, T. (2000) Ethnicity and Academia: Closure models, racism models and market models. *Sociological Research Online*, 5(2): http://socresonline.org.uk/5/2/fenoton.html.

Fernando, S. (1988) *Race, Culture and Psychiatry*. London: Croom Helm.

Finch, J. (1984) 'It's Great to Have Someone to Talk To': The ethics and politics of interviewing women. In C. Bell and H. Roberts (eds), *Social Researching: Politics, Problems, Practice*. London: Routledge and Kegan Paul, pp. 70–87.

Fine, M. (1998) Working the Hyphens: Reinventing Self and Other in qualitative research. In N. Denzin and Y.S. Lincoln (eds), *The Landscape of Qualitative Research: Theories and Issues*. Thousand Oaks, CA: Sage, pp. 130–55.

Foddy, W. (1993) *Constructing Questions for Interviews and Questionnaires: Theory and Practice in Social Research*. Cambridge: Cambridge University Press.

Fortier, A. (1999) Re-Membering Places and the Performance of Belonging(s). *Theory, Culture and Society*, 16(2): 41–64.

Foucault, M. (1977) *Discipline and Punish: The Birth of the Prison*, trans. A. Sheridan. New York: Vintage.

Foucault, M. (1986) Of Other Spaces. *Diacritics*, 16: 22–7.

Fowler, F. and Mangione, T. (1990) *Standardised Survey Interviewing: Minimising Interview Related Errors*. Newbury Park, CA: Sage.

Frank, A. (1995) *The Wounded Storyteller: Body, Illness and Ethics*. Chicago: University of Chicago Press.

Frankenberg, R. (1993) *White Women, Race Matters: The Social Construction of Whiteness*. London: Routledge.

Fraser, N. (1995) From Redistribution to Recognition? Dilemmas of justice in a 'post-socialist' age. *New Left Review*, 212 (July/August): 68–93.

Frith, H. (1998) Constructing the 'Other' Through Talk. *Feminism and Psychology*, 8(4): 530–6.

Frith, H. and Kitzinger, C. (1998) 'Emotion Work' as a Participant Resource: A feminist analysis of young women's talk-in-interaction. *Sociology*, 32(2): 299–320.

Frosh, S., Phoenix, A. and Pattman, R. (2002) *Young Masculinities*. London: Palgrave.

Gallagher, C. (2000) White Like Me? Methods, meaning, and manipulation in the field of white studies. In F.W. Twine and J.W. Warren (eds), *Racing Research, Researching Race*. New York: New York University Press, pp. 67–92.

Gatens, M. and Lloyd, G. (1999) *Collective Imaginings: Spinoza, Past and Present*. London and New York: Routledge.

Gill, R. (1998) Dialogues and Differences: Writing, reflexivity and the crisis of representation. In K. Henwood, C. Griffin and A. Phoenix (eds), *Standpoints and Differences: Essays in the Practice of Feminist Psychology*. London: Sage, pp. 18–44.

Gilroy, P. (1998) Race Ends Here. *Ethnic and Racial Studies*, 21(5): 838–47.

Gilroy, P. (2000) *Nations, Cultures and the Allure of Race: Between Camps*. London: Allen Lane.

Goffman, E. (1983) The Interaction Order. *American Sociological Review*, 48: 1–7.

Grossberg, L. (1996) Identity and Cultural Studies: Is that all there is? In S. Hall and P. du Gay (eds), *Questions of Cultural Identity*. London: Sage, pp. 87–107.

Gubrium, J. and Holstein, J. (1997) *The New Language of Qualitative Method*. New York: Oxford University Press.

Gubrium, J. and Holstein, J. (2002) From the Individual Interview to the Interview Society. In J. Gubrium and J. Holstein (eds), *Handbook of Interview Research: Context and Method*. Thousand Oaks, CA: Sage, pp. 3–32.

Gunaratnam, Y. (1997) Culture is Not Enough: A critique of multi-culturalism in palliative care. In D. Field, J. Hockey and N. Small (eds), *Death, Gender and Ethnicity*. London: Routledge, pp. 166–86.

Gunaratnam, Y. (1999) Researching and Representing Ethnicity: A Qualitative Study of Hospice Staff and Service Users. Unpublished PhD thesis, University of London.

Gunaratnam, Y. (2001a) 'We mustn't judge people ... but': Staff dilemmas in dealing with racial harassment amongst hospice service users. *Sociology of Health and Illness*, 23(1): 65–83.

Gunaratnam, Y. (2001b) Eating Into Multi-culturalism: Hospice staff and service users talk food, 'race', ethnicity and identities. *Critical Social Policy*, 21(3): 287–310.

Gunaratnam, Y. (in progress) Care and connections in racialised contexts: a multi-sited analysis in J. Fink (ed.) *Care – Personal Lives: Social Policy*. Bristol: Policy Press.

Gunaratnam, Y. and Lewis, G. (2001) Racialising Emotional Labour and Emotionalising Racialised Labour: Anger, fear and shame in social welfare. *Journal of Social Work Practice*, 15(2): 131–48.

Gurevitch, Z. (1990) The Dialogic Connection and the Ethics of Dialogue. *British Journal of Sociology*, 41(2): 181–96.

Gurevitch, Z. (2001) Dialectical Dialogue: The struggle for speech, repressive silences, and the shift to multiplicity. *British Journal of Sociology*, 52(1) 87–104.

Hall, S. (1990) Cultural Identity and Diaspora. In J. Rutherford (ed.), *Identity: Community, Culture, Difference*. London: Lawrence and Wishart, pp. 222–37.

Hall, S. (1992) The Question of Cultural Identity. In S. Hall, D. Held and A. McGrew (eds), *Modernity and Its Futures*. Cambridge: Polity Press/Open University Press, pp. 302–28.

Hall, S. (1993) Culture, Community, Nation. *Cultural Studies*, 7(3): 349– 63.

Hall, S. (1996) Introduction: Who needs identity? In S. Hall and P. du Gay (eds), *Questions of Cultural Identity*. London: Sage, pp. 1–17.

Hall, S. (1997) The Local and the Global: Globalization and ethnicity. In A. King (ed.), *Culture, Globalization and the World System*. Minneapolis: University of Minnesota Press, pp. 19–39.

Hall, S. (1999) Whose Heritage? Unsettling the Heritage, Re-imagining the Post-Nation. *Third Text*, 49(Winter): 3–13.

Hall, S. (2000) Conclusion: The multi-cultural question. In B. Hesse (ed.), *Un/settled Multiculturalisms: Diasporas, Entanglements, Transruptions*. London: Zed Books, pp. 209–41.

Hanson, E. (1994) Issues Concerning the Familiarity of Researchers with the Research Setting. *Journal of Advanced Nursing*, 20(3): 940–2.

Haraway, D. (1988) Situated Knowledges: The science question in feminism and the privilege of partial perspective. *Feminist Studies*, 14(3): 575–99.

Haraway, D. (1990) A Manifesto for Cyborgs: Science, technology and socialist feminism in the 1980s. In L. Nicholson (ed.), *Feminism/Postmodernism*. New York and London: Routledge, pp. 190–233.

Heath, C. (1998) The Analysis of Activities in Face to Face Interaction Using Video. In D. Silverman (ed.), *Qualitative Research: Theory, Method and Practice*. London: Sage, pp. 183–200.

Hemmings, C. (2002) *Bisexual Spaces: A Geography of Sexuality and Gender*. London: Routledge.

Henwood, K. and Phoenix, A. (1996) 'Race' in Psychology: Teaching the subject. *Ethnic and Racial Studies*, 19(4): 841–63.

Heritage, J. (1998) Conversation Analysis and Institutional Talk: Analysing data. In D. Silverman (ed.), *Qualitative Research: Theory, Method and Practice*. London: Sage, pp. 161–82.

Hesse, B. (1997) White Governmentality – Urbanism, Nationalism, Racism. In S. Westwood and J. Williams (eds), *Imagining Cities: Scripts, Signs, Memory*. London: Routledge, pp. 86–103.

Hesse, B. (2000) Introduction: Un/settled multiculturalism. In B. Hesse (ed.), *Un/settled Multiculturalisms: Diasporas, Entanglements, Transruptions*. London: Zed Books, pp. 1–30.

Higginbotham, E. (1992) African-American Women's History and the Metalanguage of Race. *Signs*, 17(21): 251–74.

Hill, D. and Penso, D. (1995) *Opening Doors: Improving Access to Hospice and Specialist Care Services by Members of Black and Ethnic Minority Communities*. London: National Council of Hospice and Specialist Palliative Care Services.

Hill-Collins, P. (1991) *Black Feminist Thought: Knowledge, Consciousness and the Politics of Empowerment*. New York: Routledge.

Hillier, S. and Rachman, S. (1996) Childhood Development and Behavioural and Emotional Problems as Perceived by Bangladeshi Parents in East London. In D. Kelleher and S. Hillier (eds), *Researching Cultural Differences in Health*. London: Routledge, pp. 38–68.

Hoinville, G. and Jowell, R. (1978*) Survey Research Practice*. London: Heinemann Educational Books.

Hollway, W. (2001) The Psycho-Social Subject in 'Evidence-based' Practice. *Journal of Social Work Practice*, 15(1): 9–22.

Hollway, W. and Jefferson, T. (2000) *Doing Qualitative Research Differently, Free Association, Narrative and the Interview Method.* London: Sage.

Holstein, J. and Gubrium, J. (1998) Active Interviewing. In D. Silverman (ed.), *Qualitative Research: Theory, Method and Practice.* London: Sage, pp. 113–29. .

Home Office (2001) *Community Cohesion: A Report of the Independent Review Team Chaired by Ted Cantle.* London: HMSO.

hooks, b. (1992) *Black Looks: Race and Representation.* London: Turnaround.

Huber, J. (1995) Centennial Essay: Institutional perspectives on sociology. *American Journal of Sociology*, 101: 194–216.

Humphry, D. and John, G. (1972) *Because They're Black.* Harmondsworth: Penguin.

Hurd, T. and McIntyre, A. (1996) The Seduction of Sameness: Similarity and representing the Other. In S. Wilkinson and C. Kitzinger (eds), *Representing the Other, A Feminism and Psychology Reader.* London: Sage, pp. 78–82.

Hyman, H., Feldman, J. and Stember, C. (1954) *Interviewing in Social Research.* Chicago: University of Chicago Press.

ICM Research (2002) *Muslim Poll.* www.icmresearch.co.uk.

Jackson, S. (1998) Telling Stories: Memories, narrative and experience in feminist research and theory. In K. Henwood, C. Griffin and A. Phoenix (eds), *Standpoints and Differences: Essays in the Practice of Feminist Psychology.* London: Sage, pp. 45–64.

James, N. (1989) Emotional Labour: Skill and work in the social regulation of feelings. *Sociological Review*, 37: 15–47.

James, N. (1992) Care = organisation + physical labour + emotional labour. *Sociology of Health and Illness*, 14(4): 487–509.

Jaschok, M. and Jingjun, S. (2000) 'Outsider Within': Speaking to excursions across cultures. *Feminist Theory*, 1(1): 33–58.

Jenkins, R. (1996) Ethnicity *etcetera*: Social anthropological points of view. *Ethnic and Racial Studies*, 19(4): 807–22.

Johnson, A., Anderson, A., Bradshaw, S., Field, J. and Wellings, J. (1994) *Sexual Attitudes and Lifestyles.* Oxford: Blackwell Scientific Publications.

Jones, J. (1981) How Different are Human Races? *Nature*, 293: 188–90.

Kai, J. and Hedges, C. (1999) Minority Ethnic Community Participation in Needs Assessment and Service Development in Primary Care: Perceptions of Pakistani and Bangladeshi people about psychological distress. *Health Expectations*, 2(1): 7–20.

Katz, D. (1942) Do Interviewers Bias Poll Results? *Public Opinion Quarterly*, 6 (Summer): 248–68.

Kauffman, K. (1994) The Insider/Outsider Dilemma: Field experience of a white researcher 'getting in' a poor black community. *Nursing Research*, 43, 179–83.

Kitzinger, C. and Wilkinson, S. (1996) Theorizing Representing the Other. In S. Wilkinson and C. Kitzinger (eds), *Representing the Other: A Feminism and Psychology Reader.* London: Sage. pp. 1–32.

Klein, M. (1975) *Love, Guilt and Reparation and Other Works 1921–1945.* London: The Hogarth Press.

Knowles, C. (1999) Race, Identities and Lives. *Sociological Review*, 47(1): 110–35.

Kraidy, M. (2002) The Global, the Local and the Hybrid: A native ethnography of glocalization. In S. Taylor (ed.), *Ethnographic Research: A Reader.* London: Sage/Open University, pp. 187–209.

Kurokawa-Maykovich, M. (1977) The Difficulties of a Minority Researcher in Minority Communities. *Journal of Social Issues*, 35(4): 108–19.

Labov, W. and Fanshel, D. (1977) *Therapeutic Discourse*. New York: Academic Press.

Lacan, J. (1981) *The Four Fundamental Concepts of Psychoanalysis*, trans. Alan Sheridan. New York and London: Norton.

Lankshear, G. (2000) Bacteria and Babies: A personal reflection on researcher risk in a hospital. In G. Lee-Treweek and S. Linkogle (eds), *Danger in the Field: Risk and Ethics in Social Research*. London: Routledge, pp. 72–90.

Lather, P. (2001a) Postmodernism, Post-structuralism and Post(Critical) Ethnography: Of ruins, aporias and angels. In P. Atkinson, A. Coffey, S. Delamont, J. Lofland and L. Lofland (eds), *Handbook of Ethnography*. London: Sage. pp. 477–92.

Lather, P. (2001b) Postbook: Working the ruins of feminist ethnography. *Signs*, 27(1): 199–227.

Lather, P. and Smithies, C. (1997) *Troubling the Angels: Women Living With HIV/AIDS*. Boulder, CO: Westview Press.

Latour, B. (1983) Give Me a Laboratory and I Will Raise the World. In K. Korr-Cetina and M. Mulkay (eds), *Science Observed: Perspectives in the Social Study of Science*. London: Sage, pp. 141–70.

Latour, B. (1987) *Science in Action: How to Follow Scientists and Engineers Through Society*. Cambridge, MA: Harvard University Press.

Lee, R. (1993) *Doing Research on Sensitive Topics*. London: Sage.

Lee, R. and Renzetti, C. (1990) The Problems of Researching Sensitive Topics: An overview and introduction. *American Behavioral Scientist*, 33: 510–28.

Lee-Treweek, G. and Linkogle, S. (eds) (2000) *Danger in the Field: Risk and Ethics in Social Research*. London: Routledge.

Lefebvre, H. (1991) *The Production of Space*. Oxford: Basil Blackwell (first published in French, 1974).

Leifer, E. (1988) Interaction Preludes to Role Setting: Exploratory local action. *American Sociological Review*, 53: 865–78.

Leininger, M. (ed.) (1991) *Culture Care, Diversity and Universality: A Theory of Nursing*. New York: NLN Press.

Lenski, G.E. and Leggett, J.C. (1960) Caste, Class and Deference in The Research Interview. *The American Journal of Sociology*, 65 (March): 463–7.

Levine, P. (2000) Orientalist Sociology and the Creation of Colonial Sexualities. *Feminist Review*, 65: 5–21.

Lewis, B. and Ramazanoglu, C. (1999) Not Guilty, Not Proud, Just White: Women's accounts of their whiteness. In H. Brown, M. Gilkes and A. Kaloski-Naylor (eds), *White? Women: Critical Perspectives on Race and Gender*. York: Raw Nerve Books, pp. 23–61.

Lewis, G. (2000) *'Race', Gender, Social Welfare: Encounters in a Postcolonial Society*. London: Polity Press.

Lewis, G. and Gunaratnam, Y. (2000) Negotiating 'Race' and Space: Spatial Practices, Identity and Power in the Narratives of Health and Social Welfare Professionals. Unpublished paper presented to the Social Policy Association Annual Conference, 19 July 2000, Roehampton Institute, London.

Lewis, J. (2000) Funding Social Science Research in Academia. *Social Policy and Administration*, 34(4): 365–76.

Linell, P. and Jonsson, L. (1991) Suspect Stories: On perspective-setting on an asymmetrical situation. In I. Markova and K. Foppa (eds), *Asymmetries in Dialogue*. Hemel Hempstead: Harvester Wheatsheaf.

Lorimer, D. (1978) *Colour, Class and the Victorians: English Attitudes to the Negro in the Mid-Nineteenth Century*. Leicester: Leicester University Press.

McClintock, A. (1995) *Imperial Leather: Race, Gender and Sexuality in The Colonial Contest*. New York: Routledge.

Macpherson, W. (1999) *The Stephen Lawrence Inquiry: Report of an Inquiry*. London: HMSO.

Mama, A. (1995) *Beyond the Masks: Race, Gender and Subjectivity*. London: Routledge.

Manning, K. (1993) Race, Science and Identity. in G. Early (ed.), *Lure and Loathing: Essays on Race, Identity and the Ambivalence of Assimilation*. New York: Allen Lane, pp. 317–36.

Marcus, G. (1994) What Comes (Just) after 'Post'? The Case of Ethnography. In N. Denzin and Y. Guba (eds), *The Handbook of Qualitative Research*. Thousand Oaks, CA: Sage, pp. 563–74.

Marcus, G. (1998) *Ethnography Through Thick and Thin*. Princeton: Princeton University Press.

Marcus, G. and Fischer, R. (1986) *Anthropology as Cultural Critique: An Experimental Moment in the Human Sciences*. Chicago: University of Chicago Press.

Marshall, H., Woollett, A. and Dosanjh, N. (1998) Researching Marginalized Standpoints: Some tensions around plural standpoints and diverse 'experiences'. In K. Henwood, C. Griffin and A. Phoenix (eds), *Standpoints and Differences: Essays in the Practice of Feminist Psychology*. London: Sage, pp. 115–34.

Mason, D. (1996) Themes and Issues in the Teaching of Race and Ethnicity in Sociology. *Ethnic and Racial Studies*, 19(4): 789–806.

Massey, D. (2000) Travelling Thoughts. In P. Gilroy, L. Grossberg and A. McRobbie (eds), *Without Guarantees: In Honour of Stuart Hall*. London: Verso, pp. 225–32.

Massey, D.S. and Denton, N.A. (2000) The Future of the Ghetto. In S. Steinberg (ed.), *Race and Ethnicity in the United States: Issues and Debates*. Oxford: Blackwell. pp. 114–26.

Meijer, I.C. and Prins, B. (1998) How Bodies Come to Matter: An interview with Judith Butler, *Signs*, 23(2): 275–86.

Menzies Lyth, I. (1988) *Containing Anxiety in Institutions, Selected Essays*. London: Free Association Books.

Miles, R. (1982) *Racism and Migrant Labour: A Critical Text*. London: Routledge and Kegan Paul.

Miles, R. (1989) *Racism*. London: Routledge.

Mirrlees-Black, C., Mayhew, P. and Percy, A. (1996) The 1996 British Crime Survey: England and Wales. *Home Office Statistical Bulletin*, Issue 19/96. Research and Statistics Directorate. London: Home Office.

Modood, T., Berthoud, R. and Nazroo, J. (2002) 'Race', Racism and Ethnicity: A response to Ken Smith. *Sociology*, 36(2): 419–27.

Mohanty, C. (1992) Feminist Encounters: Locating the politics of experience. In M. Barrett and A. Phillips (eds), *Destabilising Theory: Contemporary Feminist Debates*. Cambridge: Polity Press, pp. 74–92.

Montero, D. (1977) Research among Racial and Cultural Minorities: An overview. *Journal of Social Issues*, 33(4): 1–9.

Moody, J. (1997) Professions of Faith: A teacher reflects on women, race, church and spirit. In K. Vaz (ed.), *Oral Narrative Research With Black Women*. Thousand Oaks, CA: Sage, pp. 24–37.

Mulholland, J. and Dyson, S. (2001) Sociological Theories of 'Race' and Ethnicity. In L. Culley and J. Dyson (eds), *Ethnicity and Nursing Practice*, London: Palgrave. pp. 17–38.

Myers, V. (1977) Survey Methods for Minority Populations. *Journal of Social Issues*, 33(4): 11–19.

Narayan, U. (2000) Essence of Culture and a Sense of History: A feminist critique of cultural essentialism. In U. Narayan and S. Harding (eds), *Decentering the*

Center – Philosophy For a Multicultural, Postcolonial and Feminist World. Bloomington: Indiana University Press, pp. 80–100.

Nazroo, J. (1997) *The Health of Britain's Ethnic Minorities*. London: Policy Studies Institute.

Oakley, A. (1981) Interviewing Women: A contradiction in terms. In H. Roberts (ed.), *Doing Feminist Research*. London: Routledge and Kegan Paul, pp. 30–61.

Obeyesekere, G. (1990) *The Work of Culture: Symbolic Transformations in Psychoanalysis and Anthropology*. Chicago and London: University of Chicago Press.

Omi, M. and Winant, H. (1994) *Racial Formation in the United States: From the 1960s to the 1990s*. New York: Routledge.

O'Neill, M. in association with Giddens, S., Breatnach, P., Bagley, C., Bourne, D. and Judge, T. (2002) Renewed Methodologies for Social Research: Ethno-mimesis as performative praxis. *The Sociological Review*, 50(1): 69–88.

Opie, A. (1992) Qualitative Research, Appropriation of the 'Other' and Empowerment. *Feminist Review*, 40: 52–69.

Orton, S. and Samuels, J. (1987) What We have Learned from Researching AIDS. *Journal of the Market Research Society*, 30(1): 3–34.

Papadopoulos, I. and Lees, S. (2002) Developing Culturally Competent Researchers. *Journal of Advanced Nursing*, 37(3): 258–64.

Pettigrew, T. (1964) *A Profile of the Negro American*. New York: Van Nostrand.

Pittenger, R., Hockett, C. and Danehy, J. (1960) *The First Five Minutes*. Ithaca, NY: Paul Martineau.

Phoenix, A. (1987) Theories of Gender and Black Families. In G. Weiner and M. Arnot (eds), *Gender under Scrutiny: New Inquiries in Education*. London: Hutchinson/Open University, pp. 50–61.

Phoenix, A. (2001) Practising Feminist Research: The intersection of gender and 'race' in the research process. In K.-K. Bhavani, (ed.), *Feminism and Race*. Oxford. Oxford University Press, pp. 203–19. Originally published 1994, in M. Maynard and J. Purvis (eds), Researching Women's Lives. London: Taylor and Francis, pp. 49–71.

Poland, B. (2002) Transcription Quality. In J. Gubrium and J. Holstein (eds), *Handbook of Interview Research: Context and Method*. Thousand Oaks, CA: Sage, pp. 629–49.

Porter, S. (1996) Contra-Foucault: Soldiers, nurses and power. *Sociology*, 30(1): 59–78.

Potter, J. and Wetherell, M. (1987) *Discourse and Social Psychology*. London: Sage.

Price, D. and Searles, R. (1961) *Some Effects of Interviewer-Respondent Interaction on Responses in a Survey Situation*. Proceedings of the Social Statistics Section, American Statistical Association.

Probyn, E. (1993) *Sexing the Self: Gendered positions in cultural studies*. London: Routledge.

Probyn, E. (2000) Shaming Theory, Thinking Disconnections: Feminism and reconciliation. In S. Ahmed, J. Kilby, C. Lury, M. McNeil and B. Skeggs (eds), *Transformations: Thinking Through Feminism*. London: Routledge, pp. 48–60.

Quayson, A. (2002) Looking Awry: Tropes of disability in postcolonial writing. In D. Goldberg. and A. Quayson (eds), *Relocating Postcolonialism*. Oxford: Blackwell, pp. 231–50.

Quayson, A. and Goldberg, D. (2002) Introduction: Scale and sensibility. In D. Goldberg and A. Quayson (eds), *Relocating Postcolonialism*. Oxford: Blackwell, pp. xi–xxii.

Rabinow, P. (1986) Representations Are Social Facts: Modernity and post-modernity in anthropology. In J. Clifford and G. Marcus (eds), *Writing Culture: The Politics and Poetics of Ethnography*. Berkeley, CA: University of California Press, pp. 234–61.

Radhakrishnan, R. (1996) *Diasporic Mediations Between Home and Location*. Minneapolis: University of Minnesota Press.

Ram, M. (1996) Ethnography, Ethnicity and Work: Unpacking the West Midlands clothing industry. In E.S. Lyon and J. Busfield (eds), *Methodological Imaginations*. Basingstoke: Macmillan, pp. 112–30.

Ramazanoglu, C. (1989) Improving on Sociology: The problems of taking a feminist standpoint. *Sociology*, 23(3): 427–42.

Ramazanoglu, C. and Holland, J. (1999) Tripping over Experience: Some problems in feminist epistemology. *Discourse: Studies in the Cultural Politics of Education*, 20(3): 381–92.

Rappert, B. (1997) Users and Social Science Research: Policy, problems and possibilities. *Sociological Research Online*, http://www.socresonline.org.uk/socresonline/2/3/10.htm1

Reay, D. (1996a) Dealing with Difficult Difference: Reflexivity and social class in feminist research. *Feminism and Psychology*, 6(3): 443–56.

Reay, D. (1996b) Insider Perspectives or Stealing the Words out of Women's Mouths: Interpretation in the research process. *Feminist Review*, (53): 57–73.

Reay, D. (1999) Fantasies of Feminisms: Egalitarian fictions and elitist realities. *Feminism and Psychology*, 9(4): 426–30.

Reay, D. (2000) 'Dim Dross': Marginalised women both inside and outside the academy. *Women's Studies International Forum*, 23(1): 13–21.

Reed, K. (2000) Dealing with Differences: Researching health beliefs and behaviours of British Asian Mothers. *Sociological Research Online*, 4(4): http://www.socresonline.org.uk/4/4/reed.html

Renzetti, C. and Lee, R. (eds) (1993) *Researching Sensitive Topics*. Newbury Park, CA: Sage.

Rhodes, P. (1994) Race of Interviewer Effects in Qualitative Research: A brief comment. *Sociology*, 28(2): 547–58.

Ribbens, J. (1989) Interviewing Women – An Unnatural Situation? *Women's Studies International Forum*, 12(6): 579–92.

Ribbens, J. and Edwards, R. (eds) (1998) *Feminist Dilemmas in Qualitative Research: Public Knowledge and Private Lives*. London: Sage.

Richardson, R. (1999) *Islamaphobia*. London: Runneymede Trust.

Riessman, C. (1987) When Gender is Not Enough: Women interviewing women. *Gender and Society*, 1(2): 172–207.

Roediger, D.R. (1990) *Towards the Abolition of Whiteness: Essays on Race, Politics, and Working Class History*. London: Verso.

Rose, N. (1996) Identity, Genealogy, History. In S. Hall and P. du Gay (eds), *Questions of Cultural Identity*. London: Sage, pp. 128–50.

Rosenthal, G. (1993) Reconstruction of Life Stories: Principles of selection in generating stories for narrative biographical interviews. In R. Josselson and A. Lieblich (eds), *The Narrative Study of Lives*. London: Sage, pp. 59–91.

Rudat, K. (1994) *Black and Minority Ethnic Groups in England: Health and Lifestyle*. London: Heath Education Authority.

Rutherford, J. (ed.) (1990) *Identity*. London: Lawrence and Wishart.

Ryen, A. (2002) Cross-Cultural Interviewing. In J. Gubrium and J. Holstein (eds), *Handbook of Interview Research: Context and Method*. Thousand Oaks, CA: Sage, pp. 335–54.

Said, E. (1985 [1978]) *Orientalism*. London: Penguin.

St Louis, B. (2000) Readings Within a Diasporic Boundary: Transatlantic black performance and the poetic imperative in sport. In B. Hesse (ed.), *Un/settled Multiculturalisms: Diasporas, Entanglements, Transruptions*. London: Zed Books, pp. 51–72.

Sayyid, S. (2000) Beyond Westphalia: Nations and diasporas – the case of the Muslim Umma. In B. Hesse (ed.), *Un/settled Multiculturalisms: Diasporas, Entanglements, Transruptions*. London: Zed Books, pp. 33–50.

Schaeffer, N. (1980) Evaluating Race-of-Interviewer Effects in a National Survey. *Sociological Methods and Research*, 8(4): 400–19.

Schaeffer, N. and Maynard, D. (2002) Standardization and Interaction in The Survey Interview. In J. Gubrium and J. Holstein (eds), *Handbook of Interview Research: Context and Method*. Thousand Oaks, CA: Sage, pp. 577–601.

Scheff, T. (1997) *Emotions, The Social Bond, and Human Reality: Part/Whole Analysis*. Cambridge: Cambridge University Press.

Schuman, H. and Converse, J. (1971) The Effects of Black and White Interviewers on Black Responses in 1968. *Public Opinion Quarterly*, 35: 44–68.

Schutte, O. (2000) Cultural Alterity: Cross-cultural communication and feminist theory in North-South contexts. In U. Narayan and S. Harding (eds), *Decentering the Center – Philosophy for a Multicultural, Postcolonial and Feminist World*. Bloomington: Indiana University Press, pp. 47–66.

Scott, J. (1992) Experience. In J. Butler and J. Scott (eds), *Feminists Theorize the Political*. London: Routledge, pp. 22–40.

Sedgwick, E. (1993) *Tendencies*. Durham, NC: Duke University Press.

Seu, I. (1998) Shameful Women: Accounts of withdrawal and silence. In K. Henwood, C. Griffin and A. Phoenix (eds), *Standpoints and Differences: Essays in the Practice of Feminist Psychology*. London: Sage, pp. 135–55.

Shields, R. (1996) Meeting or mis-meeting? The dialogical challenge to Verstehen. *British Journal of Sociology*, 47(2): 275–94.

Shosteck, H. (1977) Respondent Militancy as a Control Variable for Interviewer Effect. *Journal of Social Issues*, 33(4): 36–45.

Simpson, J. (1996) Easy Talk, White Talk, Talk Back: Some reflections on the meanings of our words. *Journal of Contemporary Ethnography*, 25(3): 372–89.

Simpson, S. (1997) Demography and Ethnicity: Case studies from Bradford. *Journal of Ethnic and Migration Studies*, 23(1): 89–107.

Skeggs, B. (2001) Feminist Ethnography. In P. Atkinson, A. Coffey, S. Delamont, J. Lofland and L. Lofland (eds), *Handbook of Ethnography*. London: Sage, pp. 426–42.

Smaje, C. (1997) Not Just a Social Construct: Theorising race and ethnicity. *Sociology*, 31(2): 307–27.

Smith, A.W. (1993) Survey Research on African Americans: Methodological innovations. In J.H. Stanfield and M. Dennis (eds), *Race and Ethnicity in Research Methods*. Newbury Park, CA: Sage, pp. 217–29.

Smith, D. (1992) Sociology From Women's Perspective: A reaffirmation. *Sociological Theory*, 10: 88–97.

Smith, K. (2002) Some Critical Observations on the Use of the Concept of 'Ethnicity' in Modood et al., Ethnic Minorities in Britain. *Sociology*, 36(2): 399–417.

Solomos, J. and Back, L. (1994) Conceptualising Racisms: Social theory, politics and research. *Sociology*, 28(1): 143–62.

Song, M. and Parker, D. (1995) Commonality, Difference and the Dynamics of Disclosure in In-Depth Interviewing. *Sociology*, 29(2): 241–56.

Spencer, J. (2001) Ethnography After Postmodernism. In P. Atkinson, A. Coffey, S. Delamont, J. Lofland and L. Lofland (eds), *Handbook of Ethnography*. London: Sage, pp. 443–52.

Spivak, G. Chakravorty (1992) The Politics of Translation. In M. Barrett and A. Phillips (eds), *Destabilizing Theory: Contemporary Feminist Debates*. Cambridge: Polity Press, pp. 177–200.

Stacey, J. (1988) Can There Be a Feminist Ethnography? *Women's Studies International Forum*, 11(1): 21–7.

Stanfield, J. (1993a) Introduction. In J. Stanfield (ed.), *A History of Race Relations Research: First Generation Recollections*. Newbury Park, CA: Sage, pp. ix–xxv.

Stanfield, J. (1993b) Methodological Reflections: An introduction. In J. Stanfield and R. Dennis (eds), *Race and Ethnicity in Research Methods*. Newbury Park, CA: Sage, pp. 3–15.

Stanfield, J. (1993c) Epistemological Considerations. In J. Stanfield and R. Dennis (eds), *Race and Ethnicity in Research Methods*. Newbury Park, CA: Sage, pp. 16–36.

Stanfield. J. and Dennis, R. (eds) (1993) *Race and Ethnicity in Research Methods*. Newbury Park, CA: Sage.

Strathern, M. (1988) *The Gender of the Gift: Problems with Women and Problems with Society in Melanesia*. Berkeley, CA: University of California Press.

Suchman, L. and Jordon, B. (1990) Interactional Troubles in Face-to-Face Interviews. *Journal of the American Statistical Association*, 85: 232–41.

Sudman, S. and Bradburn, N. (1974) *Response Effects in Surveys*. Chicago: Aldine.

Sudman, S. and Bradburn, N. (1982) *Asking Questions: A Practical Guide to Questionnaire Design*. San Francisco: Jossey-Bass.

Tang, N. (2002) Interviewer and Interviewee Relationships Between Women. *Sociology*, 36(3): 703–21.

Thapar-Bjorkert, S. (1999) Negotiating Otherness: Dilemmas for a non-Western researcher in the Indian Sub-continent. *Journal of Gender Studies*, 8(1): 57–69.

Thomas, N. (1994) *Colonialism's Culture: Anthropology, Travel and Government*. Cambridge: Polity Press.

Thomson, Garland, R. (2002) Theorizing Disability. In D. Goldberg and A. Quayson (eds), *Relocating Postcolonialism*. Oxford: Blackwell, pp. 231–69.

Tizard, B. and Phoenix, A. (1993) *Black, White or Mixed Race? Race and Racism in the Lives of Young People of Mixed Parentage*. London: Routledge.

Tracy, P. and Fox, A. (1981) The Validity of Randomized Response for Sensitive Measurements. *American Sociological Review*, 46: 187–200.

Tuhiwai Smith, L. (1999) *Decolonizing Methodologies: Research and Indigenous Peoples*. London: Zed Books and University of Otago Press.

Turner, B. (1997) A Neo-Hobbesian Theory of Human Rights: A reply to Malcolm Waters. *Sociology*, 31(3): 565–71.

Twine, F.W. (2000) Racial Ideologies and Racial Methodologies. In F.W. Twine and J. Warren (eds), *Racing Research, Researching Race*. New York: New York University Press, pp. 1–34.

VanDyke, R. and Gunaratnam, Y. (2000) Ethnic Monitoring in Higher Education: Some reflections on methodology. *International Journal of Social Research Methodology*, 3(4): 325–45.

Van Manen, M. (1990) *Researching Lived Experience: Human Science For An Action Sensitive Pedagogy*. Albany, NY: The State University of New York Press.

Viswanathan, G. (1989) *Masks of Conquest: Literary Study and British Rule in India*. New York: Columbia University Press.

Visweswaran, K. (1997) *Fictions of Feminist Ethnography*. Minneapolis: University of Minnesota Press (first published 1994).

Waddell, M. (1989) Living in Two Worlds: Psychodynamic theory and social work practice. *Free Associations*, 15: 11–35.

Walton, H. (1986) *White Researchers and Racism*. Working Paper no. 10, University of Manchester.

Ware, V. (1992) *Beyond the Pale: White Women, Racism and History*. London: Verso.

Warner, S. (1965) Randomized Response: A technique for eliminating evasive answer bias. *Journal of the American Statistical Association*, 60: 884–8.

Warren, C. and Hackney, J. (2000) *Gender Issues in Ethnography*. Thousand Oaks, CA: Sage.

Watson, B. and Scraton, S. (2001) Confronting Whiteness? Researching the leisure lives of South Asian Mothers. *Journal of Gender Studies*, 10(3): 265–77.

Webster, C. (1996) Hispanic and Anglo Interviewer and Respondent Ethnicity and Gender: The impact on survey response quality. *Journal of Marketing Research*, 33(1): 62–73.

Wellings, K., Field, J., Wadsworth, J., Johnson, A., Anderson, R. and Bradshaw, S. (1990) Sexual Lifestyles Under Scrutiny. *Nature*, 348: 276–8.

Wengraf, T. (2000) Uncovering the General From Within the Particular: From contingencies to typologies in the understanding of cases. In P. Chamberlayne, J. Bornat and T. Wengraf (eds), *The Turn to Biographical Methods in Social Science: Comparative Issues and Examples*. London: Routledge, pp. 140–64.

Wengraf, T. (2001) *Qualitative Research Interviewing. Biographic Narrative and Semi-Structured Method*. London: Sage.

Werbner, P. (1997) Essentialising Essentialism, Essentialising Silence: Ambivalence and multiplicity in the constructions of racism and ethnicity. In P. Werbner and T. Modood (eds), *Debating Cultural Hybridity: Multi-Cultural Identities and the Politics of Anti-Racism*. London: Zed Books, pp. 226–54.

Wetherell, M. and Edley, N. (1998) Gender Practices: Steps in the analysis of men and masculinities. In K. Henwood, C. Griffin and A. Phoenix (eds), *Standpoints and Differences: Essays in the Practice of Feminist Psychology*. London: Sage, pp. 156–73.

Wilkinson, S. (1988) The Role of Reflexivity in Feminist Psychology. *Women's Studies International Forum*, 11(5): 493–502.

Wilkinson, S. and Kitzinger, C. (eds) (1996) *Representing the Other: A Feminism and Psychology Reader*. London: Sage.

Williams, R. (1977) *Marxism and Literature*. Oxford: Oxford University Press.

Willott, S. (1998) An Outsider Within: A feminist doing research with men. In K. Henwood, C. Griffin and A. Phoenix (eds), *Standpoints and Differences: Essays in the Practice of Feminist Psychology*. London: Sage, pp. 174–90.

Winant, H. (1994) Racial Formation and Hegemony: Global and local developments. In A. Rattansi and S. Westwood (eds), *Racism, Modernity and Identity: On the Western Front*. Cambridge: Polity Press, pp. 266–89.

Wise, S. (1987) A Framework for Discussing Ethical Issues in Feminist Research: A review of the literature. In V. Griffiths (ed.), *Writing Feminist Biography 2: Using Life Histories*. Studies in Sexual Politics, no. 19. Manchester: University of Manchester.

Woolgar, S. (1997) Accountability and Identity in the Age of UABs. CRICT Discussion Paper. University of West London.

Wuthnow, J. (2002) Deleuze in the Postcolonial: On nomads and indigenous politics. *Feminist Theory*, 3(2): 183 –200.

Yegenoglu, M. (1998) *Colonial Fantasies: Towards a Feminist Reading of Orientalism*. Cambridge: Cambridge University Press.

Young, E. and Lee, R. (1996) Fieldworker Feelings as Data: 'Emotion work' and 'feeling rules' in first person accounts of sociological fieldwork. In V. James and J. Gabe (eds), *Health and the Sociology of Emotions*. Oxford: Blackwell, pp. 97–113.

Young, R. (1995) *Colonial Desire: Hybridity in Theory, Culture and Race*. London: Routledge.

Zadeh, L, (1965) *Fuzzy Logic for the Management of Uncertainty*. London: John Wylie and Sons.

Zinn, M. (1979) Field Research in Minority Communities: Ethical, methodological, and political observations by an insider. *Social Problems*, 27: 209–19.

Index